Fighting back against all the odds, Teresa Cooper managed to piece together the remnants of her fragmented life to begin again and went on to have three wonderful children. Now, Teresa campaigns to bring about changes to the British legal system that will prevent many more children suffering at the hands of unethical doctors and abusive carers. She is also instrumental in providing help for victims of abuse to ensure that they can follow in her footsteps . . . and become survivors. Teresa has two sons and a daughter and lives in Essex.

TRUST NO ONE

ONE GIRL'S HARROWING AND DISTURBING
TALE OF THE ABUSE SHE SUFFERED IN CARE

TERESA COOPER

Dedication

To Deborah, who touched the hearts of those who
knew her, and to my three children, who bring me
such happiness.

———

An Orion paperback

First published in Great Britain in 2007 by Orion
This paperback edition published in 2008 by Orion Books Ltd,
Orion House, 5 Upper St Martin's Lane,
London WC2H 9EA

An Hachette Livre UK company

Originally published in hardback as *Pin Down*

A CIP catalogue record for this book
is available from the British Library.

Printed and bound in Great Britain by
Clays Ltd, St Ives plc

The Orion Publishing Group's policy is to use papers that
are natural, renewable and recyclable products and
made from wood grown in sustainable forests. The logging
and manufacturing processes are expected to conform to
the environmental regulations of the country of origin.

To protect the innocent, some of the names and details in this book
have been changed. All the events described actually occurred.

www.orionbooks.co.uk

Acknowledgements

I would like to thank my children, who have seen me through difficult times and kept me strong. Their love and support has been paramount to the mother and person I am today. They are my life and the air that I breathe and I am so very proud of the people they have become. My love is forever with them every step of the way and I wouldn't be here if it were not for their love and direction.

I would like to say thank you to my sister, whom I love dearly, and my brother, and may the future bring them much happiness.

I need to mention my eighteen pets that make my home and life complete in so many ways and fill the house with love and companionship. Not to mention all the antics they get up to, which have been the source of many magical moments for me and my children. Thank you to our vet, who does a great job.

I would like to say thank you to Clare, Amanda, Angela and Lorraine at Orion Publishing, who have been a tower of strength and support, but also for being wonderful to work with and know. Thank you to Orion for their support in bringing my book to you.

In April 2006 I also met Eve White, my fantastic agent, who has been there for me every step of the way including my highs and lows. Your support and amazing character have been exceptional.

A very special thank you to Rebecca, who has worked very closely with me on the book and our friendship is one I treasure. It has been an emotional journey for both of us and one that will not be forgotten. So much emotion went into *Pin Down*, going through the files and documents, and I couldn't have done it without her.

Acknowledgements

Jules, my best friend at Kendall House, was there for me not only at Kendall House but also since our recent reunion, supporting me, mothering me, keeping me strong and being my rock.

My warmest thank you and love to the late Mr and Mrs Whattler, who showed me the most sincere kindness and courage during the most traumatic time of my life, and to their family for all their support and care. The love I received from this special family was paramount in my life and one I will always hold dear. I will always be so grateful that the Whattlers came into my life when I was at Kendall House. Many children in the care system never have the opportunity to experience the love and care I received from the Whattlers. I know there are people out there who can give children from broken homes the support they need and work patiently with them to develop their true personality and bring out the best in them.

Much love to all my friends including Chris, Dave, Julie, Helen, Roger, Anwer, Paul, Angela and Jennifer, who have seen me through and been there for me every step of the way.

Thanks also to Church in Society, especially Adrian and David for providing information, files, listening to me when I needed someone to talk to and for their support.

To Rob, my webmaster, who has made the website **no2abuse** possible and for his continued friendship.

To John Lord for his website www.about-gravesend.co.uk, and for his support, research skills and providing me with photos and information.

To Richard Lord at Gravesend Library, who has been an asset to his profession and contributed his expertise, research and support.

Barnet Local Studies & Archives for providing photos.

To Steve at Chelmsford Library for providing information.

To the Salvation Army for their support and The Benevolent Fund for providing photos.

A special thank you to everyone who has given me support and to survivors of abuse who fight hard to help make changes.

Teresa Cooper
April 2007

CHAPTER ONE

June 1971

'Hurry up!' Mum yelled.

She grabbed my arm and dragged me up a gravel path leading to a big, old-fashioned house. On each side of the entrance there was a tall stone pillar with a stone ball on top. The house was surrounded by trees and enclosed by a high grey wall.

Clutching my favourite doll with one hand and pushing my toy pram with the other, I tried to keep up as Mum rushed towards the front door. But she was going too fast for me. I stumbled and fell, yelping with pain as the gravel cut into my knees.

'Hush, or they'll hear us!' Mum said in a forced whisper. Picking myself up, I gulped back my tears and tried to be brave.

At the entrance to the house, she took a piece of paper out of her bag and pinned it to my chest. She gave me a sad half-smile and tears welled up in her eyes. 'Make sure you're a good girl for your mum,' she said. 'I love you. Always remember that.'

I watched in bewilderment as she walked away, leaving me behind on the doorstep. She picked up her pace and started hurrying towards a car by the side of the road. I could just about make out the driver. He had a wrinkled brown face and wiry grey hair. I'd never seen him before.

I felt a lump rise up the back of my throat. 'Mum!' I called out, tears streaming down my face. Without turning back, she disappeared into the car and it pulled away, out of sight.

I didn't know what to do. I was used to Mum's erratic ways, but she'd never left me alone like this before. When would she be coming back? I sat on the doorstep and began to wait, but waiting was boring, so I started playing with the new doll that Mum had given me for my fourth birthday the week before. She was beautiful. I loved her long golden hair and gleaming blue eyes.

I noticed that Mum had left behind a black bin liner she'd been carrying. Curious, I peeped inside. It was stuffed with all my toys and clothes. I pulled a few things out and lined them up. At least I'd have plenty to play with until she came back. I was used to amusing myself and there was a lot here to distract me.

An hour passed. I wondered how much longer I'd have to wait. Suddenly the front door of the house swung open and I heard a voice behind me. Turning round, I froze at the sight of an old lady in the doorway.

'Hello, what have we got here, then?' she said in a calm, gentle tone.

I put my doll in front of my face. 'Fuck off,' I muttered.

The old lady reached down and unpinned the note from my chest. 'Now then, we don't tolerate bad language here,' she said. She took a firm grasp of my hand and led me inside the house. Within moments several children had gathered in the hallway. They stared at me, saying nothing. My legs began to tremble.

Another lady appeared. 'Who's this?' she asked brightly.

'It appears to be Derek's daughter,' the old lady said, scanning my mum's note. 'Can you stay here with her for a minute while I make a phone call?'

Holding on to my doll for dear life, I tried to avoid the stares of the other children. One of the bigger girls stepped towards me and gave me a dirty look, as if she knew me. She had long mousey hair, just like mine. A skinny boy wearing wonky glasses came up beside her. His white-blond hair was cut into a basin shape and his front teeth were missing.

'You're Teresa,' the boy said. I told him to fuck off too.

The old lady came back and knelt beside me. 'Well, young lady, we're very glad to see you,' she said. 'You've been missing for quite a while now and we've all been worried about you.'

What did she mean? I hadn't been missing. I'd been with my mum. 'Fuck off, fuck off, fuck off!' I shouted.

The children around me laughed, but the old lady's face grew stern. I ran and hid behind a big white door, shaking with fear and confusion. She followed me. 'Don't be scared,' she said. 'I'm Miss Foley, a friend of your father's. You're safe now.'

'Leave me alone!' I screamed.

The doorbell rang. Miss Foley went to answer it. A man stepped into the hallway. The girl with long mousey hair and the boy in the wonky glasses ran up to him and clung to his legs.

'Where is she?' he said. I peeped out from behind the door. He turned and walked towards me, his expression eager.

Cowering, I looked up into his face as he reached down and gathered me into his arms. His eyes were full of warmth. Tears rolled down his cheeks as he held me tightly to him.

'Teresa! My little girl!' he sobbed. 'I'm your daddy. We're so glad to have you back. Remember David and Bernadette, your brother and sister? We've all missed you so much.'

'I knew immediately it was her,' Miss Foley said.

'It's her all right,' my dad replied. 'Where did you find her? Have the police been told?'

Dad's life was too chaotic to have us living with him, so he left me with Bernadette and David at Miss Foley's children's home in Putney, South West London. I soon settled in. Even though I was only four, I was used to adapting to new situations. My life was constantly changing. At six months old, I'd been put into care for a month while Mum had an operation. Two years later, when she was again admitted to hospital, Bernadette, David and I spent a couple of months at a children's home in Tooting. Not long after that, Mum ran off with one of her boyfriends and I didn't see her again until the day she sneaked back into our flat and snatched me away behind Dad's back.

After that I lived with her in a big house in the countryside, where she was employed as a housekeeper. But she had her work cut out looking after the house and keeping tabs on an inquisitive toddler. First I broke a mirror. Then I let the dog out. Finally Mum lost the job. Shortly after that she dumped me outside Miss Foley's children's home like a piece of lost baggage.

My mother, Georgina Cooper, had not had an easy life. Her father had died young and she had struggled to look after her younger sisters in a desperately unhappy household. Unbeknown to my dad when he married her, she'd fallen pregnant in her late teens and had been forced by her mother to give up the child for adoption, against her will. Afterwards she suffered from a combination of severe post-natal depression and repressed grief. I don't think she ever really recovered. She was always very affected by her hormones.

In the early 1960s post-natal depression was dismissed as 'baby blues' and went untreated. What's more, there was still a huge stigma attached to having an illegitimate child, so there would have been no sympathy for her loss. Shortly after her baby girl was adopted, she met my father, Derek Cooper, and six weeks later they were married.

Dad was always saying that Mum was mental and had lost her marbles, but it was more a case of not getting the help she needed at that crucial time after the adoption. She took the bereavement and depression with her into their relationship and as the years passed she became totally screwed up by it. I was the last of their three children. The oldest was Bernadette. Two years later came David, and two years after him, I was born, 'on the toilet in a nunnery', as my mum described my entry into the world at St Teresa's Hospital in Wimbledon.

My father was a good man with a strong work ethic and sound morals, but a weakness for drink. He had a large family full of interesting characters, but most of them cut him off after he married Mum. They absolutely hated her and told Dad that she had been a prostitute before he met her. I don't know if it was true or not. Either way, they never had a good word to say about her.

Mum and Dad were married for about eight years before Mum left for good, taking me with her. She was petrified of Dad by the end and claimed that he had beaten her senseless countless times. In turn, Dad accused her of having affairs and said that the real reason I'd gone into care so young was because Mum had tried to suffocate me when I was a baby.

They fought like cat and dog and were always blaming each other for something or other.

'I only just managed to stop her from smothering you,' Dad used to say. 'So I was frantic when she stole you and ran off. I didn't know if I'd ever see you alive again.' It was years before I heard Mum's side of the story.

After she dropped me off at Miss Foley's, I didn't see Mum again for what seemed like ages. I missed her desperately. Even though it was good to be around other children and I enjoyed going to nursery school, nothing can replace your mum. I saw quite a lot of Dad though. He used to come round at the end of the day when Bernadette and David finished school. Dad told us that he couldn't have us to live at home with him. He said he couldn't cope, what with work and everything. He was a trained army mechanic, but he never seemed to hold a job down for long and did all kinds of work, from gardening to helping out behind the bar at the local pub.

His flat was only a couple of streets away from Miss Foley's, but it seemed like another world. Situated on the second floor of a huge 1960s concrete council block, at the top of a dark, gloomy flight of stairs, it was a boxy three-bedroom maisonette with low ceilings. Since Dad couldn't be bothered with housework, it was always a tip.

I got on well with Miss Foley. She'd known my dad for a long time and they were good friends. Although I had a few run-ins with her over the next eighteen months, she seemed genuinely fond of me. She was strict but kind, like a matron in an old film. You always knew where you were with her.

I dreaded hearing the words, 'Your dad can't make it tonight.' The only time I really felt part of a family was when he visited. The rest of the time Bernadette and David acted as if I didn't exist. Bernadette, in particular, wasn't at all sisterly towards me. From the start I had the feeling that she disliked me, and she was always my dad's favourite.

One Saturday in July, Bernadette, David and I were playing in Miss Foley's dining room, where the toys were kept. It was really hot and the windows were open to let in fresh air. I was excited because Dad was due to arrive any minute and take us home for the weekend. I tried to fill the time until he came by playing with a toy train. Suddenly David snatched the train away from me. 'Give it back!' I shouted.

He pushed me away and I fell backwards onto the floor. 'He's older than you,' Bernadette said. 'If he wants the toy you have to give it to him.'

'No!' I protested. I got up and charged towards him, intent on getting the train back. The next thing I knew I was dangling upside down out of the window, hanging precariously between wall and fence, my face dragging through cobwebs and leaves. Bernadette and David held onto my ankles, threatening to drop me on my head. I screamed for dear life.

By the time Miss Foley came to investigate the noise, they had pulled me roughly back inside.

'What's wrong with Teresa?'

'Just another one of her silly tantrums, Miss,' Bernadette said, sweet as pie.

'Calm down and be quiet,' Miss Foley told me.

'Fuck off!' I shouted hysterically.

Miss Foley pursed her lips. Taking my hand, she led me to the laundry room. 'You've got a very dirty mouth,' she said. 'Let's wash it out.' With that she shoved a big red bar of Lifebuoy soap into my mouth.

I choked and retched several times, but she kept ramming it back into my mouth. Just when I thought I was going to vomit all over her, she finally pulled it out. 'Now rinse your mouth out,' she said. No matter how much water I sluiced around my mouth, I couldn't get rid of the taste. There was soap stuck to the back of my teeth all day.

A few minutes later, Dad arrived. 'What's wrong with you, Teresa?' he asked. 'You look like you've swallowed a lemon.'

'Miss Foley washed her mouth out for saying bad words,' Bernadette said.

'Mum says those words all the time,' I said in my defence.

'Yes, you're just like your mother,' Dad sighed. 'You look like her, you sound like her and you even swear like her.'

Dad had a pretty Irish girlfriend called Martha, who used to look after us while he was down the pub. She took us to the park with her three children and fed us piles of sandwiches. Sometimes it was better to stay at Martha's house, because Dad and his drinking pals would often stay up late into the night. I was often exhausted from lack of sleep when he dropped us back at Miss Foley's on a Sunday night.

That December our Christmas treat was a trip to see *The Three Little Pigs on Ice* in Wimbledon. I was really excited as we piled into the back of the van. There were nine of us children, plus Miss Foley and another lady. Best of all, Dad was driving us.

The brightly lit ice rink was packed with noisy, expectant kids and their parents. A few minutes after we'd found our seats, the lights dipped and the arena went quiet. I snuggled up to Dad, who was sitting beside me. He gave me a squeeze. I felt so happy.

Loud music started playing and dozens of multicoloured spots of light swirled around the arena. Then the three pigs appeared in the middle of the ice, skating in time to the music, bathed in spotlights. I was entranced. It was just like something off the telly, a dream come true. I'd never seen anything so magical. When the big bad wolf came on, we were encouraged to shout out a warning to the little pigs. I screamed myself hoarse. 'Behind you! Over there!'

When the show ended, I couldn't stop clapping. I was still so caught up in its fairytale dream that I didn't watch where I was going as we filed out of our seats. Thrilled to be handed a goodie bag full of Disney toys and sweets, I dawdled behind the others while I explored its contents.

When I next looked up, everyone was gone. My heart started thumping. Where was Dad? Where were Bernadette and David? The arena was practically empty. The only people I could see were a couple of cleaners moving methodically along the lines of seats.

I ran around frantically, calling out for Dad. Finally a security guard found me and took me to the stage manager's office. It was full of people. 'Where are your mummy and daddy?' someone asked. I burst into tears. I had no idea.

A policeman turned up to question me. He grabbed a handful of sweets off a nearby counter and pushed them into my small hands. But by now I was too distraught to answer his questions. I wasn't interested in eating sweets either. I just couldn't believe that Dad and the others had left without me. I was four and a half years old.

Suddenly the door of the office opened and in came the three little pigs! Everyone laughed as they sang and danced around the room. Soon I was laughing too, especially when my idols showered me with toys and sweets. They treated me like a princess and I got to meet the other characters and explore their dressing rooms.

Eventually Miss Foley came back to pick me up. She told me off for straying, but no one told her off for forgetting me.

It was only when the police rang that anyone realised I hadn't come home with them. They hadn't missed me at all. Young as I was, this thought festered inside me for weeks.

I found it hard to believe that Bernadette hadn't noticed I wasn't in the van, but I suppose it's possible that she was distracted by the excitement of seeing the show. I wondered if she had been secretly pleased that I'd been left behind. She never bothered much with me and we rarely played together. She preferred to sit on the stairs and watch the world go by through the gaps in the banister.

Like a lot of older sisters, she seemed to take pleasure in seeing me upset, or in trouble. Aware of how much I loved my long hair, she was all for it when Miss Foley decided that I needed a haircut. She laughed as one of Miss Foley's assistants chopped it off. 'Fuck off!' I shouted, enraged. I ended up having my mouth washed out three times that day. I must have eaten a whole bar of Lifebuoy by bedtime.

A couple of days later I came across a big pair of scissors in the bathroom. One of the staff had left them on a shelf after cutting a plaster strip for another child. I picked them up and headed for the landing, where there was a good view of Bernadette sitting halfway down the stairs. Tiptoeing towards her, focused on her hair, I opened the scissors in anticipation of my first snip.

Grabbing my chance, I lunged forward and hacked a great lump of hair from the back of her head. She howled and jumped on me, trying to wrestle the scissors out of my hand. 'Stop it now, girls!' snapped Miss Foley as she rushed up the stairs to separate us. It was a wonder neither of us was injured.

Some of the other children in the home were quite disturbed. There was a horrible kid called Kevin who seemed to get a kick out of biting people, and I was one of his main targets. The staff used to press coins on my bite wounds to stop them getting infected or inflamed. It was an old wives' remedy, but it seemed to work.

I got my own back on Kevin whenever we were served liver. Like most kids, I hated liver and would do anything to avoid eating it. I pretended to like it, but when no one was looking, I'd flick bits of it off my plate so that they landed under Kevin's chair. Then he'd get told off and the staff would give him another helping.

In October 1972, when I was five years old, we went back to live with Dad. I was thrilled to be going home. 'Come back and see us soon,' Miss Foley said, giving me a squeeze when Dad came to pick us up. I felt a tug in my heart. Little did I know how much I was going to miss her in the months to come.

Things went horribly wrong almost from the moment we moved back into Dad's. He was always drunk, always legless, always aggressive and always having parties at one and two o'clock in the morning. After they'd finished down the pub, he and his mates would come back to the maisonette and sit there getting drunk all night, playing music on the old-fashioned stereo, keeping us awake. No one looked after us while he was down the pub.

He didn't wash anything. He didn't clean up. There was rarely any food in the house. Occasionally we'd come back from school to find he'd tidied up a bit and then he'd do us egg and bacon, or beans on toast, but mostly we lived off biscuits and crisps. He sometimes made an effort on Saturday. David and I would watch *Dr Who* on the old black and white telly in the kitchen while Dad chopped potatoes. David used to make me laugh by saying, 'Gobble gobble, chop chop!' but Dad always told him to shut up.

I don't have many memories from that time. Mostly I remember Dad being drunk. After a year of chaos, he approached Wandsworth Social Services and requested that we be taken into care again. That's how we ended up at The Haven children's home in Crystal Palace Park Road in South East London. He was sad to let us go, but came to visit us there at least once a month and often telephoned.

Run by the Salvation Army and housed in a huge old Victorian mansion that had once been a hospital, The Haven was a home for children aged two to twelve from all over London. We spent three years there and I liked everything about it from day one. The kids were divided according to their age and assigned to one of four groups – Eisenhower, Churchill, Schweitzer and Kennedy – and each group had its own colour and identity. I was put in Kennedy (yellow) in the charge of Captain Drummond, a really nice middle-aged woman with sparkly blue eyes.

I could see right across London from my bedroom window. I used to sit and gaze for hours at the lights at the top of the Crystal Palace transmitter, which Captain Drummond called, 'our very own Eiffel Tower'. The staff called me a dreamer, but I was also known as 'Gabby-Abby' because I talked too much. I couldn't help it. I'm a Gemini and we chat for England.

The Haven staff seemed genuinely to care. When I fell off the roundabout in the back garden or was stung by a hornet or bitten by the cook's dog, they were full of sympathy and took me straight to the doctor. Punishments for bad behaviour never went beyond being sent to your room or made to sit on the equivalent of a 'naughty step'. I never saw any violence or abuse the whole time I was there.

There was a trampoline in one of the rooms and one day

I fell off it and landed on the floor right next to Captain Drummond, with a view directly up her skirt. 'I can see your knickers!' I shouted gleefully.

She didn't see the funny side. 'You mustn't say things like that,' she said sternly and sent me to my room.

We went on loads of trips. One year we bundled into a coach and went to the annual Policeman's Ball in Kent, a charity event that raised money for children's homes, among other causes. There was a long line of tables piled high with puddings and sweets, so we kids had a wail of a time. Dickie Davies was there, the sports presenter with bushy eyebrows. Bernadette thought he was lovely, so she wasn't best pleased when he picked me up and made a fuss of me.

Every September we'd go to a children's party at the Miss World contest in London, organised by Eric and Julia Morley. I loved it. It was like a fairytale adventure. The Morleys took a lot of interest in us and I think they donated money to various children's homes as well. We didn't actually watch the contest, although we did get to meet the contestants. They would come downstairs loaded with presents to watch us eat jelly and ice cream and play party games. They were stunning! David fell in love with one of them and she gave him a signed photograph.

I imagined Mum to be beautiful like the Miss World contestants. By now I was finding it hard to picture her, but in my dreams she was a long-lost princess. I was sure that one day she would arrive at The Haven, dressed in a beautiful gown and a tiara. Then she'd shower me with gifts and sweep me away to a life of luxury in a far-off palace.

One day she really did come to visit. Although she wasn't wearing a shimmering dress, she was even more beautiful than I had imagined her to be. She was tall and slim with short blonde hair and amazing blue eyes. She was very loving too, and wouldn't stop kissing and cuddling me. A lifelong fan of Avon products, she brought us a wonderful selection of shampoos and bubble bath, along with a ring with a ladybird on it for Bernadette and a Noddy ring for me. We went to the dinosaur section of Crystal Palace Park and spent a happy afternoon in the sunshine. Then, just as suddenly as she had arrived, she was gone. I can still remember how hollow I felt after she left.

At first I really missed her, but I was young and there were plenty of distractions. Next door to The Haven there was an old people's home and if we were good we were allowed to go and visit the residents. Bernadette hated it, but I'd have my hand up immediately when the staff asked us if we wanted to go. The old people were always pleased to see us. I had a great time moving from one old lady's lap to another, chatting away and eating the sweets they'd saved for me.

We were taught that God was love and He was everywhere. This made sense to me because there was a real atmosphere of love among the staff and children at The Haven. I definitely felt loved while I was there. We said grace before each meal and the Lord's Prayer every night before bed, and the staff often used to sing us to sleep. I always prayed for Mum to come back soon.

Every week we went to Sunday school, where we were taught Bible stories. Captain Drummond used to give me a coin to put in the collection box at church, but one day I kept it and spent it on gobstoppers and bubblegum on the way home instead. I buried my goodies at the foot of one of the tall fir trees that lined the pathway leading back to The Haven, but when I went back later to collect them they were gone. I was convinced that it was God's way of punishing me.

Once a year we held a fete in the back garden. We'd knock on doors all around Crystal Palace and ask people for their empty jam and coffee jars, which we soaked in a great big sink of water to get the labels off. Then we'd decorate the lids, stick new labels on, fill them with bath salts and sell them at the fete. We made all kinds of things to raise money for the home, and the locals would come along to support us.

At Easter some benefactor or other would donate a massive Easter egg covered with sugared flowers, as big as a person. The staff broke it up into huge thick pieces and divided it among us. One day I slipped into the room where the pieces were kept, took a great big piece and ran off with it. Coincidentally I went down with a horrific bout of gastric flu later that day, which I was convinced was another punishment from God. The vomiting and diarrhoea went on for days and days and throughout it all I prayed intensely for God's forgiveness. I vowed never to steal again.

Each year at Christmas an enormous fir tree was delivered on a big army truck – a present from the Queen, so the staff said. There were lots of beautifully wrapped presents for everyone, donated by various children's charities. The tree was always unbelievably tall, like something from the land of giants in a fairytale. The whole building exploded with excitement when it arrived. We all rushed into the hall to help decorate it.

One year I was hanging silver baubles on the tree's lower branches when Captain Drummond called me into her office. Bernadette and David were already standing in front of her desk.

'I've got some wonderful news for you, children,' she said. 'You're going home to your father's house for Christmas!

We'll be really sad to say goodbye to you, but won't it be lovely to be living as a family again?'

Two days later, Dad bundled us and our Christmas presents into a blue car. Captain Drummond and several other members of staff came to see us off. One of the staff – a woman named Katherine – was in tears as she waved goodbye. As the car drew away, she broke into sobs. I remember thinking how nice it was to feel loved.

CHAPTER TWO

January 1977

Dad hadn't paid the gas and electric bills, so the flat was freezing cold. The sitting room stank of booze and fags. The carpet was sticky, the atmosphere depressing.

Dad wasn't just drunk in the evenings anymore. He was drunk all day and all night, every day, for long stretches at a time. Almost every penny he got from the social and his jobs on the side went on getting pissed. He didn't think to go and buy food. The fridge was always empty. There was a constant rumbling in my belly. Birthdays and Christmas didn't figure at all. I don't remember even seeing Dad on my tenth birthday, let alone getting a card or present.

Dad's method of laundering our clothes was to throw them into a bucket to soak and then forget about them. Days, sometimes weeks later – whenever the smell of stale water became overpowering – he'd rinse them out in the sink. Everything I wore reeked of damp, mould or dirt. In the absence of hot water, I rarely bathed or washed my hair. Before long I was skinny, scruffy and filthy.

At fourteen, Bernadette was old enough to disappear off to her friends' houses, leaving David and me to fend for ourselves. Every morning we woke up hungry. If Dad was in a particularly good mood, he might go out and buy food for breakfast. The rest of the time we had to beg him for money for chips, and when he couldn't or wouldn't give us any, we had to improvise.

We did a lot of out-of-season carol singing, which yielded results even in the height of summer. People gave us money, socks, old jumpers and fruit. Mostly, all we could afford to buy was biscuits.

One day David took a chisel to the iced-up freezer compartment at the top of the fridge, but all he found was a packet of ancient sausages, so we fed them to the cats that roamed outside a little old lady's house next door to the flats. With her straggly silver hair and baby blue eyes, the old lady was very intriguing. She had the most unlikely son – a biker who wore tasselled leather jackets and looked like a member of Hell's Angels.

I loved her cats, especially the one I named Blackie. He purred a lot and was so silky to touch. He would come running to me every time I called him from outside the flats, and then he'd follow me along the wall and the fence to the base of a huge tree, where I'd sit and stroke him. He was my only real friend and I felt peaceful around him.

Dad didn't like me touching the cats because I kept getting ringworm from them, but I didn't care. I didn't get love from my dad. I didn't get it from my sister and the other kids in the flats were always taunting me. So I found my world in those cats, especially Blackie.

One day he stopped coming when I called. I never found out why. I felt very alone without him and kept going back to the wall to look for him, but he never appeared again. I cried for weeks over Blackie.

When we didn't have any money and Dad was down the pub, David would sit me on the photo booth outside the local Asian deli, which had a wall running along beside it. 'I'm going in the shop for something to eat,' he'd say. 'When I shout "run", run!'

Sure enough, a few moments later he'd come bolting out of the shop clutching a packet of biscuits, which were the easiest thing to snatch because they were closest to the door. I'd jump off the photo booth onto the wall and sprint around the corner to a nearby block of flats, where we'd eat the biscuits in a reeking stairwell. The shopkeepers always chased David, but they never caught him.

He didn't steal for the sake of stealing. He had to steal, to keep himself – and me – alive. But it definitely set him down the wrong path. One freezing cold winter's day when we were absolutely starving, he went through Dad's pockets while Dad was out cold on the sofa, pissed as a cricket. It was a dangerous game to be playing, because if Dad woke up there would be all hell to pay. But what was the alternative? Not realising that he was taking the biggest note of the lot, David tentatively pulled a twenty-pound note out of Dad's trouser pocket.

It was snowing as we trudged towards the chip shop opposite Dad's local, the Fox and Hounds. We bought a bag of chips each, which felt like luxury because we usually had to share a bag. I can still remember how delicious every mouthful tasted. It was the best meal ever. Next we went on the bumper cars at the little fairground next to the pub, something we'd always longed to do. I loved the crazy rush of adrenalin as I crashed around that little rink. We buried the rest of the money in the snow round the back of the pub, for safekeeping.

Back at home, Dad was shouting and crying, going mad about the missing note. 'What have you done with it?' he screamed at us. 'I need that money! Give it back now!'

After forcing a confession out of us, he marched us up to the Fox and Hounds and made us dig through the snow. We searched for ages but the money was either gone or lost. He gave us a hiding when we got back to the flat. Then he went back to the pub and got pissed again.

Dad hit us a lot. Not just the odd slap – he would really lay into us. Once he broke a tennis racquet over my head. Usually he'd start on me first. His excuse would be that I resembled Mum in some way: I sounded like Mum; I cried like she did; I looked like her. He hated being reminded of Mum. David often came to the rescue. He would stand in between us and take the blows that were meant for me. Dazed and distracted, Dad would then focus his drunken aggression on my brother instead.

A beating usually meant being smacked around the head, kicked, pushed and thrown against the wall, but occasionally Dad took it even further. When the police told him that David had stolen a bike, he threw him over the banisters, dragged him into the bathroom, grabbed him by his head and smacked his face into the sink. I looked on aghast as the skin on my brother's face split across his eye and started spurting blood. It was like a horror film. The blood went everywhere.

One particular time, Dad was beating me so hard and swearing so vehemently that his false teeth shot out and landed on the floor. It was totally unexpected. He stood stock still with a look of amazement on his face. I was really hurting, but I couldn't help laughing, and once I'd started I couldn't stop. Even Dad had to laugh, right in the middle of hitting me. For a change I was off the hook without David having to step in between us.

Dad had his good moments though. One happy incident can see you through twenty bad ones, which is why when I look back, the good outweighs the bad. At Easter he went into the sweet shop halfway down Putney Hill and bought us a Kinder Egg each. We sat for hours playing with the toys we found inside. In the early summer we went on a day trip to Brighton with his new girlfriend, Bella. He was happy that day, so we all had a really good time, even David.

My brother was a mass of contradictions. He stole for me and shielded me from Dad, but he could also be really mean to me, so it was sometimes hard to know where I stood with him, or what he was going to do next.

I loved all kinds of animals, so I was thrilled when we found a live newt at Kingsmere Pond on Wimbledon Common. Dad said we couldn't take it home, but unfortunately for the newt we smuggled it into the flat anyway. If I'd known what David had planned for it I would have thrown it back into the pond.

At home David moved the kitchen table into the sitting room, placed a bowl of hot water on the floor and spent the next hour knocking the poor animal off the table into the water. I begged him to stop – I was so upset that I became hysterical – but he just kept telling me to shut up. Eventually he got fed up because the newt had no life left in it. I tried to stroke it back to life. It twitched a bit and then died.

I buried it in an Altoids Mints tin in the gardens behind the flats. A few days later I noticed that its little grave had been disturbed and went to investigate. Suddenly my brother and his friend Paul appeared out of nowhere, brandishing the poor, dead, rotten, disinterred newt. They held me down and tried to force it into my mouth but I fought them off and ran away.

David was attracted to danger. He was always throwing himself off great heights, whether it was scaffolding or the top diving board at Putney Swimming Baths. One day he jumped off a high wall and broke his ankle severely. I was inside with Dad when the neighbours came to tell us that he'd been injured. Dad was too pissed to go and see what had happened, so I went instead. I found David lying on the ground, screaming in agony. 'Wait here, I'll get help,' I said, sprinting back to the flat.

Dad was still slumped in his chair, barely conscious. I tried to pull him up, but he was too heavy for me. 'David's really hurt,' I yelled. 'You've got to do something!' Dad was furious that he had to take my brother to hospital, because it meant less drinking time down the pub.

When they came home several hours later, David had a plaster cast on his leg. But the next day, while Dad was at the pub, he hacked it off with a pair of scissors. Dad went mad, whacked David and took him back to the hospital, where they put on another, thicker cast.

A week or so later, he cut it off again. This time the doctors were so annoyed that they put on a fibreglass cast. Undeterred, David borrowed a saw and sawed it off.

'Doesn't it hurt?' I asked.

'Does it matter?' he said. He just didn't care about anything.

Of the three siblings, I think David probably had it the hardest. We all knew that Bernadette was our dad's favourite. Dad didn't provide David and me with basic food, but he bought Bernadette clothes and dolls and paid for dancing and trumpet lessons. It was no secret that I was Mum's favourite. She constantly assured me – on the phone or during her occasional visits – that she was trying to get herself into a stable and settled position, so that she could have me to live with her. But both Mum and Dad rejected David, which must have been very difficult for him.

His reputation for being bad and wild didn't do me any favours with the kids on our block. Wearing shabby, unwashed clothes didn't help either. The other kids were wicked to us and called us every name under the sun. We were scum to them. They scared me because whenever they saw me they'd spit or shake their fists and threaten violence. Not one of them ever had a kind word for me – more likely I'd get a slap. So I'd sit on the stairs of the flats, paralysed by fear, unable to go up or down. No one ever wanted to play with me, not even the girls my own age.

Our next door neighbour always talked to me like I was dirt. I used to get scared walking past her door. Most of the adult neighbours were polite to me, but she wasn't. She would stand in the doorway and stare me out as I walked past, so I'd wait in the stairwell until she went inside before I ran into Dad's. She knew we were beaten at home and yet she was still horrible to us. I was terrified of her son. He used to chase David around and beat him up. Her daughter was always getting me into trouble with the other kids.

Down the stairs lived a girl called Susie. She was the same age as me and went to the same school. One day her mum Barbara told her to invite me out for the day. They also invited another girl called Jill. We took a picnic to Box Hill. It was a beautiful sunny day.

As soon as we arrived, Susie and Jill sent me to Coventry. It's a horrible feeling when someone won't say a word to you or even look at you. I spent most of the day talking to Barbara while Susie and Jill played badminton and styled each other's hair. Then a man wearing a black protective glove walked past. Perched on the glove was a huge, chained falcon. It fascinated me so much that I stopped caring that the girls weren't talking to me.

Towards the end of the afternoon I stood up and launched myself down the hill at breakneck speed. The feeling of freedom was exhilarating. I was intoxicated by the fresh air and sense of wide, open space. Except when Dad took us to visit our nan at Roehampton Vale, I rarely went further than the local high street and pub.

We had regular visits from a social worker from Wandsworth Social Services – a kind lady called Nicky Fletcher. She meant well, but I don't think she realised quite how bad things were for us at home. Dad always knew about her visits in advance, so he'd make sure he was sober – and the flat relatively tidy – when she came to see us. Still, she knew enough to realise that there was no chance of Dad taking us on holiday, so she arranged for Bernadette, David and me to join The Haven's annual holiday in Hastings.

It was the long hot summer of 1977 and I had just turned ten. We spent every day on the beach, building sandcastles and playing rounders. At night we camped in a church hall. I loved every minute of it. But on the last day the mood suddenly changed. I was happily playing a ball game near the cabin on the beachfront, where the staff were listening to the radio and making sandwiches and tea. A little boy started screaming that a dog had run off with his ice lolly, which I found hilarious. I turned round to tell Captain Drummond, but inexplicably she and the other staff had tears streaming down their faces.

'What's wrong?' I said, feeling alarmed as they began to bawl their eyes out.

'The King is dead!' Captain Drummond wailed.

'Oh,' I said. 'Come and play ball?'

They were all absolutely devastated. Everyone on the beach was. I couldn't understand it, because apparently none of them had actually known this Elvis bloke they called the King. A real sense of mourning descended on our group and the staff rounded us up and took us back to the church hall. To me, it just seemed a waste of a good afternoon on the beach.

Back at home, Dad was now getting so out of it that he could hardly make it back from the pub. He was constantly falling over and hurting himself. Worried that he might do himself an injury, I started waiting outside the pub doors at closing time until he staggered out. He'd hang on to me as we weaved our way up Putney Hill. It was a long, tiring walk and an embarrassing one, because everyone we passed stared at us. That's when I first realised what a spectacle we were to other people, the scrawny little girl and her drunken, lurching old dad. Bernadette wouldn't go near him in public.

Dad was loved by everyone at the Fox and Hounds, where he often helped out behind the bar. Dad's friends loved me too and sometimes I used to sneak into the pub and watch them playing cards. I was thrilled when Mary, the landlady, taught me how to knit. My first solo attempt was a baby's booty. When it was finished, I rushed to the pub to show everyone. To my dismay, Dad and his friends cracked up laughing. 'Wow!' Dad said, slipping it on his foot. 'When are you going to knit me the other one?' My beginner's lack of perspective meant that I hadn't calculated the dimensions very well.

Around this time, Nicky Fletcher went on maternity leave and was replaced by a new social worker, Elizabeth Pryde. Mrs Pryde definitely disapproved of my trips to the pub. I'll never forget the day I met her. Slim, with blonde bobbed hair, she turned up at the flat wearing a green skirt, a green top, green tights and green shoes. I took an instant dislike to her. Dad did too. He said she was the spitting image of the leader of 'the flaming Tory Party'. David called her 'the leprechaun'. I just thought she looked like a big bogey.

Mrs Pryde was always nice to us in front of her colleagues at the Social Services offices in Putney, but she was another person on home visits. David and I went to her office to ask for money for food a couple of times, but she told us to go away.

When Dad admitted that he was again finding it hard to cope with us, Mrs Pryde arranged for David and me to go into temporary care. I went to Westdean Close Children's Home in Wandsworth, and David went to Blackshaw Road in Tooting. Bernadette was allowed to stay at home because Dad said she wasn't any trouble.

The home at Westdean Close was a big modern building on two floors. I have no idea why I was sent there because it was totally wrong for me. The other kids were quite a bit older than I was and they were a rough, tough bunch. Luckily they decided to take me under their wing and treat me like a baby sister. I dread to think what might have happened if they'd turned against me.

The staff were OK, apart from Tony, a slightly creepy man of about thirty. Tony constantly gave the impression that he was sneering at me. He made a lot of snide remarks about my appearance and took pleasure in pointing out how immature I was for my age. He also seemed to enjoy telling people I was mad. I don't think he really meant it, but it upset me a lot because Dad was always saying that Mum was mad.

Everybody at Westdean smoked. Cigarettes were stolen moments of sophistication, rebellion and secret pleasure. Sharing a fag was a way of bonding. They called it 'two-sing'. Not long after I got there, a couple of girls pushed me up against a wall, put a cigarette in my mouth and lit it. Some of the other kids gathered round to watch me have my first smoke. 'Make sure she inhales!' one of the boys said.

Already pale with fear at being picked on, I went green as I choked on the cigarette's acrid fumes. Feeling panicked, I sucked in as much fresh air as I could before giving it another go. It was important to pass this initiation test. Smoking was cool and I really didn't want to come across as a loser. After a few more puffs, the smoke began to go down more easily. 'You're getting the hang of it,' one of the girls said approvingly. Before long I was totally addicted and spending my school lunch money on packs of ten Embassy.

The Westdean kids broke all the rules. They used to run off secretly at night and meet up with the kids from David's home, which was somehow connected to ours. One night they took me along with them to a park in Tooting. We had to climb over a really high wall to get in. Not having seen David for a few weeks, I was actually quite pleased to clap eyes on him for a change, but he didn't hang around. He and the rest of the gang ran off to another part of the park, leaving me on a bench with a couple of cigarettes and a guy called Bradley.

Bradley and I two-sed the cigs and then he tried to kiss me. 'Omigod,' I thought as his tongue emerged from his mouth and began probing my lips. 'What's he trying to do?' It wasn't anything like the scenes I'd watched between Scarlett O'Hara and Rhett Butler in *Gone with the Wind*, my favourite romantic film. I kept my lips pressed firmly together.

'What's wrong?' he asked.

I searched desperately for something to say, some way of distracting him. Just in time I saw a plane moving across the sky. 'Look! An aeroplane!' I said. I began to chatter about planes, airports, holidays, other countries – anything to delay another uncomfortable kissing moment. As I rambled on, I kept thinking, 'What am I doing here? Why did they leave me with him?' By the time the others came back, I think poor old Bradley was glad to get shot of me.

Around this time Elizabeth Pryde paid me another visit to say that she had arranged for me to be fostered. I was glad to get away from Westdean, but my time with the foster family was very brief. It was a loving family environment – a couple, their two daughters and another foster girl – but I felt uncomfortable. I just didn't fit in. They seemed to expect me to slot automatically into their routine. Suddenly I was supposed to go to a posh school, wearing a smart new uniform, and then come home, do my homework and go to bed. It was a life I'd never had, a life I wasn't used to, and I didn't know how to adapt.

One of the daughters secretly smoked and so did the other foster girl, who had been with them for some time. I shared a bedroom with her, and when she offered me a drag on the cigarette she was smoking out of the window, I accepted. Just after she'd put it out, the mother stormed into the room demanding to know which one of us had been smoking. I got the blame and was subsequently asked to leave. It seemed totally unfair, but I was actually quite glad to get out of there, even if it meant I had to go back to Westdean.

By now I'd moved to Mayfield secondary school in Wandsworth. Bernadette was there too, but a lot of the time she wouldn't acknowledge that I was her sister. The girls in my class didn't want to talk to me either. The only friend I made was a girl called Penny, who was quite scruffy as well, which is probably why we bonded.

Although I could be a real chatterbox, I was often quite withdrawn at school, especially if I'd been home for the weekend and had the bruises to show for it. It's hard to act normally when it hurts to sit down and I think the other kids picked up on that. I was always being bullied.

But on a good day, I really enjoyed some of the lessons. I loved all the practical subjects, like cookery, art and dress-making, and I liked writing essays and poems. My maths was above average and my French was actually quite good. 'Bonjour, Papa,' I used to say when I saw Dad. 'Ça va bien?'

I was proud of my ability to conduct basic conversations in French. I knew how to ask someone their name, what time it was and how to get to the nearest train station. I could chat about food, the weather, school and my family. I knew the words for all the colours, days of the week, months and most everyday household items. I dreamed of going to Paris and practising my new-found language skills. I imagined myself walking through the streets wearing a black beret. 'Je m'appelle Teresa,' I'd say to the people I met. 'Comment t'appelles-tu?'

There were some crucial gaps in my knowledge though. My ignorance of biology meant that I thought I was dying the day I started my period. Unfortunately, creepy Tony was on duty that day.

'I'm bleeding!' I told him, filled with panic. 'I need to go to hospital.'

'You're absolutely bonkers, aren't you?' he said. He loved saying it. He knew how much it upset me. 'Listen, everyone,

Teresa's becoming a woman!' he declared, with a horrible grin on his face. It sounded ominous. I hoped it didn't mean I'd suddenly turn into my mother.

It wasn't long before he had told everyone in the home about my transition to womanhood. Unlocking the supplies cupboard, he took out a couple of sanitary towels and threw them at me. 'Go and put one of these on,' he said, turning his back and walking away.

I gathered that I wasn't going to die, aged twelve. The opposite, in fact – I was growing up. But I still didn't know what to do with a sanitary towels. Back then they involved loops and belts and things – and I was too embarrassed to ask anyone. So the next day in school I just sat there and bled, doubled up with stomach cramps.

When I asked to be excused and got up from my seat, Mrs Brown, the Maths teacher, noticed the stain on my skirt and realised what was going on. She arranged for me to be taken to the medical room to be cleaned up. The school nurse gave me a fresh skirt and showed me how to use a sanitary towel. 'You're having a period,' she said. 'It's very normal.' What a relief it was to hear those words!

Back in class, the girl behind me prodded me. 'Why didn't you tell us you were in a children's home?' she said. Mrs Brown gave me a reassuring smile. She'd obviously told them a bit about my background while I was in the medical room. The girls in my class were much friendlier after that, which made life a bit easier.

One morning the fire alarm went off. We all had to evacuate the building and line up in the playground. After a few minutes, a rumour went down the lines that someone had set fire to the dining room. Then, sure enough, the fire engines arrived.

Next, everyone was speculating about the identity of the culprit. News travels fast in schools. Within a day we all knew who was responsible. 'Have you heard? It was Bridget.' At the time I couldn't put a face to the name. Little did I know that both would come to haunt me in the not too distant future.

At home, where I spent most weekends, Dad was more aggressive than ever, and the beatings he gave us more violent. When David and I sensed the onset of a ferocious mood we would run and hide in the junkyard opposite the flats. The only way in was through a corrugated iron fence, which Dad was never able to negotiate. Instead he would smash himself against it and scream, 'I'm going to kill you!' He was really scary. On the other side of the fence, we quivered with fear.

Amid the debris of metal sheets, broken glass, steel pipes and tools there was a rusty old wreck of a caravan. We took to spending our evenings inside it, with only a candle for a light. Later we progressed to sleeping there, even though it was freezing. Most of the time Dad didn't even notice we were gone.

He often threw us out in a drunken rage. Once we went to Nottingham to try to find Mum, who had written to us from a Nottingham address. With two pounds between us, we took the bus to St Pancras and got on the train, only to be met in Nottingham by the transport police. They tried tracing Mum, but she'd moved on without leaving a forwarding address, so they rang Dad. A social worker took us back to London the next day. We comforted ourselves with the thought that at least we'd got a bed for the night and some hot food, courtesy of Social Services.

Dad chucked us out one freezing cold November night.

We took refuge in the caravan, but after a couple of hours we were chilled to the bone. There was no choice but to brave Dad's moods and go back to the flat. We could see lights on, but there was no answer when we knocked on the door and the piece of string with the key hanging inside the letterbox had been removed. Assuming Dad was comatose, we lay down and fell asleep outside the front door, exhausted.

The next thing I knew I was being shaken awake by a policeman. 'All right, love?' he said. It was three in the morning. Apparently one of the neighbours had rung to report us. It took another hour to rouse Dad. For once I was glad to slip between the filthy, smelly sheets of my bunk bed.

As the situation at home spun out of control, life at Westdean took a sudden turn for the worse. Creepy Tony took to coming into my bedroom and sitting on my bed at night, which made me feel extremely uncomfortable. Something about his dark presence felt wrong. One night I woke up to find him there again and I freaked out, absolutely petrified. I started screaming at him to leave me alone.

'Be quiet!' he hissed, but he couldn't quieten me down. I began sobbing uncontrollably.

Sally, another member of staff, came to investigate the commotion. 'What's up with Teresa?' she asked.

'I have no idea,' Tony said. 'You know how mad she can be.'

'I am not mad!' I yelled. 'You scared me! I woke up and you were on my bed!'

Again I thought about all the times that Dad had described Mum as mad. He was always saying it. Since he constantly reminded me that I was just like Mum, and sometimes added that I was mad like Mum, Tony's comment had hit a nerve. I knew I wasn't mad, but there are only so many times you can be told you're insane before you start worrying about it. Images of Tony on my bed kept flashing through my mind. What had he been doing before I woke up? Had he even touched me? I couldn't remember. All I knew was that my instincts were on high alert.

In his report on the incident, Tony described me as 'a wicked child'. He no longer came to sit on my bed, but I never really felt safe from him or his nasty jibes. I begged Mrs Pryde to send me somewhere else, somewhere like The Haven or Miss Foley's, where I'd be happy again. Unmoved, she told me there was nowhere else for me to go.

CHAPTER THREE

When I did finally leave Westdean Close a couple of months later, I couldn't get out of there fast enough. I was ready and waiting by the front door with my suitcase before the staff even had a chance to tell me to pack. I didn't bother saying goodbye to anyone. I had no friends there.

Bernadette and David were back at the flat in Raynors Road, so I went home to the usual chaos. But this time Mrs Pryde pushed Dad into taking us to be evaluated at the Roehampton Child Guidance Clinic, where we had regular family therapy sessions with Dr Williams, a consultant psychiatrist. I didn't mind going, but the meetings always seemed to end the same way, with Dad and Bernadette ganging up against me and David, calling us mad.

'She's crazy like her mother,' Dad kept telling the doctor.

'And every bit as annoying,' Bernadette would add.

I hadn't seen Mum for more than four years and couldn't recall whether I resembled her or not. I could only assume they were right, and act accordingly, so when Dr Williams asked me awkward questions about the past, I babbled a load of rubbish to avoid giving a straight answer. I wasn't going to tell him about Dad's violence or Bernadette's indifference to me, especially not in front of them. So I just chatted away about the first thing that came into my head, just as I imagined my 'mad' mother would.

Although he tried not to show it, I think this tried Dr Williams's patience sorely. But what was he expecting? He was never going to get me to grass up my own family while we were all in the same room together. I knew that if I told him about Dad hitting us, I'd get a beating when we got home. David could easily turn on me too, so I didn't want to say anything about his behaviour. As for Bernadette, I couldn't help craving her love, even though she had never shown me any, so I wasn't going to complain about her either.

Dr Williams came to the conclusion that it would be better for David and me if we didn't live at home. David went to Dunstable Road Children's Home in Twickenham, but Dr Williams said he was finding it hard to settle on somewhere for me.

'You're an intelligent girl, Teresa, but not very easy to evaluate,' he sighed.

Finally, he arranged for me to make a visit to the adolescent unit at Long Grove Psychiatric Hospital in Epsom.

'But I'm not ill!' I said.

'It won't be forever. Just take a look round and see how you find it,' he suggested.

During this time Dad was going through a really dark phase. His drinking was getting worse, he wasn't earning any money and he was always in a bad mood. So when Mrs Pryde joined Dr Williams in pressuring me to go to the adolescent unit at Long Grove, I decided to give it a try. Anything was better than living at home.

The unit was located in the centre of the hospital. It wasn't a secure unit as such, but it was locked at night, probably to protect us as much as to keep us there. We were allowed into certain parts of the hospital grounds, but I didn't venture far. There were all these mental patients wandering around and I found it a bit scary.

There were about thirty of us in the unit. The other kids were really nice to me. I was twelve and they were all around fifteen and sixteen, so again I suppose I was a bit like a little sister to them. Certainly I seemed to bring out their protective instincts and no one picked on me too much.

The unit was T-shaped, with two dorms on opposite sides of a corridor, the boys' dorm on the right and the girls' dorm on the left. The beds in each dorm were partitioned off with curtains. Beyond the girls' dorm at the far end was a fire door marked 'exit'. To my horror there were also two padded cells hidden away in their own little corridor. Down the left side of the corridor were toilets, bathrooms and doctors' rooms. At the end of the corridor was a play area with a pool table in it, a dining room, a smoking room and a back door leading to the garden where we would sit and play on a makeshift tyre swing.

Every morning before breakfast there was a group meeting in the games area. I often took my knitting along with me, which annoyed some of the kids because all they could hear was the click-click of the needles. I was always hungry and my stomach used to make loud growling sounds too. In the end, I was told not to bring my knitting anymore, but they couldn't do anything about my rumbling tummy.

I made two good friends at the unit – Esther and Sally. Esther was stocky, with greasy shoulder-length hair, and looked a bit like a boy. I liked her from the moment I met her, even though she didn't utter one word in all the time I knew her. If she needed to give an answer she would either nod or write things down. I used to sit on a chair in her cubicle with my feet up and chit-chat away to her for hours. It was great for me, because I love talking! She'd just smile at me as if to say, I'm enjoying just listening to you.

Something awful must have happened to turn Esther mute, but I never found out what it was. A lot of the kids at Long Grove were severely traumatised. Some of them – boys included – had been violently raped or attacked at a very young age. In comparison to most of them, I was the lucky one, and it seemed odd that Dr Williams had wanted to place me there.

I remember asking Dr Staple, the consultant psychiatrist, why I had been sent to Long Grove.

'It's not ideal. It's just a temporary measure,' he told me. He was worried that I was too young to be mixing with the others and agreed that I did not have the same issues and problems.

'So why am I here?' I asked again.

'Good question!' he said, fiddling nervously with his moustache. I never did get a proper answer.

The staff were OK to me, but Esther was petrified of them. She had a phobia about grease, which they tried to cure by smearing butter and lard on her arms. It was awful to watch her being pinned to a chair and made to face her biggest fear. It was torture for her. Things got even worse when they started taking her over to the main hospital, where they gave her drugs and electric shock treatment. It was cruel of them to subject her to added trauma. She used to come back to the unit in a terrible state, crying hysterically. I hated the way they treated her.

They seemed to find Esther's silence very frustrating. One staff member in particular – a guy called Neil – was nastily aggressive in his attempts to force her to speak. One day I came across him shouting at her and another girl, Chrissie, over something they were supposed to have done wrong. He was threatening Esther with a spell in one of the padded cells if she didn't answer him. It looked as if he was about to hit her.

I launched myself at him. 'Don't you dare hurt her!' I yelled.

He turned and grabbed my face. As I pulled away from him, he dug his nails in and dragged them along one of my cheeks. I felt a burning sensation, but had no idea of the damage he had done until Chrissie screeched, 'Oh my God, your face!' There were huge raw stripes down my cheek. He had ripped off practically all the skin on one side.

The police were called in and they interviewed Esther, Chrissie and me. Neil was suspended and I went home for a few days. Dad was shocked to see me. My face looked really bad, all scratched up. It took weeks and weeks to heal properly.

In June we went on a camping trip to Dover. The weather wasn't great but we had a good laugh. On the morning of my thirteenth birthday, some of the lads dragged me out of bed and threw me into the sea. That was my birthday treat. They ripped my tent in the struggle, and of course that night it belted it down with rain. I woke up at 4 a.m. in a soaking wet sleeping bag in a drenched tent. Dripping with rainwater, I made my way over to the staff tent and slept the rest of the night there.

I was small for my age and very skinny, but at least I was officially a teenager. It was 1980, the Specials were big and Sally and I fancied ourselves as rude girls. I dyed my hair every colour under the sun and wore a pair of two-tone burgundy trousers with a white stripe down each side. Sally had a fantastic black and white checked skirt.

Like every other teenage girl, I dreamt of love and romance, and I started getting crushes on every other male I came into proximity with. When I confessed as much to Dr Staple, he told me not to worry. It was totally normal for a girl my age, he assured me.

I had a big crush on a skinhead boy called Kevin. He and his best friend Andy were kings of the castle at the unit. Kevin, especially, was everybody's idol. I was mad about Matt, one of the teachers, too. But my biggest crush was on Bill, one of the porters. Bill was probably in his early thirties, but he was very sweet and charming with me, so when he asked me if he could give me a kiss, I let him. I didn't understand the problem with the age difference. I just thought he was a really nice person. Since I didn't get any attention from the boys in the home because they were into the older girls, it felt good to have someone showing an interest in me. It made me feel special. Then one night a member of staff caught Bill tapping on the girls' dorm window, trying to attract my attention. I never saw him again after that. I think he might have been sacked.

Mum got in contact again and I was allowed to meet up with her. By now I hadn't seen her for five years. It was hard not to be nervous. She was very good-looking, my mum. I was dazzled by her appearance. She flung her arms around me and called me her 'darling girl'.

'Don't worry, I'll get you out of that place,' she told me. 'I want you to come and live with me when I'm settled. Would you like that?'

'Yes please, Mum, as soon as possible,' I said. I didn't see or hear from her again for months.

Dad was a regular visitor though. Sometimes he turned up smelling of booze and other times he only stayed half an hour, but I was always glad to see him. One day I had some exciting news for him.

'Dad, I'm in a show they're putting on!' I told him.

'Are you playing the back end of a donkey?' he joked.

'No, I'm the lead!'

Dad's face was a picture as I explained that a staff member had heard me singing alone in the games area one day. She had immediately complimented me on my voice. At first I hadn't known what the hell she was on about. I'd always thought my voice was terrible. But the next thing I knew I was learning lines and songs and dances – and two weeks later I was up on stage in front of an audience playing Pandora in a musical called *Pandora's Box*.

After the show, a lot of people came up to me and told me I had a wonderful voice. I didn't know how to react. I wasn't used to being told I was good at anything.

Although life wasn't too bad for me at Long Grove, I was restless and longed to be free. Sick of rules and regulations, I ran away one night with Esther and two other girls. It was spooky making our way through the hospital, listening to patients crying and moaning in their wards, knowing that some of them were really dangerous. We got out of a window and scurried over to the shrubbery on the other side of the lawns. I was so tense as we made our way through the bushes that I jumped at every tiny rustle, creak or twig snapping. I kept expecting one of the mental patients to leap out of nowhere and murder me, which the others found hilarious.

It took ages to get out of the grounds. Well, it felt like ages, but perhaps it was only about fifteen minutes. Once we were beyond the gates, we set off in the direction of Epsom train station. It was a very long walk along dark roads and unlit alleyways. It seemed to last forever. But finally we got there, only to find that the station was closed for the night. It was pitch black and deserted.

'We'll have to sleep here and get the first train that comes in the morning,' I said, looking around for a timetable.

Esther nodded and made signs to the effect that we weren't bloody well going back to the unit! It didn't matter that we had no money and no plans to go anywhere particular. We just wanted to jump on a train and get away, even if it meant bunking the fares.

I saw a car approaching. 'Quick! It might be the police,' I whispered. We had already discussed what we would do if a police car passed us. Because Esther looked like a boy, we'd decided to try and pass ourselves off as a drunk couple out late. We put our arms round each other and pretended to kiss. The other two did the same. The police car drove straight past us.

'We fooled them!' I said, laughing.

A few minutes later the car returned for a second look. Busted! The policemen took us straight back to the unit. The staff weren't too bad with us and as I went off to sleep, back in my narrow bed in the girls' dorm with the curtains drawn around me, I couldn't help giggling about Esther's sudden sex change.

At Christmas I was permitted to go and stay with Mum for a few days in Brighton, where she was working as a housekeeper. Bernadette, David and I took the coach from Victoria. I sat next to David. Bernadette found a seat at the back of the coach and pretended not to know us. Mum met us at the other end. She was so happy to see us. It was the first time she'd had us all together since we were small and she was determined to enjoy every minute.

Mum's joy was infectious and we had a lot of fun. On

Christmas Day we wore paper crowns and pulled crackers. There were lots of presents too. After a proper traditional turkey lunch, Mum and Bernadette dressed David up as a girl in a dress and a fur coat. They even did his make-up. He looked ridiculous by the time they'd finished with him. I laughed until the tears streamed down my cheeks. Later on I got legless on sweet wine and threw up all over the bathroom floor. I was mortified, but nothing could dent Mum's good mood. As she helped me to clear up, she told me that she was going to apply for custody of me.

'I want you home with me,' she said, giving me a hug.

On Boxing Day we went to visit some of her friends. They were Indian and gave us a fantastic Indian meal. In the afternoon David and I walked down to the seafront and watched the waves. It was great to spend time with my brother again. He had put me through hell on many occasions, but I loved him all the same.

The following day we returned to London by coach and I reported back to the unit at Long Grove. After such a lovely time with Mum, I really resented being in an institution again. I took to tattooing myself with Quick Ink, a needle and a matchstick, and joined up with a gang of kids to raid the staff bar beer supply.

In late January, Sally heard that her brother had committed suicide by taking an overdose. She was devastated.

'I've got to get home and see my parents. Will you help me get out of this place?' she sobbed.

'I'll come with you, if you like,' I offered. We sneaked out of the unit later that evening and caught the train to London.

There was a heavy atmosphere at Sally's parents' house when we got there. Her mother looked almost mad with grief and shock. Her father sat pale and staring at the wall in the sitting room for hours on end. I wanted to get away, but I felt bad about leaving Sally, so I agreed to stay the night.

When we got back to Long Grove the following day, Dr Staple called me into his office. 'In view of your latest attempt to abscond from the unit, I have written to Wandsworth Social Services to say that it's time for you to leave us,' he said. He went on to explain that I didn't have the kind of problems that the unit specialised in dealing with and he had decided to exclude me. He said that the unit was geared towards helping children with severe trauma and mental health issues, which was not how he would describe me. In his opinion I had coped pretty well with a difficult childhood. There was nothing wrong with my mental health and I did not need psychiatric help.

According to Dr Staple, my problems were social, in which case it was recommended that I go out into the world and live as normal life as possible, going to a normal school and making friends.

'I have suggested to Social Services that they look into the possibility of sending you to a state-run boarding school if you can't live at home. Either way, we are going to have to say goodbye to you.'

After ten months at Long Grove, I was finally moving on. Although it was hard saying goodbye to poor Esther and Sally, I was hugely relieved to be leaving, not least because I didn't want to risk getting the same kind of treatment they were doling out to Esther. She wasn't the only one either. During my time at the unit I saw other kids being punished and given drugs, so I had every reason to want to go. Or so I thought.

Less than a week later I was in court to answer Wandsworth Social Services' application for a full care order. I didn't want to be there. I didn't think it was right. I hadn't done anything wrong and I couldn't understand why it was happening.

The judge explained what a full care order was and asked me if I was happy about it. I wasn't happy about it at all and said so. It just seemed weird. Wandsworth had stripped my mum of her custody rights and handed me to my dad, knowing that he was violent and a drinker, so what did they care?

In the end I didn't have a choice. The judge read out some sort of section and told me that Wandsworth Social Services would now be my full carers instead of my dad. He didn't say that this gave them the right to do what the bloody hell they liked and I didn't realise that I was now completely in their power.

At first I was placed with Miss Foley, at her new children's home in Briar Walk, Putney. It was nice to be back under her wing. She was always very kind to me and trusted me with the little kids. I used to walk them down to the local shop to buy sweets.

It was lovely to be near Dad again too. He was working at the Fox and Hounds and I'd wander down there to play dominoes and rummy with him and his friends. Dad and I used to sit at the piano and sing 'Blue Moon' together. I played the melody and he played the low part. I also helped him to collect up the glasses and clean the mirrors with vinegar. We had such a lovely time. His friends were always very nice to me, even when I thrashed them at cards. I started thinking that I was quite a fun person, someone whose company people might enjoy. It was a real boost to my self-esteem.

Occasionally Dad took me to the working men's club balls

in the function room at Putney Swimming Baths, and to dances at the Conservative Club (even though he voted Labour religiously). He and his friends taught me to waltz and fox trot and a little cha cha cha. I loved it. I wasn't a bad dancer. I would even go so far as to say I was quite graceful.

Social Services were not happy about me going to see Dad at the pub. 'It's a bad influence,' my social worker told him with a frown.

She kept on at me about going to boarding school. 'But I like the way things are,' I told her. Dad and I were bonding finally. He didn't hit me anymore. Life was better than it had been for a long while.

'You can't stay at Miss Foley's forever. It's only a temporary option, and you know it.'

She told me about a small, specialised boarding school in the middle of the Kent countryside that took girls aged thirteen to sixteen. It was run by something called the Council of Social Responsibility.

'There is so much more space and greenery than there is in London, and it's near the sea,' she said. 'I've got a girl who is doing really well there. It's a very relaxed, happy place and there are no more than fifteen girls, so everyone gets lots of attention.'

It sounded good. I had always craved attention. I pictured long walks on the beach and through fields. I imagined myself sitting in the middle of a happy, laughing group, playing cards and telling jokes and stories. I told her I'd think about it.

Meanwhile Mum sent me a note telling me to meet her outside Miss Foley's. I wasn't supposed to see her without permission, so I had to sneak away without telling anyone where I was going. That day she wasn't the happy manic person we'd spent Christmas with. She seemed very nervous and distressed and kept clutching my arm as she spoke.

'Are those bastards getting you down?' she asked.

'Who do you mean, Mum?'

She shook her head sadly. 'There's no hope for you, Teresa. I'm sorry to say it, but it's true. I know what's going to happen to you. No one will ever want you. You're going to spend your life being shunted from pillar to post like an unwanted piece of baggage. You're just no good.'

Her words really upset me. I began to cry. 'I don't understand. Why are you saying this?'

'It's all over,' she went on. 'Nobody is ever going to love you. You're very ugly, you know. I can hardly bear to look at you sometimes. Ugly, ugly girl! I don't want you to suffer any more. No one cares about you, so I've come to give you something that will help you. If you don't do as I tell you then you will suffer. Promise me you'll do as I say. Promise me!'

'I promise, Mum,' I replied through my tears. She was still my princess on a pedestal and I believed every word she said. I would have done anything for her.

She rifled through her handbag and pulled out a box of pills, which she pressed into my hand. Staring intensely into my eyes, she said, 'In the medicine cabinet at Raynors Road you will find a brown bottle of pills with a white label. Your dad is never without them. I want you to swallow them along with the pills I've just given you.' She took hold of my shoulders and gently shook me. 'Listen to me, Teresa, it's for the best. You'll be better off. And it's not a bad way to go.'

She went on and on, begging me to take the pills and end my life, until I was distressed to the point that I could no longer think clearly. Eventually we said goodbye. Drying my tears, I headed off to the Fox and Hounds to ask Dad for the key to the flat. I didn't mention that I'd just seen Mum.

'What do you want?' he said, handing over a bunch of keys.

I tried to seem casual. 'Oh, just some clothes.'

At the flat I headed straight to the medicine cabinet. It was funny – I'd never really noticed it before and I'd certainly never opened it. I took all three of the tablets in the bottle Mum had described, plus the ones she had given me. Then I sat down and wrote a note to Bernadette, telling her that I was going to die.

I dropped the keys off with Dad on my way back to Miss Foley's. I also gave him the note addressed to Bernadette, telling him not to read it. He was honourable like that; I knew he wouldn't open it. He gave it to Bernadette when she passed by the pub.

Back at Miss Foley's, I went into my room and lay down. Some time later, a member of staff called Mark came into my bedroom and asked if I was all right.

'Not really,' I said. I felt woozy and had stomach ache.

'Bernadette has rung and she's very concerned about you. She thinks you might have taken some tablets. Have you?'

'Yes, but I'm OK though.'

'You don't look OK. What have you taken? Show me. They could kill you.'

I didn't understand the permanence of death. I just knew that my mum wanted me dead and I was trying to please her by doing what I'd been told to do. I thought it would please both Mum and Dad.

Mark took me to hospital, where the doctors concluded that what I'd taken was not enough to do any real damage, mainly because the pills Mum had given me were laxatives. The pills in Dad's medicine cabinet were tranquillisers though, so it was lucky there had only been three in the bottle.

I went to sleep at the hospital and woke up amazed that I hadn't died. Seeing a nurse, I thought, 'Hang about, this isn't heaven!' The whole incident had given me a bit of a fright as well as a bad tummy. I asked for my mum but she wasn't there, even though Miss Foley had rung and told her what had happened. I didn't see her for a while after that. It was hard not to hate her.

What was her motive for persuading me to commit suicide? I've often wondered. Perhaps she felt that if she couldn't have me, why should anyone else? Or maybe she wanted to save me from the same mental health system that had let her down so badly and destroyed her soul? It's impossible to know. She was a sick woman who had been in and out of hospital for nearly two decades.

I told Miss Foley the truth of what had happened. I'm not sure if she believed me that Mum had told me to do it, but we had a good talk in the sitting room and she gave me a lovely cuddle.

'There are to be no more secret meetings with your mum,' she chided gently.

At our next meeting, Mrs Pride my social worker informed me that it was time to make a decision about boarding school.

'What are my choices?' I asked.

It was Kendall House – the wonderful haven in Gravesend, Kent – or nothing, she said. 'There's a space for you now and I believe you will be happy there.'

Miss Foley seemed less certain that it was the right place for me. 'Are you sure?' she asked. She was frowning. She seemed anxious.

'I need to be around other girls my age, and it will be good for me to be in the countryside,' I explained, parroting the official Social Services line. 'You know how much I love animals and nature.'

It was only later, when it was too late to change my mind, that David warned me not to trust Social Services. 'I wouldn't believe one word they say,' he said. My heart began to thump. He was right, of course. They had only started being nice to me when the business of boarding school had come up.

The day before I left for Kendall House I received a letter from Mum. Inside it, she had enclosed a St Christopher pendant on a silver chain. 'St Christopher is the patron saint of travellers,' she'd written. 'He will protect you on your journey.' I was wearing it as I got into Mrs Pryde's car. Mark loaded my bags into the boot and we set off. Miss Foley waved until the car was out of sight.

CHAPTER FOUR

25 June 1981

The journey seemed to go on for ages. I was gasping for a cigarette to calm my nerves, but Mrs Pryde had made me put my packet of JPS in the boot. I kept asking her to pull over.

'Not much further now,' she said in the singsong tone she always used with David and me in front of her colleagues at the Putney Social Services office.

'I'm thirsty,' I said. 'Please can we stop for a drink?'

'Hang on, we're nearly there!' she chirped.

Something didn't feel right. She was being too cheery, too pleasant. I began to tense up. What if Kendall House wasn't as nice as everyone had made out? My heart pounded as we sped out of London through the suburbs and into Kent, passing towns and fields along the way. Finally, we drove along a tree-lined street and pulled up outside a big detached red-brick Victorian house. It had a grey slate roof and huge bay windows above and on either side of an arched doorway. The windows were hung with drab net curtains. It wasn't a bit like I had imagined and didn't even remotely resemble an idyllic mansion in the countryside.

'Here we are! Kendall House!' Mrs Pryde was still speaking in that false tra-la-la voice, as if we were friends on a lovely day out.

She got out of the car. I stayed put. Feeling really uptight, I said I wasn't going anywhere until I'd had a fag. She went up to the front door and knocked.

'Come along, Teresa,' she coaxed. 'You can have a cigarette the moment we're inside, I promise.' She took my bags out of the boot and dumped them on the doorstep. Reluctantly, I got out of the car.

I could hear the clink of keys and locks turning as we waited outside the double doors at the entrance to the building. 'This isn't how you described it,' I said. She said nothing.

Eventually the doors swung open and a middle-aged woman appeared in the doorway. 'Welcome to Kendall House,' she said. 'I'm Kate.'

'Hi,' I mumbled, trying to force a smile. I'd been in and out of homes all of my life, but this was different. I had a very bad feeling about it. My heart was racing as we stepped inside.

Kate briskly locked the front door behind us. Directly in front of us was another door, also locked. For the moment we were trapped. She sorted through a big bunch of keys, found the one she was looking for and skewered the keyhole. We entered a long hall with several doors leading off it.

'Teresa, you come with me,' Kate said. 'Mrs Pryde will log you in and go through the necessary paperwork in the office.'

Mrs Pryde halted outside the first door on the right, and knocked. A key turned. The door opened. Kate led me down the hall and through a heavy wooden door, which creaked as she pushed it open. We came to another door. She jabbed it with a key. 'Here we are,' she said. 'The staffroom.'

'Why are so many doors locked? Is there a problem with burglaries in this area?' I asked.

'Let's start getting you organised now, shall we?' she said brightly, totally ignoring the question.

'Can I have a cigarette, please?' I said. 'I was promised I could have one as soon as we got here.'

She smiled. 'I'm sorry, but girls are not allowed to smoke on the premises.'

My heart sank as she told me that cigarettes were a privilege that had to be earned. 'Kendall House has a system of rewards and punishments to encourage good behaviour in the girls,' she explained, going on to list some of the other so-called privileges, which ranged from walks to family visits.

'You can't stop my dad coming to see me!' I protested. 'He'll bust his way in if you try.'

Her eyes narrowed. 'In the beginning, nobody is allowed visitors or phone calls,' she said. 'You'll need time to settle in. But after that, if you behave well, you'll be able to ring him and arrange a visit.'

My head swam. I couldn't bear the idea of not seeing my dad, let alone not speaking to him. He wasn't the greatest father, but I loved him all the same.

'He said he'd come with my sister Bernadette next weekend,' I said, hoping that this would somehow change her mind. 'Mrs Pryde said it would be fine.'

'Well, I can assure you that it's not going to happen,' Kate said sternly.

Tears pricked my eyes. 'Why not?' I asked. 'He's my dad. I should be able to see him, and my sister too.'

She smiled. 'It's one of the rules. It's the same for everybody. All the girls have to obey them, not only you.'

A lump rose in my throat. The urge to talk to Dad was overwhelming. 'Can I just ring him and give him the number here, then?'

'No, sorry, that's not allowed. I'll drop him a line later with all the necessary information.'

The door opened and another woman entered the room. 'Ah, Mrs Kale,' said Kate. 'This is Teresa, the new girl. Will you stay here with her while I go and find Benita?' She turned to me. 'Mrs Kale is one of the staff here.'

Mrs Kale took a packet of cigarettes out of her bag. I watched avidly as she lit up. 'Please let me have one,' I begged. 'It's my first day and my social worker promised I could have a fag when we got here. She promised!'

She smiled kindly. 'Girls are not allowed to smoke on the premises, but on this occasion I'll make an exception,' she said, offering me one of her Bensons.

Finally, a cigarette! I puffed it gratefully.

'It won't take you long to learn the ropes,' said Mrs Kale. 'But there are certain things you should know straight off. Firstly, you have to put your coat and shoes in the coat cupboard around the corner.'

'I see,' I said, although I didn't see at all.

She extended her arms as if to take my long navy coat. I shrugged it off my shoulders and gave it to her. She gestured to my feet. 'What?' I said.

'Your shoes.'

'Yes?'

'Take them off.'

I stared down at my scuffed black court shoes. 'But they're the only ones I've got.'

'You're not allowed to wear shoes in the house and all coats and shoes are locked in the coat cupboard. I'll find you a pair of slippers once you've taken those off.'

Reluctantly, I stepped out of my shoes. 'Why aren't we allowed them?' I asked.

'Oh, lots of reasons, but mostly because of noise and dirt,' she replied.

'I'll need them when I go out.'

'Yes, but only when you've earned the privilege of going out.'

Again, that word 'privilege'. I didn't understand the way it was being used. To me, a privilege was something special, something good, not a basic right like wearing shoes, or going to the corner shop. But before I could argue, she was telling me more about the rules at Kendall House. She seemed to enjoy it.

Girls were banned from discussing their lives before Kendall House, she told me. This made it easier for everyone to make a new start, with a clean slate. 'No one can judge you on your past if they don't know anything about it,' she said. I wasn't sure what she meant. Why would anyone judge me on my past? I hadn't done anything wrong.

'One moment, Teresa,' she said. She left the room, taking my coat and shoes with her. When she returned she was clutching a pair of old-biddy slippers with plastic bottoms. She began to recite a litany of rules. Phone calls from family members were only allowed on Fridays. The laundry room and kitchen were out of bounds, as was the dining room, except at meal times. No eating between meals. No food allowed in the dorms, schoolrooms or sitting room. On and on she went. I found it impossible to take everything in.

'Understood?' she asked, when she had finished explaining bath times and restrictions. I nodded dumbly, trying to hold back the tears. 'Don't worry, you're not the only new one,' she said. 'Another girl arrived yesterday, so perhaps you can help each other to settle in.'

Kate returned with Benita, a grim-faced Asian woman of

around twenty-five wearing drainpipe jeans and high heels. Benita told me to open my bags and show her what was in them. I watched as this complete stranger rummaged through my clothes, fingered my underwear and inspected the contents of my sponge bag. She confiscated my cigarettes, matches, money and aspirins, before reciting another bunch of rules.

'At the end of the day, you must hand in your knickers for laundering to the member of staff on duty,' she said. 'When you come on your period, just let a member of staff know and you'll be given a sanitary towel.'

Soon it was back to 'privileges' again. Watching television, listening to music, reading books and magazines, using pens, paper or drawing materials, even attending lessons – these were all concessions that could be given and taken away. Punishments included being made to wear our nightclothes during the day. After a while I stopped listening. I couldn't digest any more rules.

A wave of tiredness washed over me. 'Would it be all right if I went and lay down for a bit?' I asked.

'Of course not, don't be a baby,' Benita said. 'You're not allowed into the dorms until bedtime. Now come with me.'

She showed me around the ground floor, repeating Mrs Kale's warnings about the rooms that were out of bounds. The front room and dining room doubled up as school-rooms, she explained. The bathroom was next to the laundry. She stopped in front of the only unlocked door we'd come to so far. 'And this is the girls' sitting room.'

Hesitantly, I stepped through the doorway. With its plastic, foam-filled chairs and old cheap carpet, the girls' sitting room reminded me of a hospital waiting room. There were about seven girls gathered around the television, and one girl was sitting in the corner, rocking and staring into space. Benita came up behind me and introduced me. 'Hello,' I said shyly. There was a tremor in my voice.

'Yeah, hi,' someone said. The atmosphere seemed heavy with unspoken tensions. Only a couple of girls bothered to look away from the TV. One of them wrinkled her nose and then turned back to the screen.

'Sit down and watch some television, Teresa,' Benita said, walking away. She looked at her watch. 'Tea is in just over half an hour. I expect you're hungry after your journey.'

My stomach churned. Food was the last thing I wanted. 'What are you watching?' I nervously asked the group.

'Telly, thicko. What does it look like?' said a small dark-haired girl, raising a couple of half-hearted laughs from the others.

Fighting the urge to run out of the room, I went to sit down. As I walked towards a spare seat, a leg shot out and smashed into my shins. I tripped and pawed the air, just catching myself before I fell.

A heavy-set, muscular girl in a nearby seat screamed with laughter. 'Watch your step, new girl,' she said. 'You don't want to go arse over tit, now.' Sucking air in through her teeth, she turned to face me. 'Not that you've got much in the way of arse or tits,' she added, looking me up and down disdainfully.

She flicked a glance at the thin black girl sitting next to her. The girl gazed at me, saying nothing. There was a hardness in her expression that chilled me to the bone. I made a mental note to stay out of her way.

Feeling totally unwelcome, I slipped out of the room. I was unsure of where to go next or what to do, so I climbed the stairs leading to the next floor and sat halfway up, watching the goings on below through the bars in the banister. A couple of girls passed me on their way downstairs, staring me out as they went by. Whispering and giggling, they headed towards the sitting room.

I heard someone say, 'Look what the cat's dragged in,' but I wasn't sure if it was me they were talking about.

Resting my elbows on my knees, I covered my face with my hands. Tears trickled through my fingers. I wasn't good at making friends at the best of times, but it looked like it was going to be virtually impossible at Kendall House. The girls were all so hostile. So much for my dreams of cosy chats and walks on the beach. I longed to be back at Miss Foley's where the staff were caring and the kids were nice.

Suddenly I was aware of someone standing at the bottom of the stairs. I peeped through my fingers. My heart thumped. It was the stocky girl from the sitting room.

'Aw, diddums,' she said, her voice dripping with sarcasm. 'Don't you like your new home? Missing your mummy and daddy, are you? Well you'd better get used to it!' The last part was shouted, like the punchline of a rowdy pub joke. She scrunched her face into an ugly grimace.

I buried my face in my lap and tried to pretend she wasn't there.

'It's teatime, crybaby,' she snarled.

'I'm not hungry,' I said.

'Think you've got a choice, do you?' she laughed. 'Haven't they told you what they do to you if you don't behave? You've got a big shock coming then. This place is your worst nightmare. If you break the rules they drug you and lock you up.' She paused.

'I don't care,' I said, even though her words had made me shiver. I thought about Esther at Long Grove, and how badly affected she was by her sessions in the hospital. I remembered the change in some of the other kids too.

'And guess what?' she went on. 'I'm even worse than your worst nightmare. So you'd better come down and eat your tea. You need to keep your strength up, because I'm going to get you later.' She punched the air with her fist and began to beckon me downstairs, laughing like some demented witch.

Just then, someone called out, 'Bridget!'

She froze, mid-cackle. 'Yes?'

The scary black girl was standing in the hall. 'Leave her alone,' she said.

Bridget raised her thick arms as if she had a gun pointed at her. Suddenly she didn't look so tough. 'I'm not doing anything! I'm just calling her for tea,' she said defensively.

The black girl said nothing more, but watched stonily as Bridget turned away from the staircase and sauntered in the direction of the dining room. 'Thank you,' I said softly, but she didn't respond. I waited until she had gone into the dining room before I left my safe place on the stairs.

Tea was a miserable affair. Desperately trying not to cry, I silently pushed piles of stewed meat and veg around my plate, feeling dazed. No one made conversation with me, not even Bridget, who was too busy trading insults and threats across the room with the others to pay me much attention. Once I caught the other girl – Maya – staring at me. Although she didn't say a lot, I sensed that Maya was top dog among the girls. They were nervous around her, jumpy. When she made a joke, everyone laughed. When she offered an opinion in her soft low voice, everyone agreed with her.

Halfway through the meal, a girl on the same table as me abruptly pushed back her chair. 'I can't stop shaking,' she moaned, staring down at her hands. They were trembling like mad.

'Shut your gob, Jane, you drama queen,' someone said.

'No, but look!' she wailed. She appeared to be transfixed by the sight of her shaking hands. She tried to stand up, but collapsed back onto her chair. 'I feel so weak, so weak . . .' Her voice trailed off.

I didn't know what to do. The girl was obviously ill, but no one seemed to care. 'Are you OK?' I asked.

'I feel like I'm dying,' she whispered feebly. 'They're killing me. Kendall House is killing me.'

'Hurry up and die, then!' Bridget shouted. The rest of the girls laughed.

I was shocked by their callousness, but didn't feel brave enough to speak out. Moments later, Benita came in and hustled Jane out of the room. I noticed that she had trouble walking and had to lean on Benita for support.

As soon as tea was over, I went back to my place on the stairs. A couple of girls shoved past me on their way up to the first floor. One of them flicked my face. 'You're in trouble,' she said with a sneer. 'Bridget's got it in for you.'

I heard Benita calling me. It was time to show me around the rest of the house, she said. I asked if Jane was feeling any better. Fine, she replied matter-of-factly. She led me upstairs, her bunch of keys jangling. On the first floor landing, she unlocked a door on the left – a schoolroom. Straight ahead was the washroom and toilets, also locked. Next to the washroom was Miss Woods's office. Miss Woods was the superintendent of Kendall House. I would meet her in the morning.

On the right, next to Miss Woods's office, I noticed a wooden door with a small window in it. It looked like a police cell door. I asked Benita about it.

'Oh, that's the detention room,' she said breezily. 'Hopefully you won't be spending much time in there!'

We went up some more stairs. The higher we got, the shabbier the decor was. Downstairs everything was polished and spick and span, but up here the paint on the walls was chipped and there were patches of threadbare carpet. We came to a thick fire door. As Benita unlocked it, I heard the sound of a baby crying. I jumped. It was so unexpected. 'What's that?'

Benita explained that Deborah, one of the girls, had just had a child. For the moment, mother and baby were staying in the room known as Sick Bay, which was on the right as you came up the stairs. A group of girls was fussing over them in a big way, especially Maya, who I later learned was good friends with Deborah. I noticed that Sick Bay also had a wooden door with a peephole window in it.

To the left there was a toilet, which was locked, and a bedroom where the night staff slept. There was also a nurse's room, another staffroom and a girls' dormitory. Up a few more stairs, on the top floor – the shabbiest floor – there were two more dorms, a fire escape and a staff bedroom. The rooms all had to be unlocked in order for me to see inside them. Every window was nailed shut. There was no fresh air. Most of the rooms smelled of stale bodies.

'Is this some kind of prison?' I said. 'Because if it is, I think there must have been a mistake. I haven't done anything wrong. I'm not supposed to be locked up.'

'I'm sure it's for your own good, Teresa,' Benita said. 'Just wait until you settle in. You'll find it's not so bad.'

I shook my head. She was wrong. I knew I'd never get used to being trapped inside this building, nor would I be able to accept it.

Then, on the way downstairs, she started talking about how some of the girls were allowed to keep hamsters and rabbits. My heart soared. It was a ray of hope. I told her about how much I loved animals.

'Will I be allowed to have a pet?' I asked. I thought about Blackie, the old lady's cat that had meant so much to me at the flat in Putney. I knew that having a pet to love could make all the difference.

'You're a real little softie at heart, aren't you?' she said with a note of dislike in her voice.

I flashed back to Bridget's raised fist. The girls at Kendall House were obviously a bunch of hard nuts, so perhaps I'd better start giving the impression that I had a tough side too. 'I can be quite hard too,' I said, but it sounded feeble. I had never been the aggressive type and I had a feeling I never would be. Still, something told me I wasn't going to survive very long if I didn't try to stand up for myself. I'd better save my soft side for the hamsters and rabbits.

I made my way to the girls' sitting room, telling myself to be brave. Just then, Bridget came rushing past. She collided with me and punched me hard on the arm. Bursting into tears, I retreated to my place on the stairs.

I cried myself to sleep that night. Staring through the darkness at the only photograph I possessed, a framed picture of Dad, David, Bernadette and me, I thought about how much I missed them. 'Please don't leave me here,' I prayed. 'Someone, please, please, rescue me.'

'Shut up or you'll get a slap,' said Zara, the girl in the bed next to mine. I buried my face into my pillow and tried to muffle my sobs.

CHAPTER FIVE

'Get up, you lot,' Benita growled. She yanked open the curtains next to my bed. Sunlight streamed into my eyes. I was already awake. I'd hardly slept. My head was throbbing.

'You'd better not snivel and cry like that again tonight, or I'll strangle you while you're asleep,' Zara threatened from her bed. I said nothing. I couldn't tell if she was serious or not. She got up and put on a dressing gown. 'Come on, it's time for morning wash.' She aimed a kick at my bed on her way out of the room.

Eyes still puffy from crying through the night, I followed her to the washroom on the first floor, where some of the girls were lined up in front of the basins along the wall, washing themselves down. I was horrified by the lack of privacy. There was no way I was going to strip off and scrub my privates in front of everyone.

When the first lot of girls had finished at the basins, the next lot stepped forward. Keeping my eyes averted from the girls on either side of me as they pulled their nightdresses off, I washed my hands, cleaned my teeth and splashed water on my face.

Turning to leave, I came face to face with Bridget, who was standing behind me, her broad, muscly arms crossed over her massive bust. 'And where do you think you're going, smelly?' she said, grinning nastily.

'To get dressed,' I said, trying to pass her.

She took a step to the side and blocked me. 'But you haven't finished washing.'

'I have,' I said firmly.

'Suit yourself then, you dirty bitch.' She pinched her nose and scrunched up her face. 'No one's going to want to sit next to you in class!'

I got dressed and walked miserably down to breakfast, tummy rumbling. In the dining room there were boxes of cereal lined up on the counter near the hatch. Plates piled with cold toast sat uninvitingly on the table, with another plate covered in small squares of butter alongside it.

'Is this it?' I asked Zara, pointing at the plates of toast.

'Yeah,' she said despondently. 'Don't eat it all at once.'

After breakfast I was called into the office and introduced to Miss Woods, the elderly superintendent of Kendall House. With her fluffy, scarecrow-style grey hair and thin, pursed lips, she reminded me of an uptight matron in the *Carry On* films.

'Can you tell me why I've been sent here?' I asked. 'I'm not violent. I've never broken the law. I really shouldn't be in a lock-up.' My voice cracked with emotion.

'I expect it all seems a bit strange just now, but you'll soon settle in,' she said, handing me a brown envelope with my name written on it. 'Here's your medication. Get yourself a glass of water from the tray over there.'

'What's it for?' I said, opening the envelope. Inside were four tablets, two blue and two white.

'Just swallow them down.'

'I don't understand. I'm not ill. I don't need any medicine.'

She sighed. 'It's for your own good, Teresa. Hurry up, now. Dr Peri's here and he wants to see you.' She picked up a tray holding a teapot and tea things, a plate of biscuits and two dinky cups.

Reluctantly I swallowed the pills and followed her up to her office, where a fat, smartly dressed man with dark skin was sitting in a comfortable armchair. Miss Woods set the tray of tea down on a small table in front of him. I hovered in the doorway, not wanting to go any further. There was something about this man that made me feel very uncomfortable.

'You must be Teresa,' he said, his chin wobbling as he spoke. 'I'm Dr Perinpanayagam – Dr Peri to you. Come in and sit down.'

I disliked him immediately. Everything about him struck me as repulsive, from his beady little eyes and fleshy lips to his enormous Buddha-like belly. The hairs on the back of my neck stood up as he beckoned me inside the room. I took a small step forwards. Again he told me to sit down. I refused. I definitely wanted to remain standing.

Miss Woods pulled up a chair and sat down right next to Dr Peri, her legs spread so wide that I could see right up her skirt. I looked away, shocked.

Dr Peri asked if I was settling in. I told him I hadn't slept all night. 'I'm not supposed to be here, but no one will listen to me,' I said. 'Why have I been given pills? I'm not ill. I don't need medicine.'

He raised one eyebrow. 'If you are not supposed to be here, why did Social Services send you here?' he asked.

'God knows,' I burst out. 'I didn't know it was like this or I would never have come anywhere near it.' He shook his head, as if in disbelief.

I listed my objections to the rules and restrictions. 'I want my shoes back,' I said, tears streaming down my cheeks. Getting more and more worked up, I complained about the other girls, the lack of privacy and the attitude of the staff. 'Please let me out of here!' I begged. 'I'm not a criminal and I'm not aggressive like the others.'

Dr Peri raised the palms of his hands. 'Now calm down, young lady,' he said in an infuriating tone of voice. He was so smug, so patronising. 'I have read your medical and social history and I know all about you, so obviously I am in a position to tell you what is best for you. Firstly, I can assure you that everyone is here to help. What is more, the rules were made to make life easier for you, so you had better start cooperating.'

'No,' I wailed. 'You don't understand! There's been a terrible mistake. I shouldn't be here. I'm used to being free. I've never been locked up before.'

He glanced at the file on his lap and started wagging his finger at me. 'Do not try all this pretending, because it will not work with me. It is all very well to act the poor little innocent girl, except that I happen to know that you were excluded from the adolescent unit at Long Grove Hospital. So you are not so innocent after all.'

'I am! Why are you trying to twist everything?' I sobbed. 'I got excluded because there was nothing wrong with my mental health. It was the wrong place for me, like Kendall House is the wrong place for me!'

He gave me a menacing look and told me to keep my voice down. 'If you keep up these hysterics I will have no hesitation in admitting you to one of my beds in the psychological unit at Stone House Hospital,' he said. 'And you do not want that, do you?'

I immediately fell silent. There was no point in arguing,

especially if he had the power to make things even worse for me. Clearly I was never going to get a straight answer out of him. He didn't care about me. No one cared about me. Trying to talk to the staff at Kendall House was like banging my head against a brick wall. They weren't going to let me go. I was stuck here until they sent me somewhere else, or I escaped.

'In the meantime, I am prescribing you a mild sedative to help you sleep at night,' Dr Peri went on. 'You seem extremely excitable.'

'I don't want your medicine,' I said.

He leaned back in his chair and rubbed his blubbery stomach. 'The sedative will help you. You will feel a lot better when you are sleeping properly.'

'I don't want it. I won't take it.'

His eyes flickered with reptilian indifference. 'You do not have a choice,' he said. He waved an arm at me. 'You can go now. You are dismissed.'

As I turned and left the room, I heard him sneer, 'Believe me, Doris, she will show her true colours in time.'

A few moments later, Miss Woods followed me out of the room. 'Now hurry along and get to school. You're due in RE with Mrs Petsworth downstairs,' she said. I glared at her, my eyes welling up again, but she took no notice.

Brushing away the tears, I made my way down to the classroom at the front of the house. As I opened the door, I locked eyes with Bridget, who was sitting in the back row. In a repeat of the pantomime that she'd acted out in the bathroom earlier, she screwed up her face and pinched her nose.

'Ah, come in, Teresa,' Mrs Petsworth said warmly, gesturing to a spare seat. 'We were just talking about the origins of Christianity.'

I sat down and tried to focus on the class. Having spent three years at a children's home run by the Salvation Army I knew a little bit about the struggles of the early Christians, and Mrs Petsworth seemed impressed by my knowledge. But she was an uninspiring teacher and it wasn't long before my concentration began to wander. I still wasn't feeling fully awake and my mind was fuzzy, which I put down to my sleepless night.

At break time I wandered back to my spot halfway up the stairs. As I sat there with my head against the banisters, I became aware of a presence at the bottom of the staircase. I looked up fearfully, expecting to see Bridget. To my relief it wasn't her, but a girl I hadn't noticed before. She had a sweet face and lovely almond-shaped eyes. 'I'm Emma,' she said with a friendly smile. 'Why do you keep going up there? Come down and chat to me.'

I was so grateful for those few friendly words that I could have hugged her. I stood up and followed her into the girls' sitting room. Within a few minutes of talking to her, I had a much clearer idea of how things worked at Kendall House, including the rules that could be bent and those that couldn't. She warned me against a few of the staff members, especially a nurse called Harriet, who could be really mean, and the biology teacher, Mrs Tarwin.

When I mentioned my run-in with Bridget in the washroom, she told me not to worry too much. 'That's just talk,' she said. 'Don't get me wrong. Bridget's a scary bitch. But she won't do anything bad without Maya's permission. Maya's the queen bee here. If she hasn't taken against you, then you're safe.'

She went on to repeat some of the rumours about Maya and the things she'd done in her time at Kendall House, which included beating up several girls and sexually abusing at least one. When I thought about Maya's cold staring eyes, the stories weren't hard to believe, even though she didn't exactly have an overpowering physique. 'She may be thin but she's vicious,' Emma warned. 'Whatever you do, don't get on the wrong side of her.' Even the thought of it made my blood run cold.

As for Bridget, she was a big bully and best avoided. Everyone was convinced she was a lesbian. 'The staff love her, especially Janice, one of the nurses,' Emma said. 'Know what I mean?' She nudged me and gave me a knowing look.

'So do Bridget and Maya . . . ?'

'I don't think so. They're not friends,' she said, grimacing.

Emma didn't seem to care that we weren't supposed to discuss our lives before Kendall House. She gave me a brief run-through of the other girls' histories. One of them had been sent there for arson, another for assault. There was a compulsive thief, a mugger and a girl who was so promiscuous that her parents had given up on trying to control her. Someone else had made repeated attempts to kill herself.

'And Bridget?' I asked.

'She set fire to a school in Wandsworth.'

I thought back to Mayfield School and the day we all drilled into the playground because a girl called Bridget had set the dining room ablaze. It had to be the same girl.

'What about you?' Emma asked.

I shook my head. 'I just can't understand why I'm here. I've never broken the law or stolen anything. I've never hit anyone, never even had a boyfriend. I took a sort of overdose a few months back, but the pills were mostly laxatives, so they didn't do any harm. So I have no idea what I'm doing here.'

She beckoned over a girl who had just come into the sitting room. 'This is Jules. She's new too.'

I liked Jules on sight. She was smaller than I was, with curly brown hair and kind brown eyes that twinkled with humour. Jules was as bemused as I was about being sent to Kendall House. She had arrived there the day before me and hated it as much as I did. 'I'm not like the other girls, either!' she assured me.

I glanced over to the far corner of the room, where a petite girl with curly, bright ginger hair was sitting in a chair, rocking and making moaning noises. 'We're nothing like her, that's for sure,' I said. 'She was there yesterday too. What's wrong with her?'

'Georgie?' said Emma. 'She's harmless, but she's not all there, if you get my meaning. She's a lot older than the rest of us, at least twenty. Sophie says she was sent here because she kept trying to have sex with strangers and there was nowhere else for her to go.' She tapped her forehead. 'She shouldn't be here. But none of us should. It's a hellhole.'

I thought about the girl with the trembling hands in the dining room the previous evening. 'What about Jane?'

Emma mimed giving herself an injection. 'Drugged up,' she said.

Just before lunch, I was called in to see Mrs Ryfield, the head teacher. Slim and extremely tall, with a beehive hairstyle that exaggerated her height, Mrs Ryfield wore old-fashioned glasses with winged frames. To me she looked like a towering, elongated version of 1960s pop singer Mary Wilson.

'I thought it would be good to have a little heart-to-heart,' she said. She asked how I was finding Kendall House.

'At last!' I thought. 'Someone who is going to listen.' I let loose a torrent of questions and complaints. 'What was I doing here? Why were they giving me pills? Who was Dr Peri? Why were all the doors locked?'

Her kindly expression disappeared and she raised her hand. 'That's enough. Everyone has to go through the privilege system. By taking this attitude you're not helping yourself and you're certainly not helping anyone else.'

I bowed my head, hopes dashed. No sympathetic ear here then.

After lunch I was called into the downstairs office by a mixed race member of staff named Harriet, whose light-skinned face was sprinkled with freckles. There was a line of girls in front of me, and Harriet was handing each of them a brown envelope and a glass of water. 'Drink them down quickly,' she said when it came to my turn. 'You don't want to be late for lessons.'

Although I remembered that Emma had warned me not to tangle with Harriet, I couldn't help saying, 'Why am I being given these pills? I don't want them.'

'Hurry up, I said!' Her dark eyes flashed and another cold shiver ran through me. I gulped down the pills and went upstairs to the maths class.

I was good at Maths, even though I didn't particularly enjoy it, and at first Mrs Connolly seemed pleased with my contributions to class. 'Well, at least someone knows their long multiplication!' she said approvingly.

Then, about half an hour into the lesson, thick waves of tiredness began to flow through me. My eyelids started drooping and my vision blurred. 'Teresa?' Mrs Connolly said, waiting for the answer to a simple equation.

I shook my head in an attempt to clear my mind. 'Sorry, I'm feeling exhausted all of a sudden,' I explained. 'I didn't sleep much last night. It must be catching up with me.'

'Try a bit harder. It's an easy one.'

I did my best to concentrate on the equation, but the symbols in my exercise book were wobbling in front of my eyes. 'I can't do it,' I said weakly. I was sorely tempted to lay my head on the desk and go to sleep right then and there.

The next lesson was needlework, also taught by Mrs Connolly. I loved making things – needlework was one of my favourite subjects – but I could hardly keep my eyes open as I practised my cross stitch on a piece of square cotton. I was also beginning to feel a bit sick.

Towards the end of the afternoon I started to brighten up and managed to tune back in to what Mrs Connolly was saying. It was a relief to feel the sharpness returning to my brain, to be able to think straight again.

I sat next to Emma and Jules at tea. Jules was really upset. She kept bursting into tears and saying, 'I can't stand it here. I've got to get out.'

'Are they giving you tablets?' I asked.

'Yes. They're making me feel bloody awful.'

On our way to the girls' sitting room I heard my name being called. 'Not again,' I thought. 'Please, no more pills.' Pretending I hadn't heard, I sat down in front of the TV with the others. Adam Ant was on *Top of the Pops*. Jules's sadness melted away and a soppy look appeared on her face.

'He's revolting! You can't like him,' I teased.

'I love him. Don't you say a word against him!'

A figure appeared at the door. It was Harriet. 'Teresa! Jules!' she barked. 'Come into the office now.' Jules left the room. I stayed put.

Emma nudged me. 'You'd better go,' she whispered. 'Harriet can be a real bastard when she wants to be.'

I traipsed along to the office, where Harriet handed me another brown envelope with my name on it. 'How much longer am I going to have to take these tablets for?' I asked.

'Just do as you're told and you won't have any trouble.' She turned away to busy herself with paperwork.

Half an hour later, back in the sitting room, the intense waves of tiredness returned. My hearing kept zoning in and out and I started nodding off in front of the television. I couldn't keep up with what was happening on screen. The other girls broke into laughter, but I didn't get the joke.

'Are you OK?' Jules asked.

'I feel really weird,' I said. The words came out slurred. My mouth was dry; my tongue felt fat.

I stood up and walked up and down the hall outside, shaking my head from side to side. It felt like someone had taken out half my brain and stuffed rags in its place. My neck was floppy. My limbs felt heavy. I desperately wanted to lie down. Instead I staggered to my place on the stairs, where I sat, slumped, with my head resting against the banisters. I hardly noticed when Bridget walked past and gave me a kick. It didn't even hurt.

Sometime later – maybe an hour or two – my head began to clear again. I got up and went to look for a member of staff. That night a woman called Maggie was on duty. She was slim, with blonde bobbed hair and a kind face. I found her in the sitting room. 'The pills they're giving me are making me feel really ill,' I told her. 'I shouldn't be taking them. They're sending me to sleep.'

Maggie said I'd get used to the effects in time. 'You're a bit of a fusspot, aren't you?' she said.

I shook my head. 'I was fine until I started taking the tablets. Now I feel terrible.'

She told me to take it easy. After all, she said, it was only my second day at Kendall House. 'That's what's worrying me,' I told Jules later. 'If I feel like this now, how will I be in a week's time?'

'I'll go mad if I don't get out of here soon,' she whispered. 'Will you come with me if I find a way to escape?'

I didn't hesitate. 'Yes! Don't go without me.'

'I won't.' She squeezed my arm. 'We're in this together.'

At nine o'clock, after we had been given hot milk drinks and a piece of fruit, I was called into the office and given another brown envelope. Harriet watched carefully as I swallowed four pills, plus the extra one that Dr Peri had prescribed to help me sleep. Half an hour later I dragged myself up to the top floor and collapsed on my bed. I don't remember drifting off. In the morning I awoke from a dreamless oblivion to the sound of Zara shouting that some bitch had stolen her hairbrush.

CHAPTER SIX

I still felt really woozy. I told Harriet that I didn't want to take any more tablets. She was unsympathetic, so I threatened to starve myself unless I was taken off them.

'If you don't cooperate, you will be punished,' she warned. I tried keeping the pills on my tongue so that I could spit them out later, but she forced me to swallow them while she watched.

The house had emptied out. It was a Saturday and most of the girls had gone to their parents or to foster placements for the weekend. Bridget and Maya were still lurking around though, so I kept a low profile. Bridget had made it clear that she was going to beat me up at the first opportunity and although Maya appeared not to have a problem with me, I didn't want to take any chances. All I could do was hope that Jules came up with an escape plan sometime soon.

When I caught up with her, she said that she had checked all the windows in the house and that every single one was nailed shut. 'Don't worry though, I'll find another way to get out of here,' she said.

She sauntered over to talk to Paula, the member of staff on duty in the sitting room. Soon they were laughing and chatting away, much to my amazement. So far I had only seen Jules being rude or sullen with the staff. I moved closer so that I could listen in. First, they discussed various Kendall House rules and privileges. Then Jules casually asked if any of the girls had ever tried to escape. Paula said that it wasn't unknown for girls to run away, but they were always caught, brought back again and punished.

'So, how do they get out and where do they go?' Jules said. She caught my eye and quickly looked away.

'What does it matter? They never get far,' Paula replied. She cocked her head and wagged a finger at Jules. 'Don't even think about trying anything silly unless you want to spend a week in your nightclothes.'

After lunch, Bridget and Maya were allowed out for a walk and a cigarette. This really annoyed us. 'It's not fair! I'm dying for a fag. I haven't had one for days,' I said.

We confronted Brenda, another member of staff. 'We haven't been allowed out since we got here,' Jules complained. I backed her up, arguing that it was unhealthy to stay inside all the time.

Brenda smiled. 'You know that newcomers aren't allowed out,' she said, adding that if we were good girls we would eventually earn the privilege of a walk.

At this, Jules started to get really worked up. She swore at Brenda and said she'd smash a window if she didn't get permission to go out soon. For the second time that day I threatened to go on hunger strike. Brenda reacted coldly and threatened Jules with the detention room if she continued using bad language. Jules swore under her breath and said she couldn't give a fuck where she was sent. Brenda must have heard her because she grabbed her by the arm and yanked her towards the door.

'Get off!' Jules yelled, pulling away.

Brenda stumbled. Surprise flickered in her eyes. 'Why, you little . . . ! You'll soon find out what we do with nasty little rebels like you.' She pulled Jules roughly out of the door and marched her off. Within a few minutes she was under lock and key on the first floor. I felt so sorry for her.

I mooched around for the rest of the day, experiencing intermittent patches of drowsiness, just like the day before. They wouldn't let me see Jules. I kept asking, but the answer was always no. Eventually I managed to sneak upstairs just before tea. From the landing, I could hear her crying and banging on the door. She was begging to be let out. I tiptoed forward and knocked softly on the door. 'It's me. Teresa,' I whispered.

'Teresa!'

I sat on the floor and began talking to her, reassuring her that nothing she'd done deserved such bad treatment. Not even liking Adam Ant! That made her laugh and by the time Benita found me and sent me downstairs, she'd started to calm down.

After tea, my nose clogged up and I felt like I was going down with flu or a bad cold. Harriet smeared my throat and nose with Vick's Vapour Rub and took me up to my dorm, unlocking and locking doors as we went.

'It's the medicine. I'm sure it's making me ill,' I told her.

'What nonsense. It's just a summer cold.'

The next morning Jules was visibly shaken after a night spent in the detention room. Her eyes were really swollen. She said she'd cried for most of the night. 'It was horrible, like being in a prison cell. But I don't care how much they try to break me, they won't stop me from getting out,' she kept saying.

My flu symptoms had improved slightly, but I was feeling

very run down. Every time I had another dose of medicine, my head and limbs felt slower and heavier. I wondered whether eventually I'd come to a complete halt, like a wind-up toy that's lost its key.

Bridget was spending the rest of the weekend at Janice's house – Janice was the nurse that Emma had told me about – and Maya was out with another member of staff, so there were only three girls left in the house: Jules, Georgie and me. We spent the morning in the sitting room, listening to records. Georgie hogged the record player, playing her Culture Club records over and over again until I felt like snatching them from her and breaking them over my knee. She was totally obsessed with Boy George and rocked and dribbled more than ever while she listened to him.

My moods were all over the place. One minute I was calm and the next I felt like slashing my wrists or throwing myself out of a window. 'This place is going to drive me around the bend,' I told Jules.

'I'll already be there when you get there,' she said with a sigh.

The next few days went by in a blur of pills, lessons and rules, punctuated by terrifying encounters with the other girls. Some of them could be really scary. Every time Bridget passed me in the corridor she'd start on me, and she was always hissing threats about knocking my teeth in and beating me up. A girl called Sophie K said she'd rip my tongue out if I complained about any of her favourite teachers or staff members, and Zara kept taunting me that I was a baby. But Zara could also be unexpectedly nice, so I never knew where I was with her.

One morning, about a week after I'd arrived at Kendall House, I woke up in floods of tears. I couldn't stop crying. It was weird. It felt more like a physical than an emotional reaction. I went on weeping all through the morning wash and was still crying at breakfast.

'Shut up, for God's sake!' Zara yelled at me. 'You're always crying. What's wrong with you?'

'I don't know,' I wailed. 'I can't stop.'

'Have they got you on them blue and white pills?' she asked.

'Yes,' I said, going into another heaving round of sobs.

'It's a side effect of them pills,' she said. 'It'll wear off by this afternoon.'

What she said made sense, but it didn't stop me bursting into tears at unexpected moments. I was all over the place. Of course I had plenty to cry about, but this felt as though it wasn't really me crying, rather a distant, shell-like version of me. I felt so weak too. The more tears I shed, the more it seemed as if my life was draining out of me.

By lunchtime when the mood finally lifted, I felt knocked out. 'You were right about it wearing off,' I told Zara in between yawns. 'How did you know?'

'I've been on bloody pills for a year and a half. I hate them.'

I shuddered. The thought of spending years feeling floppy, emotional and fuzzy-headed frightened me. I felt I'd rather die than endure that.

'Why are some girls on pills and others not?' I asked. She couldn't say.

The favouritism at Kendall House was obvious for all to see. Maya was always being asked into the staffroom for tea, or to have a cigarette. The staff seemed to dote on her. Bridget was another of their pets. They weren't drugging her. In fact, she seemed to be more on their side than ours. Every morning she stood on self-appointed inspection duty in the washroom, arms crossed, eyes trained on the girls. She had no shame about stripping off and making a meal of washing herself with a flannel down below, sound effects included, and she made no attempt to disguise how much she enjoyed watching us undressing and washing our privates.

I was so uncomfortable with the way she stared that I just cleaned my teeth and splashed water on my face. When she reported me for being unhygienic, I was given several lectures on cleanliness by Shirley. Shirley was one of the nicer members of staff, but she was strict as well.

I refused to obey the rule that said you had to give your dirty knickers to a member of staff at the end of every day. Instead I washed them myself and put them to dry on the radiator, hidden under my towel. Jules did the same. It just didn't feel right to give them to the staff, especially when there were men on duty. Of course, Bridget reported me for this as well, and when Shirley asked me about it, I felt totally tongue-tied. It was degrading to be questioned about such personal things.

Humiliation was an everyday part of life at Kendall House. Since we weren't allowed to keep a store of our own sanitary towels, I had to tell a member of staff when my period started. Unfortunately, the only person available that night was a tall, greasy-haired man called Philip.

'I need a sanitary towel,' I mumbled.

'On your period, are you?' he said.

No, I want to wear it as a hat, you idiot!

'Yes,' I said, cringing.

'Come back to me with some proof and I'll give you an ST.'

'Proof?' I couldn't even begin to imagine what he meant.

'Stains on your knickers, for instance.'

'No way!' I protested.

We got into an argument and I angrily stood my ground. Finally Benita turned up and took me into the staffroom, where the sanitary products were locked away in a cupboard.

'This time I'll let you off. Next month you will be required to prove that you are menstruating,' she said.

'No.'

'Fine. Bleed all over the place, then; it's your choice.'

'But why?'

Her reply was mystifying. 'The girls are known for abusing certain hygienic products like STs,' she said. 'They ask for more than they need and then they misuse them, which is a terrible waste of money. They're not cheap, you know!'

She handed over a thick Dr Whites towel with loops on each end. I wasn't sure how you secured them to your knickers and asked if the loops were supposed to attach to something. She said that the belts that held them in place were prohibited and I'd have to improvise.

'Has anyone ever tried to hang themselves with a sanitary towel belt?' I asked. 'I suppose there's a first time for everything!'

I asked how she expected me to 'improvise'. 'I'll leave that up to you,' she snapped.

Inevitably the sanitary towel kept riding down my knickers and I ended up leaking. Just as inevitably, Bridget noticed the red marks on my clothes and made endless nasty comments about my standards of hygiene. Even though I had frequent baths, she held her nose and screwed up her face every time I entered a room. I began to hate her for it.

After two long weeks at Kendall House, they let me phone Mum and Dad. I tried the Fox and Hounds number first, hoping Dad would be there, as there was no phone at home. It rang and rang, but no one picked up.

Next I tried Mum. 'Hello, love,' she said. 'How are you doing?'

A lump formed in my throat and for a moment I wasn't sure if I'd be able to speak. 'Oh, Mum!' I croaked.

She instantly picked up on my distress. 'What is it, Teresa? What's wrong?'

Suddenly it all came flooding out. 'Mum, I hate it here!' I told her about Bridget, Dr Peri, the locked doors, the pills – everything.

'I knew it! I knew they were going to lock you up,' she said angrily. 'Find a way to escape and once you're out, ring me and I'll tell you how to find me.'

'I will, Mum,' I'd said, my heart leaping with hope.

Two days later, I was finally allowed out through the kitchen into the back garden. Having been cooped up inside for so long, the garden felt like another country, another planet. I kept taking in long, deep breaths of fresh summer air. It felt so good to be out in the open, even though the garden was enclosed by a huge metal fence, about twelve feet high. Turning my face up to the sky, I forgot my troubles for a few moments and relished the warming sensation of sunshine on my face. I stretched out my arms and twirled in a circle, enjoying the sense of space and freedom. As I spun around, I kept hearing Mum's voice urging me to run away.

Harriet doped me up again after lunch. Then Kate sent for me. 'Janice says you behaved very well in the garden this morning, so I'm going to let you come out and spend your pocket money with us this afternoon.' She looked at me expectantly.

I took the hint. 'Thank you!' I said, perking up at the thought of a change of scene.

My weekly pocket money allowance had been set at seventy-five pence. Out of that I had to buy some personal products, including soap, shampoo and deodorant from the Kendall House supply. The shampoo came in Sunsilk sachets that cost five pence each. The deodorant was called Mum, somewhat ironically. Although it didn't work very well, we all loved it because it came in pretty pastel pink or blue and had a lovely scent.

I'd already spent most of my first two weeks' money, but I just about had enough left for a packet of cigarettes, or almost. Zara and Sophie C agreed to chip in so we could buy a pack of twenty.

We went into town and wandered around the shops in the local high street, waiting for a chance to sneak off and have a smoke. Kate kept her beady eye on us though. I thought we'd never be able to give her the slip. Finally, she was distracted by a discussion with a shop assistant about whether stripes or plain material worked better for curtains. As she eyed up several bolts of cloth, Sophie C nudged me and nodded towards the shop door. I nudged Zara and raised my eyebrows, but Zara shook her head and motioned to us to leave without her. We tiptoed out of the door. As soon as we reached the pavement outside, Sophie C broke into a run. I sprinted after her with no idea of where I was going, nor did I care.

I'd hardly had any exercise for weeks and was quickly out of breath. 'Where are we going?' I asked, panting.

'Fags first, then my mum's.' She disappeared into a sweet shop and came out with twenty Embassy.

We got a train and a bus to her mum's house, where her mother welcomed us with open arms and gave us a slap-up meal. I rang my mum on the number she had given me, my heart thumping. But Mum sounded flustered and told me to stay at Sophie's for now. She was changing jobs again, she said. 'So it may take me a little while to get settled and ready for you.' I felt sick with disappointment, but tried not to let it show.

Towards evening, my mind started feeling a lot clearer than it had been for the previous fortnight. 'Give me another fag,' I said to Sophie C. 'They're making me feel much better.'

'You'll have to go back tomorrow or the next day, girls,' Mrs C said, sighing. 'They'll definitely come looking for you here.'

'Can't you hide us somewhere?' I pleaded. I hated the idea of being locked up again.

'I'm afraid not, love,' she said with regret.

We stayed up late watching telly and larking around. It was wonderful to be able to do and say what we wanted, even if it was only giggling at a silly joke as we drifted off to sleep in Sophie's bedroom. For once I didn't feel totally conked out, just pleasantly, naturally tired.

I woke up in the middle of the night to the sound of loud knocking. Someone was at the front door. A couple of minutes later I heard the rumble of low male voices and Mrs C saying, 'Not at this time of night, surely?'

Heavy footsteps pounded up the stairs. Sophie's bedroom light snapped on. Two burly policemen dragged us out of bed and took us downstairs into a waiting police car. Mrs C came outside with a carrier bag. It had our clothes in it. 'Aren't you even going to let them get dressed?' she said.

'No point,' one of the policemen said. 'They're going straight back to bed.'

I thought this meant they were going to take us back to

Kendall House. I begged them not to. 'They're drugging me,' I said. 'They're turning me into a zombie!' Neither of the policemen replied.

They put us in a dirty holding cell at Bromley Police Station. It stank of vomit. No one checked up on us all night. In the morning they sent a policewoman to let us out. We told her about being forced to take medicine at Kendall House. She seemed to take a keen interest and I began to hope that she might follow up on our complaints. But when she came back she said that she'd been told we were psychiatric patients, so it made sense that drugs were being used on us.

'I'm not a psychiatric patient!' I said.

'Me neither!' said Sophie.

The policewoman shrugged. 'Sorry, girls, I'm afraid I can't help you.'

Some hours later, Kate drove us back to Kendall House in silence. Tears dripped down my cheeks at the thought of being forced to take more pills. Finally I said, 'Why did you tell the police we were psychiatric patients? You more or less said we were mental, didn't you?'

Kate sighed. 'Teresa, were you or were you not a patient at the Long Grove Adolescent Unit?'

'But they chucked me out because it was the wrong place for me! I'm not mad. Dr Staple said I wasn't mad. I shouldn't be on pills. There's nothing wrong with me.'

'Pipe down, for goodness' sake,' she said. She turned on the radio and hummed along to an old 1950s track.

Miss Woods gave us a right telling off when we arrived. We were ordered to bathe and get into our nightclothes again. 'Am I supposed to go to lessons in my nightie?' I said.

'You're not going to lessons. Oh no, you're coming with

me.' She grasped me by the wrist and led me upstairs to the first floor.

It wasn't until we reached the top of the stairs that I realised where she was taking me. 'Don't lock me up. No!' I pleaded, trying to pull away from her and run back downstairs. Remembering how Jules had looked after a night in the detention room, I dreaded having to go through the same experience.

'Did you think you weren't going to be punished? What a very stupid girl you are, then. Now don't go kicking up a stink and making my job harder. You know it won't do any good.'

Harriet appeared on the landing and stood with her arms crossed as Miss Woods unlocked the door to the detention room. 'In you go, then.'

'No, please!'

Harriet stepped forward and gave me a violent push. 'Get in there!' she ordered.

I took a couple of steps forward, even though every part of my body was silently screaming at me to make a run for it. Harriet pushed me again and suddenly I was through the doorway. The door flew shut and the lock immediately turned. I was trapped.

The detention room was tiny and claustrophobic, with minuscule plastic windows high up on the wall. It contained nothing but a built-in wooden cabin bed. Miss Woods told me to bang on the door to attract the attention of a staff member when I needed the toilet. The rest of the time I was supposed to keep quiet and stare into space, except when they brought me more tablets to take. Books and writing material were banned. A little later, I asked if I could work on my sewing. The answer was no.

'Have you locked Sophie up too?' I said.

'Sophie is being dealt with,' Harriet replied tersely. She refused to elaborate further.

I cried myself to sleep and woke up in the early afternoon feeling alone and sorry for myself. I hadn't heard from my dad or Bernadette since I'd arrived at Kendall House. David was in a new home and couldn't be contacted. My mum was going God knows where. Nobody cared about me.

I was allowed downstairs to eat tea before being taken back up again. Kate came in for 'a chat'. I told her how scared I was of some of the girls and said I was going to tell Elizabeth Pryde about all the threats Bridget had made.

'Mrs Pryde is Bridget's social worker as well, didn't you know?' Kate said.

I bit my lip. Just my luck.

I spent a fitful night in the detention room, obsessed with the thought that the door was locked and I couldn't get out. What if there was a fire? Would I be forgotten in the scramble to evacuate the building? I kept turning the possibilities over and over in my mind, and when I did sleep, I had vivid nightmares about being trapped in a coffin or underwater. At one point I woke up and sat bolt upright. The walls of the already cramped room felt as if they were closing in on me. I got out of bed and banged on the door. 'Help! Let me out!' I shouted. No one heard. No one came. I started screaming, but nothing made a difference.

I woke up feeling groggier than ever. I wasn't allowed to get dressed. That 'privilege' had been taken away from me, so I went downstairs in my nightdress once the staff had unlocked the door. After breakfast, I had to line up and swallow the usual dose of tablets, even though I complained that they were making me ill. I had a constantly runny nose and was getting a lot of headaches.

In Mrs Nuttall's drama class, my head began to throb again. Mrs Nuttall had given me a good part in the play reading, but I kept stumbling over the words.

'Come on, Teresa, you can do better than this!' she said.

I threw my copy of the play on the floor. 'I can't do anything on these pills!' I howled. 'I can't think straight. Everything's blurry. It's horrible. I think they're trying to drive me mad.'

My head was swirling and my thoughts were jumbled. 'I hate it here,' I went on, desperate to make her understand what I was going through. 'The staff think I'm crazy. The girls want to beat me up. No one likes me because I'm new. My dad doesn't want to know. My mother has disappeared again. My brother's locked away. My sister doesn't care. All I want to do is kill myself!'

My legs began to feel wobbly. I sat down. I rested my head on the desk and drifted off to sleep.

After lunch, and more pills, I went to the bathroom and splashed water on my face in an attempt to wake myself up. But crushing tiredness overcame me during that afternoon's cookery lesson and I lost my sense of coordination, spilling stewed prunes all down my nightdress.

I expected Mrs Ryfield to be cross, but she said, 'Don't worry, let's get it in to soak before it stains.' She led me down the hall, unlocked a door and handed me over to Dot, who was in charge of the laundry.

'Dear oh dear,' Dot said kindly, inspecting my nightdress. 'Were you trying to drown yourself in prunes?'

I laughed weakly. She helped me to get cleaned up and gave me another apron. Just then, I heard a miaow. I scanned the room eagerly and spotted a cat poking its head through a hole in the wall, a plump tabby with a really pretty face.

'There's Buttercup,' Dot said. 'That's odd. She usually hides from strangers, but she doesn't seem to be so scared of you.'

'Perhaps she can tell how much I love cats,' I said. I knelt down and called her over, but she just watched me warily.

Buttercup lived in the laundry with the other Kendall House cats, but she was special. Like me, she was scared of everyone apart from Dot. It took me ages to gain her trust. She was incredibly shy. At first she would just peer through the hole in the wall when I called her name. She watched nervously as I knelt and talked to her, and resisted all my attempts to coax her to come nearer.

As time went on, she grew braver and crept closer and closer to me, until one day she finally sat on my lap. I felt immense happiness in that moment. She was very loving, and would purr and rub her head against my face. She gave me love in a place that was cold and cruel. But the moment another girl came into the laundry, she'd be gone. She was as lonely and scared as I was.

I told Dot about my love for animals and she asked whether I had a hamster yet. 'I'm getting one next week, if I'm good,' I said, smiling for the first time since I'd been brought back to Kendall House. I was thrilled when she said I could come back and see Buttercup soon.

My euphoria was short-lived. There was a strange atmosphere in the sitting room after school and when I asked Zara what was going on, she ignored me. Neither Emma nor Sophie C would talk to me either. I noticed that they were sucking up to Bridget more than usual, telling her how nice she looked and asking what she wanted to watch on TV.

'Bad news: Maya's gone,' Jules whispered a few minutes later. 'She's left Kendall House for good. Bridget is queen bee now.'

My heart fluttered with fear. Now I understood why none of the other girls were talking to me – Bridget would have told them not to. Jules said she'd stick by me though. I was so grateful. Having a friend by my side made all the difference.

As the evening wore on, it became clear that we'd both been sent to Coventry. We tried not to take any notice and settled down to do a jigsaw puzzle, but it was hard to pretend we didn't care. I kept worrying that the girls in Jules's dorm would turn her against me during the night. She said I was being silly, but I knew how hard it was to stand up to that kind of pressure. If she were anywhere near as scared of Bridget as I was, then she wouldn't hesitate to do what Bridget told her to.

For the second night in a row I was forced to sleep in the detention room. I tossed and turned in the thin, hard bed, unable to calm my anxiety. Now that there was no one to stop Bridget bullying me, there was no telling what she would do.

My fears were confirmed in the washroom the next morning. 'Smelly cow!' she shouted as I cleaned my teeth. 'I'm in charge here and I'll beat you senseless if you don't wash yourself properly today. Get undressed right now.'

'I've already washed myself,' I said.

She stepped forward and slapped the back of my head. 'Don't you fucking talk back to me, you little bitch!' she yelled. 'You'll do as I say or I'll kill you.'

I believed her. There was something so twisted and thuggish about Bridget that I wouldn't have put anything past her, not even murder. I took off my nightdress and wrapped a towel around me in an attempt to stay partially covered up while I washed my body.

'What are you trying to hide?' she crowed. 'Do you think anyone wants to look at your ugly, scrawny body?' She went into a rant: I was mad, I was ugly and no one liked me. I was thick. I stank. If I didn't hurry up she was going to smash my head against the wall. I left the bathroom in tears, dreading the rest of the day.

Next I was summoned to Miss Woods's office, where Dr Peri delivered a lecture on obedience from his usual comfy armchair. Wearing nothing but my nightdress, I stood before him as he explained the consequences of breaking the rules. He shook a fat finger at me. 'I will permit you to get dressed today, but only because this is the first time you have absconded,' he said. 'If you do it again you will be punished a great deal more severely.'

Something told me that I was supposed to be grateful and express my thanks. But I wasn't, so I didn't. He waved me away when I asked if I'd be allowed to stop taking tablets four times a day.

No one spoke to Jules and me at breakfast. It was a horrible feeling having ten girls stare through you as if you weren't there. Jules tried to reassure me. 'It won't go on forever. They'll pick on someone else in time,' she said. I wasn't so sure. The glint in Bridget's eyes had been there from the moment I'd first met her. I couldn't see it disappearing any time soon.

CHAPTER SEVEN

Dad was given permission to visit the following Sunday. 'Teresa, what's happened to you? You're so thin and pale. You look awful!' he said.

'Oh Dad,' I said, breaking into uncontrollable tears. 'This place is terrible. Can't you get me out of here?'

He was appalled to hear about the pills they were giving me. 'I'll ring Social Services and give them a piece of my mind,' he promised. 'They've no right to be drugging my daughter.'

When he left an hour later, he was full of assurances that he would also be phoning Miss Woods to complain about the way I was being treated. 'See you soon,' he said. 'Hang on in there. I'll sort them out.'

I didn't have a lot of faith in Dad's ability to change the situation, but it was the only hope I had, tiny as it was, and like a drowning man clinging to a matchstick, I hung on to it for dear life. Then, less than a week later, the matchstick floated away when he rang to say that he was being evicted from the flat. He sounded really low. 'I've got my own battles to fight for now,' he said dejectedly, 'so you'll have to look after yourself for the time being.'

I wasn't sure how long I could go on. Life was getting worse every day. Bridget's grip on the other girls was so powerful that they ignored me most of the time. Even Jules was finding it tough to stand up to them, just as I'd predicted. I didn't hold it against her. When you've got a gang of girls constantly pushing you one way, it's very hard to keep going in the other direction.

I never knew when or where to expect some kind of assault, whether verbal or physical. Violence could erupt at any time, often at totally random moments. It wasn't only directed at me. There was constant in-fighting among the girls. It seemed as if there was always someone punching or kicking someone else, and scraps would start at dinner time, bath time or bedtime – even first thing in the morning. On more than one occasion Zara slapped me as I got out of bed. 'I've just about had enough of your bloody crying,' she'd say.

One afternoon I was last in line for my pills behind Sophie K, who was in a foul mood. She told Harriet that she was not going to take her tablets. 'I won't take mine either,' I said, hoping that Sophie would appreciate the back up, even though I found her a bit intimidating. She was blonde and of medium build, with a great big scar on her face that she got in a car accident before she came to Kendall House.

'Shut up, Teresa!' she shouted. The next thing I knew she had leapt at me and was ferociously pulling my hair, trying to rip it from my scalp.

Harriet separated us, with the help of Ivy and Benita, who took me upstairs and made me change into my nightclothes. 'Why isn't Sophie being punished?' I asked. Surely they had noticed that she'd started it.

'If you make trouble, you get trouble,' Benita said cryptically.

My stomach twisted. I didn't bother to argue. Even the staff seemed to be turning against me.

Although it was a struggle to keep myself alert when I was being drugged four times a day, the fear-fuelled adrenalin that constantly pumped through me seemed to run counter to the effects of the pills. I became nervy and jumpy and hypersensitive to the slightest noise or movement, even when I was really drowsy. I could always sense when someone was coming up behind me; I didn't have to hear them first.

When two new girls arrived – Nicole and Tina – I half-hoped that Bridget and the others would forget about me and start picking on them instead. Unfortunately, it didn't work out that way. Nicole was very, very pretty and Bridget seemed to be enchanted by her from the start. Her eyes lit up when Nicole first appeared in the girls' sitting room and I noticed how she would stare at her whenever she was near, greedily taking in the girl's cute symmetrical features and glossy dark blonde hair.

As for Tina, she was small and thin and looked like she couldn't hurt a flea, but in her case appearances were definitely deceptive. Word soon spread that she'd been sent to Kendall House for attacking a girl with a hot iron. According to the rumour, she'd held the girl down and pressed the iron against her cheek, scarring her for life. Nobody dared to ask her about it, but from the start it was obvious that she was a hard nut, despite her tiny frame. She seemed OK at first, but she soon developed a habit of creeping up behind me and launching herself onto my back, clinging on like a crab, biting and pulling my hair. She did it to everyone.

In the end, it got to the point where every time I walked away from her, Tina was hanging off my back. She was that bad. You could beat the shit out of her – you could probably take the head off her body – and she would still hang onto your back. Small as she was, she was frighteningly disturbed. Nothing and no one seemed to scare her, not even Bridget.

Two days after Sophie K attacked me, Harriet ordered me to get out of my nightie and get dressed. 'Ever been to Dover?' she asked.

I thought back to the old songs Dad and his friends had sung around the piano at the Fox and Hounds. 'No. Are the cliffs really white?'

'Well, you'll soon find out, won't you?'

Sure enough, after lunch several girls plus Harriet and Brenda piled into Fred's van and drove along roads signposted with pictures of ferries.

'Let's stow away to France,' I whispered to Jules. 'They've got great beaches and je parle bien français.'

She laughed. 'I'd rather go to Holland and cycle through fields of tulips.'

As we drew into Dover, chattering about our dreams of escape, Fred started making suggestive jokes about running away with sailors. Sophie K rolled her eyes. I remembered hearing that Fred was known for making innuendoes about sex. Harriet and Brenda laughed though. They seemed to find him funny.

Fred was engaged to Janine, one of the staff at Kendall House, and I'd already seen him a few times. He was very unattractive. With his thin lips, weak chin and greasy black hair, he looked like Dracula on a bad day. To add to that impression, he often wore sunglasses, even when the weather was dreary.

The van pulled up in a car park near the docks. Before we got out, Harriet laid down the law. 'We stick together. Any funny business and we go straight back to the house.'

'We'll be as good as gold, don't you worry,' Sophie K said, sounding like butter wouldn't melt in her mouth.

But the instant we got out of the van, Sophie made a bolt for it, sprinting out of the car park at full pelt. I watched her go, amazed. She was running fast enough to win an Olympic medal. Brenda and Fred pursued her, leaving the rest of us with Harriet, who made us get back in the van and wait until they caught up with Sophie. We ended up playing I spy for the next hour. Some trip that turned out to be. I didn't even get to see the white cliffs.

Sophie was picked up trying to hitch a lift at the ferry exit. 'I nearly made it,' she said under her breath, as Fred and Brenda bundled her back into the van.

'Better luck next time,' we commiserated.

On the drive back to Gravesend we silently hatched another plan to escape, this time involving the whole group. Pulling up outside Kendall House, Sophie C gave everyone a discreet thumbs up. I drew in a deep breath and got ready to run.

As Fred let us out of the back of the van, we burst out onto the pavement and hightailed it off in different directions. 'Go, go, go!' shouted Sophie K.

I lost sight of her and Jules, but Sophie C and I linked up and legged it as fast as we could towards town, with Brenda following hot on our heels. Adrenalin pumped through me as my feet pounded on the pavement, and although the unused muscles in my thighs soon began to ache, my legs went on pumping away, fuelled by desperation. But then, as we raced down Cobham Street, Sophie stumbled over a small pile of bricks on the pavement. I tried to steady her, but lost my footing and tripped, landing painfully on my knees. Thirty seconds later Brenda had us firmly in her grip.

'You'll be in your nightclothes for a week this time,' she gasped angrily.

Back in the dorm at Kendall House I heard that Sophie K and Jules were still missing. A wave of depression swept over me at the thought that Jules might get away for good. Of course I would be glad for her if she managed to escape, but how would I survive without my only true friend? As I changed into my nightie and tried to prepare myself for another tortured night in the detention room, I was overwhelmed by a sense of hopelessness. What was the point in going on?

I picked up the framed photo by my bed and stared at the smiling faces of my family. Why had everything gone wrong for us? It seemed so unfair that other girls my age were living happy, settled lives within loving homes, while I was shut away in a lock-up for delinquent girls – for no other reason than that there had been nowhere else to send me long term. A surge of bleak fury went through me and I threw the photo to the floor. The frame cracked and shards of glass flew everywhere. I burst out crying.

In a jumble of self-pity and anger, some kind of hazy logic told me that perhaps it would just be easier to end things now. After all, anything was better than being stuck in Kendall House, and I was sure that nobody would miss me when I was gone. I reached down and picked up a sliver of glass. It felt sharp and lethal against the tips of my fingers. I jabbed my wrist with it. Tiny droplets of blood formed on my pale skin.

Suddenly something snapped inside me and I began to slash my arm, all the way up to the elbow and biceps. Soon the whole arm was running with blood and my hands were covered in cuts and grazes. I hardly felt any pain; my nerves seemed totally numb. Instead it felt a little as though I had lanced a boil, releasing a build-up of misery and tension. It was a relief to express how much I was hurting inside, even if it meant turning my pain and anger in on myself.

Harriet found me lying on the bed in a daze. 'Teresa!' she shouted. 'What have you done, you stupid girl?'

She cleaned me up, using cotton wool and witch hazel, while Miss Woods swept up the glass. 'Here, drink this,' Harriet said, passing me a glass of cloudy hot water.

'What's in it? I don't want any more medicine.'

'It's a vitamin drink. It'll stop you feeling so weak.'

I took a sip. It tasted very odd, like a mixture of cough syrup and almonds. 'It won't knock me out, will it?' I asked, but she wouldn't say. Thirsty from the exertions of the afternoon, I drank the rest down in one, and twenty minutes later, I fell into a state that wasn't so much a sleep as a coma. I was dead to the world for the next fourteen hours. Annette – another member of staff – had to shake me awake the next morning.

My eyelids felt heavy; my limbs were like lead. I dragged myself down to breakfast but kept dropping my knife as I tried to spread butter on my toast.

'You don't look well,' Jules said. Neither did she. They'd grabbed her and Sophie K about an hour after they'd caught up with Sophie C and me. She had spent the night in the hated detention room, drugged up to the eyeballs.

'I feel like I've been hit with a sledgehammer. God knows what was in that drink Harriet gave me!' I said.

'Me too,' she added wearily.

I shambled along to the music class in my nightdress. I got on well with Miss Shilling, the music teacher. She knew how much I enjoyed the subject, so she usually gave me a certain amount of leeway when I grew sleepy in class. But today she seemed surprised by my inability to join in with recorder practice. The most I could do when she asked me a question was smile stupidly at her, and I kept nodding off.

Art with Mrs Nuttall was no better. My painting skills were reduced to toddler level and I tipped over two tumblers of water. In the end Mrs Nuttall suggested that I sit quietly with a book. I didn't care one way or the other. Nothing seemed to matter.

Later in the day my mood switched from dopey to jittery and I went up onto a nervous high. I'd lost my appetite and hadn't eaten all day, so I was already buzzing from lack of food, as well as the after-effects of the previous night's medicine.

Jules was my partner for the afternoon disco and ballroom dancing class in the front room. Our attempts to rumba were a complete disaster; it was the drugged leading the drugged. She went one way and I went the other and we kept bumping into each other and treading on each other's toes, much to the chagrin of Mr and Mrs Harding, the older couple taking the class. Worse still, because I was feeling so jumpy, I kept missing beats and jigging around to try and make up the rhythm. In the end, Jules took over and yanked me around the cramped dance floor, taking care not to hurt my bandaged arm.

Dad and his friends had taught me to waltz and foxtrot at the working men's club balls, but my fogged brain could scarcely recall the steps. I looked over Jules's shoulder to try to get some tips from the other girls. They were no help. We were like a bunch of elephants and one-legged giraffes.

But catching sight of Bridget's huge backside swinging from side to side under her grey skirt, I couldn't help giggling. There was something absurd in the way she danced. For one, it's impossible to look tough doing the cha cha cha. What's more, she was a really rubbish mover.

I wasn't the only one who found Bridget's dancing funny. Every time she swung her backside, the room rippled with suppressed laughter. She could sense it too. If she caught anyone looking at her, she would get a right cob on. 'What you staring at?' she'd hiss. It was so hard not to laugh in her face.

I thought Jules and I looked rather glamorous waltzing in our brushed cotton pink nighties and dressing gowns, but the floaty look didn't suit the next stage of the class, which was disco dancing. Every week, Mr and Mrs Harding brought along the same record – the cheesy 1980s track, D.I.S.C.O by Ottawan – and played it over and over again. We were supposed to perform a routine with arm movements that spelt out the word 'disco'. It was like the YMCA routine, and I could never get it right.

Jules constantly had to nudge me and shove me in the right direction, which had us in fits of laughter. Added to that, I couldn't help watching Bridget out of the corner of my eye. For some reason it was important to her to suck up to Mr and Mrs Harding and she tried diligently to get her moves right, even though she had not one ounce of dancing talent.

'Watch this!' Sophie K whispered to Jules and me about halfway through the lesson. She stood behind Bridget and imitated her, exaggerating her clumsy movements. Everyone laughed. Suddenly Bridget whipped round to face her and pushed her backwards, screaming obscenities.

'Stop that now!' Mrs Harding said, putting out a frail arm to restrain Bridget.

''You can fuck off too, you daft old bitch,' Bridget shouted, totally forgetting to suck up. Mrs Harding recoiled in horror.

'Don't speak to my wife like that!' Mr Harding protested. 'And don't ruin the class for the rest of the girls. Everyone else is having a lovely time, aren't they?'

'No, we hate it! Why do you make us do the same stupid dance every single week?' yelled Sophie C. Mrs Harding started saying something, but Sophie told her to shut up, 'you old bag'.

Soon most of the girls had joined in, subjecting the couple to a barrage of shocking insults and bad language. They quickly fled the room and reported us to Mrs Nuttall, and for the rest of the afternoon we were made to sit in silence. By then I was feeling sleepy again, so I was glad of the break, and anything was better than hearing that damn D.I.S.C.O. track on repeat. It was like some horrific form of torture. Even to this day I could recite the lyrics in my sleep.

That evening Mrs Pryde rang and left a message to say that David was being sent to Feltham Borstal for burglary. I was devastated for him. Everyone knew how rough borstal was. As the tears flowed, I knew I was crying for myself too, because this meant that David wouldn't be able to visit me now. We probably wouldn't see each other for ages.

Even though my brother was often mean to me, we had been through a lot together and I missed him. I couldn't understand why he hadn't written to me as he'd promised he would. (I found out later that Kate was withholding his letters. Her excuse was that she thought they would distress me.) Harriet found me sobbing in the dorm and I told her how worried I was about him. The more I talked about him and the rest of the family, the more upset I became. Eventually she forced me to drink down another glass of hot vitamin drink. I went out like a light again, back into the same dreamless, lifeless sleep as the night before.

I woke up at dawn, feeling on edge. The sky was orange and pink through the cracks in the curtains. I got up and started to pace the dorm, but five minutes later a wave of tiredness swept through me and I slept again. My jaw ached when I finally got up for good. 'You were grinding your teeth,' Zara said when she saw me rubbing my jaw. 'We all do it. It's the pills.'

The contents of the brown envelopes Harriet was giving me had begun to vary. Along with the blue and white tablets there was sometimes a yellow one and other white and orange pills of varying sizes. I asked Harriet repeatedly, but she wouldn't tell me what they were for, or why I was supposed to take more of them some days than others.

I started getting rashes and dry patches on different parts of my body. My right ear was constantly itchy and flaky. My hair lost its sheen and my mouth filled up with ulcers. Worst of all, I began suffering from what felt like period pains – but all through the month, not just when I was menstruating. They would start as a dull ache in my lower back and then gradually encircle me, creeping across my stomach until I had a ring of pain around me. Sometimes the pain in my kidney area would get so bad that I'd be doubled up, unable to go on with what I was doing.

The staff and teachers were totally unsympathetic. 'Always moaning and groaning, aren't you?' Mrs Petsworth used to say, tutting away.

One morning Mrs Macdonald flashed up a card with 'hypochondria' written on it. She asked the class if they knew what it meant. 'Teresa's a good example of a hypochondriac,' she said with a superior smile. It didn't seem fair. My symptoms were very real – and very worrying – to me. I knew I wasn't being paranoid.

Harriet made me take more and more of her lethal hot water concoctions. It didn't matter how hard I tried not to drink them – spitting, dribbling and spilling them were just some of my avoidance tactics – she always made sure that enough went down to zonk me out.

Increasingly I didn't make it to breakfast. One of the staff would come into the detention room or my dorm and rouse me around lunchtime. Even then it would be hard to wake me. I started falling asleep in class and my crying fits became more frequent and intense. I kept picturing David trying to tough it out at Feltham Borstal. It upset me to imagine how unhappy he would be there and I guessed he was probably be feeling suicidal, like me. I hated to think of Dad being evicted from the flat too. Where would he go? And what about Mum?

I had a fantasy that one day soon the family would come together again and we'd all live happily ever after. Dad would go to work and Mum would cook delicious meals. Bernadette and I would swap clothes and make-up and then we'd all sit around the telly in the evenings, laughing and joking. David would get a job and a girlfriend, and on Saturdays they'd take me skating, or to the cinema. I'd have lots of friends and Mum would make them welcome in our house, cooking them meals and fussing over them, and me.

Apart from when I was lost in my dream world, life was bearable only when I was in the laundry with Buttercup the cat, or helping to clean out the other girls' hamsters. I was always begging Miss Woods to let me have a hamster of my own. 'I'll look after it so well! I'll feed it and make sure its cage is always clean!'

'You have to earn that privilege, as you well know,' she'd say primly. 'You won't be getting one unless your behaviour improves considerably.'

She kept dangling it like a carrot, and then telling me that I'd ruined my chances. She didn't seem to understand that a lot of the time it felt as though I didn't have much control over the way I behaved or reacted. I didn't want to fall asleep in class any more than I wanted to slur my words or forget what I was saying mid-sentence, and yet I kept being told off for all three. However hard I struggled to be normal, my mood swings were becoming more extreme, and I could swoop from a state of deep sadness to hysterical laughter in the blink of an eye. I started harming myself with whatever I could get my hands on, from plastic and glass to the edges of pieces of paper.

I constantly thought about suicide. I couldn't see any point in living through this hell, without an end in sight. I pictured death as a blissful escape. It seemed as if things just couldn't get any worse. How wrong I was. In fact things were about to get a lot, lot worse, beyond my darkest imaginings.

CHAPTER EIGHT

I began to forget my French. Just over a month into my time at Kendall House, I could no longer recall words that had come easily to me before, or translate basic sentences like, 'The book is on the table.' To me, this was proof that the daily cocktail of pills was affecting me in a very harmful way.

'The tablets are making me stupid!' I complained to Mrs Nuttall. 'Don't you remember how good my French used to be?'

'I just don't think you're trying,' she said condescendingly.

Nothing I said made a difference. It was like living among Martians. I was trapped in a twilight zone where I could not make myself heard, or believed. I felt totally helpless. There was nowhere to turn, and no one willing to listen. I couldn't see the point in going on.

In despair, I grabbed a plastic pen, snapped it in half and plunged it into my arm. Blood dribbled down my skin, but I didn't care. I didn't feel any pain.

'Stop that at once!' Mrs Nuttall cried out, rushing towards me. 'Where did you get that pen?' She tried to snatch it from me. I pushed her away.

'Leave me alone,' I said. 'It's my pen. I can do what I want with it.' I jabbed my arm again. The pen began to splinter.

'Teresa, don't!' She left the room, swiftly returning with Harriet.

'Give me the pen,' Harriet ordered.

'No. Don't come near me.'

Harriet lunged at me and tried to grab the pen, but I shoved her back. Her dark eyes flashed with anger. She pressed her lips together into an uneven grimace.

'Go away! I've had enough of being controlled,' I said.

I slashed at my arm with a piece of jagged plastic, fast and furious. Soon there was a criss-cross pattern from the top of my left arm right down to my wrist. Thin streams of blood dripped into my hand. Watching them, I felt a temporary sense of peace, beyond pain.

I wanted to stop, but I was scared of lashing out. I knew it was wrong to hurt other people. It was far better to take it all out on myself. I felt desperately unhappy and lonely, and so small and insignificant that it was almost as if I didn't exist. I had no mind of my own anymore. I was nothing.

Shirley entered the room. 'Now, Teresa, please . . .' she said in a placatory voice. Harriet lunged towards me again and I screamed loud and hard, drowning out whatever it was that Shirley said next.

Harriet wouldn't give up. I could see she wanted to fight. Now Shirley came for me too, grabbing for my arms and trying to pull them behind my back. But I wouldn't give in. The fear of being restrained gave me unexpected strength and I struggled furiously, punching and kicking in every direction. Mrs Macdonald appeared out of nowhere and tried to pounce on me, and at some point Mrs Petsworth joined the fray. Her long thin arms kept reaching out to grasp me, but I slapped them away.

Miss Woods and Matthew, who was the part-time book keeper at Kendall House, burst into the room and rushed at me. Matthew was thin and wiry, but very muscular. He punched me hard in the back, winding me. I fell forwards, face down, with my arms outstretched and flailing. 'Pin her down!' Miss Woods shouted. 'Quick, Harriet, inject her.'

I was still kicking and yelling as they yanked my arms behind me. Matthew took hold of my hands and pressed them against my lower back. A heavy weight landed on my left leg, squashing it. I realised that someone was sitting on me to keep me down. Someone else sat on the other leg. A hand kept pressing my head down. I heard my jaw crack as they pushed my face hard against the ground. I tried to resist and push up with my neck, scared that my face would smash into the floor again. Someone grabbed my hair and jerked my head upwards. A fist thumped into the middle of my back. My chest felt like it was caving in. I couldn't breathe or swallow. I was terrified.

I didn't want to live, but if I was going to die it would be at my own hands, not theirs. An even heavier weight pressed down on me. My ribs were hurting badly. I screamed out but they kept on pressing me down. I felt sick. Vomit rose up my throat and I started to choke. My hair stuck to my face. It was drenched in tears. I begged them to get off me. I screamed out that I would do anything they wanted me to.

'It's a bit late for that now!' Harriet said gleefully. She seemed to be enjoying the drama.

I heard Ivy's voice, and then Miss Woods's. Someone pulled my nightie up to waist level, exposing my legs and bottom. A rough hand started fumbling with my knickers. Terrified, I struggled harder, jerking and wriggling as much as I could. I was desperate to get away, out of their clutches.

My knickers tore as they were violently pulled down. 'No!' I cried out. 'Get off! Help me, someone!'

'Stay still,' Harriet ordered. 'Just lie back and think of England. What's the point in struggling? There!'

A sudden, searing pain shot through my bum down my legs and up through my back. I screamed with every last bit of energy I had, petrified that they were trying to kill me. For a brief moment my body vibrated with the most intense pain and fear I'd ever experienced. Then I felt a potent mixture of drugs pumping through my system, immobilising me, shutting me down on all levels. My scream floated away into thin air, no longer loud or powerful. I heard myself whimper a couple of times.

They got hold of me as I went limp and dragged me like a rag doll through the corridor, not caring when my head knocked against a door. I could see and feel what was going on, but at the same time it felt as if I wasn't in my body. I saw several girls watching with wide, horrified eyes as they yanked me through the hall and up the stairs, like a pig to slaughter. My last thoughts were a jumbled mixture of confusion and hatred. And then I was out, dead to the world.

I woke up in the detention room, with Shirley standing over me. At first I couldn't think who she was. Petite, with plain, open features and short, curly, fair hair, she brought to mind a farmer's wife I had once seen interviewed on TV. Her arm was in a sling. 'You're a very naughty girl, aren't you?' she said.

I shook my head, unable to remember how I'd ended up in the room, or why. I tried to speak, but my mouth was as dry as a desert and my throat was sore. My body felt tender and bruised all over, as if I'd just gone ten rounds in a boxing ring. My arm was bandaged. A nerve in one of my eyelids kept flickering. I had a really bad headache and my brain was barely functioning.

With great effort, I managed to swallow. 'What happened?' I asked in a small, ragged voice.

'Come off it, Teresa, are you trying to tell me that you don't recall punching Harriet in the ribs, or hurting my elbow?'

I frowned and slowly shook my head again. 'No. I don't.'

'Well, I am in a lot of pain because of you. Every time I move my arm it hurts, and it looks like I'm going to be wearing this sling for at least a fortnight. So, what have you got to say for yourself?'

A surge of guilt overcame me. I hated the idea of causing anyone pain. It had never been in my nature to hurt anything. I loved animals. I loved people. I loved kids. I was that way inclined. To hurt someone was a major thing. 'Is it broken?' I asked.

'As it happens, it's not, but that's no thanks to you, madam!'

'I'm so sorry,' I croaked. 'I can't remember anything, but I'm sure I didn't mean to do it.'

'Sorry is better than nothing, I suppose,' she said. 'But it's not going to make my elbow better, is it? And it's not going to heal poor old Harriet's bruised ribs either.' She tapped her temple, as if pointing to her brain. 'You are just going to have to think harder about the consequences of your actions in future, aren't you? Perhaps this will teach you not to misbehave, eh?'

Hot tears welled up in my eyes. 'I'm sorry. I didn't realise I'd done it.'

'So will you promise me that we won't have hysterical scenes like that again? No more slashing your arms with pens, no more fighting with members of staff. If you want to stay friends with me, you're going to have to be a good girl from now on. Do you understand?'

I nodded, still unsure which hysterical scenes she was referring to. My mind was a haze and I was feeling incredibly small and weak and powerless. Right then I would have agreed to anything in order to get a bit of comfort or care. But suddenly I flashed back to the memory of someone pulling down my knickers. A mishmash of images crowded into my mind and I began to piece together what had gone on. Shuddering, I reached out and touched Shirley's arm. 'They hurt me,' I said. 'You hurt me.' As the full horror of what had happened came back to me, I shrank away from her, reliving my fear.

'No, Teresa,' she scolded. 'We simply stopped you from harming yourself.'

'But I ache all over.' I pulled up my nightdress to inspect my legs. My knees were black and blue. There was a hand-shaped bruise on my thigh.

'I'm not at all surprised. You wouldn't let us help you, so we had to use a certain amount of force. It was only for your own good, you know.'

Again those words: 'for your own good'. It was the catch-all reason for everything they were doing, from drugging me to locking me up, from taking away my shoes to pinning me down. But there wasn't any good in it. Everything was getting worse. I'd never self-harmed before Kendall House. I hadn't experienced all-day crying fits. I'd been a healthy girl with a good appetite and a clear complexion. I may have been messed up by my family situation, but I'd still managed to be happy and chatty most of the time. Yet now I had slash marks and scars up and down my arms. I was always in tears.

My appetite was tiny, my skin was covered in rashes and I was miserable most of the time. I told Shirley how unhappy I was feeling.

'Well, how do you think I feel?' she said with a poor-me smile, looking down at her trussed up arm.

I felt another pang of guilt. 'I'm so sorry, sorry, sorry! I'll never do it again, I promise.'

'That's what I like to hear,' she said, beaming. 'Now, if you're good I'll pop back later and give your hair a brush and tidy you up a bit. Would you like that?'

'Yes, please,' I said, my voice choking. More than anything, I wanted to be looked after.

I was alone for the next few hours, drifting in and out of sleep. I felt increasingly guilty about Shirley and hoped she believed me that I hadn't meant to hurt her. On the other hand, it confused me that she had joined the others to help pin me to the ground and inject me. What's more, she hadn't shown any sympathy for what I had been through. I was literally covered in bruises, from head to toe, but she hadn't batted an eyelid when I showed her the marks that she and the others had left.

Miss Woods came in for a chat. I tried to sit up, but my back was stiff and ached terribly. 'It really hurts. I think I need a doctor,' I said.

'There you go again, attention-seeking at every opportunity!' she tutted. 'You're unbelievable, you are, and after hurting Shirley like that too!'

'I didn't mean to! I said I was sorry.'

All the guilt trips they were throwing at me just made me feel worse about myself. I wanted to self-harm even more than before. I was useless. No good. Bad.

I fell back onto my hard pillow and stared at the ceiling

while she lectured me about my behaviour. She finished up by saying, 'I will be confiscating your pens and we will be monitoring all of your personal possessions. You have forfeited the right to be responsible for them yourself.'

'But I need pens to do my homework,' I said.

'Don't concern yourself with school for the time being. Far more important is learning how to get the best out of Kendall House, and you can do that by going right back to basics. So, no school tomorrow – I've told the teachers that you can have a few days off. We don't want you getting upset over your failures again.'

I thought back to Mrs Nuttall's class. 'I've forgotten how to speak French,' I said. 'I used to be really good, but I can't remember a thing anymore.'

Miss Woods pursed her lips. 'We can't all be clever, you know. But Mrs Connolly tells me that your needlework is excellent, so why don't you concentrate on the practical subjects when you get back to school?'

She just didn't understand. I tried to explain that the medicine was affecting my learning abilities, but suddenly I felt very tired and couldn't remember what I wanted to say. I tried to speak, but all that came out was a burble of mixed up French and English. My brain felt as if it had been liquefied. My thoughts were a swirling mass.

Finally I was able to say something coherent. 'I'm so scared. What's happening to me?'

Miss Woods stood up. She looked down at me with hard eyes. 'You are learning some of life's most important lessons, including how to cooperate,' she said. 'Yes, it can be difficult to adjust, but life will be impossible for you here if you don't learn how to live peacefully.'

A little later, Harriet came in with a handful of tablets.

She too was full of recriminations. 'How could you treat Shirley like that? Have you seen her poor arm? What disgusting behaviour! You should be ashamed.'

I burst into tears. 'I've said I'm sorry, and I am, I really am. I didn't mean to hurt her.'

After she had left I fell into a deep sleep. In my dreams, I was pursued by monsters wielding enormous hypodermic needles. As they got closer to me, I realised that Matthew and Harriet were among them, their features distended and distorted. Matthew was waving a pair of blue knickers. 'Lie back and think of England!' Harriet kept shouting. I woke up shivering and drenched in sweat.

When Harriet woke me up the next day, I was still feeling very groggy. 'Chop chop!' she said, throwing some of my clothes down on the bed. 'Get dressed. We're going out for a walk.'

'Is Shirley's arm better?'

'It's still extremely painful. She had to go to hospital to have it X-rayed in case it was broken. Honestly, how could you have done such a nasty thing?'

Once again I said how sorry I was. I still felt really bad about it. My stomach made a growling sound. I rubbed it. 'I think I'm hungry.'

Harriet gave me a slanted look. 'You do pick your moments, don't you? Shirley tried waking you for breakfast and for lunch, but she couldn't rouse you. Go and get a snack from the kitchen, but hurry up. I haven't got a lot of time for our little outing.'

'Where are we going?'

'You'll see when we get there.'

It took me ages to put on my clothes. I was a fumbling wreck – all fingers and thumbs, as my nan would have said –

and by the time I was ready to go out I had lost my appetite. My mind kept zoning in and out and I forgot what I was supposed to be doing half the time. Harriet became very impatient and rushed me along on our way into town. It was hard to keep up with her.

First we went to the chemist. I gazed longingly at the lipstick samples while Harriet discussed something with the pharmacist. Next we went to a hardware shop to pick up a couple of things. I began to wonder why Harriet had brought me with her. It wasn't as if she needed someone to help her with the few things she'd bought.

As if sensing my confusion, she said, 'Didn't you say you wanted a hamster?' She pointed at the pet shop on Philip Street.

Had I heard right? At first I couldn't believe it. But sure enough, she took me into the pet shop and told me to pick out a hamster. I went straight for the loudest and liveliest, a gorgeous little thing with light ginger fur and beautiful dark eyes. He was squealing like a nutter, full of energy, and running maniacally around his cage. I was even more impressed when I put my finger in the cage and he bit me. A true fighter, he wasn't content with just one bite. He sank his teeth in and hung on for dear life. I was determined to get him to like me.

'Isn't it sweet?' Harriet said. 'You should call it Ginger.'

She had to be joking. 'No, I'm going to call him Dynamutt. Yes, Dynamutt.' I laughed. It was thrilling to have my own pet. 'Because he's like a teeny, weeny explosive miniature dog!'

Harriet looked puzzled. 'Dynamutt? No, that's no good. Call it Ginger. That's a much better name.'

'Is he my hamster?'

'Yes, it's yours for as long as you tend to it and treat it well.'

'Then I get to choose the name. And it's Dynamutt.'

She pressed her lips together. How could she argue? She paid the shop assistant and we took Dynamutt back to Kendall House. He shrieked all the way. Perhaps he sensed what was in store for us both in the coming weeks.

Back inside the house, Harriet told me to put Dynamutt with the other hamsters on the bottom shelf of a built-in wall unit in the sitting room, and then to get back into my nightclothes. 'Please don't put me back in the detention room!' I said.

'Miss Woods says you can sleep in the dorm tonight, but only if you're good and take your pills.'

I groaned, although anything was better than being cooped up in that claustrophobic hellhole. But, as it turned out, I wouldn't have known much about it either way. The medication Harriet gave me after tea put me out like a light. I slept for fourteen straight hours and woke up at eight thirty the next morning with what felt like a head full of sand.

I didn't feel well enough to go with the other girls on their trip to the Isle of Grain that afternoon, but when they came back, I joined them in the sitting room to watch a film. Tina and Bridget kept interrupting the TV to say nasty things. 'I'm going to get a hamster,' Bridget said. 'I'm going to train it to fight your hamster and sink its teeth into your hamster's neck and suck out all its blood.'

I shuddered at the thought of my lovely Dynamutt being in danger. 'You're not coming anywhere near him,' I said. 'Only Jules is allowed to feed him when I'm not there.'

Bridget switched channels on the television. 'Hey! I was watching that,' Sophie K said.

'Ya boo sucks,' Bridget spat at her. Turning to me again,

she said, 'First I'm going to kill your hamster and then I'm going to kill you. Ha!'

I shut my eyes and clapped my hands over my ears, unable to bear the cruelty in her gaze, the sadistic satisfaction in her voice. 'Fuck off, fuck off, fuck off!' I mumbled, returning to my childhood mantra. I spent the rest of the evening sitting halfway up the hall stairs.

Two days later I was called into Miss Woods's office. Mrs Pryde was sitting in the leather armchair that Dr Peri favoured, with Bridget opposite her. Bridget was drinking from one of Miss Woods's dinky cups. There was a tea tray between them and they were laughing together about something. It was a very cosy, intimate scene, unlike any meeting with Mrs Pryde that I could ever imagine. I stood at the doorway wondering when they would notice me.

Just then Bridget looked up. 'Uh-oh, here's trouble.'

Mrs Pryde looked at her watch. 'Time's up now, Bridget. See you next time,' she said. Bridget scowled at me as she left the room.

'So, Teresa,' my social worker said, barely smiling. 'How are you getting on, then?' Looking vaguely bored, she settled back into the chair to hear what I had to say.

I begged her to take me away from Kendall House. 'I'm being drugged and bullied. I'm losing my mind!' I told her.

About five minutes into the conversation, she held a hand up to silence me. 'It's going to take time to settle in. Let's review things in a couple of months,' she said. She wrote a brief scribble in her notepad.

My heart thumped. 'No!' I protested. 'I'll be dead by then. I'm dying, Mrs Pryde. I'm sure of it. I can't think anymore. I'm battered and bruised and I feel ill almost all of the time. You've got to get me out of here now!'

She rapped her fingers on the arm of the chair and gave me one of her disapproving smiles. Glancing at her wrist again, she said, 'At least let's leave it until my next visit. I'm very pressed for time. I've got another appointment.'

'But you have to save me! I am being drugged to death.'

She sighed. 'Always so dramatic! Teresa, this is all in your head. Dr Peri is a highly respected psychiatrist who knows what he is doing. You must do whatever he says is best for you, for your own good. Whatever he says is right. Just remember that. Now hurry along and get back to school.'

'But I've only ever seen Dr Peri twice, for about five minutes in total!' I protested. 'He can't see what the drugs are doing to me. He doesn't bother visiting to evaluate me. How can he know what's best or isn't?'

I told her about how I had forgotten my French and most of my Maths. She rolled her eyes and assured me that I was in expert hands.

'Trust those who are older and wiser than you are,' she said, putting away her notepad. 'Time to go.'

I eyed the tea tray. 'Don't I get any tea?'

She gave me a tight smile. 'Too late, I'm afraid! Goodbye.'

That night I lacerated my left arm with a tiny shard of glass I found on the floor. As I slashed at my skin, I realised that I hated what I was becoming. It was almost second nature to hurt myself in moments of despair. It was like the next step on from crying – a release, but something I would rather not do.

Ivy dressed the wounds with Savlon cream and a crepe bandage. 'This is very silly behaviour, Teresa. If you're not careful you will scar your arms, which you will regret when you have a nice boyfriend one day.'

I had no idea what she was going on about. Boyfriend?

She was talking about a world I didn't inhabit, a place where mums baked cakes for their kids and boys asked girls to the cinema. Later Harriet made me sleep in the detention room, 'for my own good', although I saw it as a punishment. I banged the walls and shouted for ages, hoping someone would come and let me out, but no one did. I was desperate to go to the toilet and had to hold it in all night, which was very uncomfortable.

The next morning my head felt full of fog. My hands shook as I washed. I kept missing my teeth and cut my gum open with my toothbrush. A member of staff called Trinny was on duty, a very overweight older lady with white hair. I showed her my shaking hands and told her how bad I was feeling.

'Have you been glue sniffing?' she asked.

'No!' I said. The idea was almost laughable. Why would I want to get high on solvents when I was already out of my head on the drugs they were giving me? It didn't make sense.

Trinny dismissed my worries and told me to go to school. Feeling weak and dizzy, I stumbled into Mrs Macdonald's class and slumped in a chair. 'Why do I feel ill all the time?' I asked. Mrs Macdonald ignored me.

I began picking at the bandage on my arm. It felt uncomfortable. I wanted to take it off. A wave of tiredness swept over me. I put my head on the desk and went to sleep. When I woke up, I went to complain to Mrs Ryfield.

'I'm being over-drugged.'

'That can't possibly be the case. Dr Peri does the prescribing and he knows what's most suitable for you.'

My vision blurred. I found myself squinting at her. 'I'm not myself on these tablets. They are turning me into a zombie,' I said.

'Let's just wait and see, shall we? It's all for the best. Now go and get that bandage on your arm re-dressed.'

Kate took me to the nurse's station on the second floor, where Miss Woods changed my bandage. 'No more of this, Teresa! You've only got two arms and they've got to last you a long time,' she scolded.

That night I pulled off the bandage and re-opened the wounds with a piece of paper, adding a thousand tiny cuts to the pattern of despair on my arms. I wished I were dead.

Over the following weeks, my aches and pains got worse. My head throbbed and my eyes became highly sensitive to light. My stomach pains were excruciating at times; I frequently felt sick and feverish. My hands shook, my knees felt weak and often I didn't have the strength to walk even a few paces. I was always hitting tired patches, forgetting what I was saying mid-sentence or simply losing the energy to go on with whatever I was doing. I started to hallucinate and every movement I made was in slow motion. I trembled with cold a lot of the time. My nose was constantly runny and my eyes watery.

'It's hell, Dad!' I said, the next time he came to visit.

'Don't you worry, I'm going to write to our MP about it, get you off the drugs,' he promised.

I wanted to believe him, but he reeked of alcohol and I figured that he was unlikely even to remember the visit when he got home, let alone his promise to help.

I hated saying goodbye to Dad. I often wondered if we would both manage to survive until the next time we met. His life seemed so precarious, what with all the drinking, and I felt close to death a lot of the time. But at least he had his freedom. At least he could walk out of Kendall House and go where he pleased. I had no independence whatsoever.

I couldn't even go to the toilet without asking a member of staff to unlock the door for me.

We went on occasional trips and outings, but they were carefully monitored and restricted. The staff would bring along our medication and feed it to us in the most unlikely places, and they were always barking orders and shouting at us, so we rarely had any fun.

In early September, Fred and Maggie took Emma and me to Camber Sands in Kent. The weather was still good and it was fantastic to be able to stare at the wide horizon, dreaming of escape from Kendall House. My eyes were so unused to seeing beyond the walls of the building that it took a bit of time for my focus to adjust, but soon they were greedily taking in the open space.

My mood changed when I put on my swimming costume though. I could feel Fred's vampire dark eyes on me, his gaze lingering for far too long on certain parts of my body.

'Teresa may be skinny, but she'll soon get her curves in all the right places,' he said as I came out of the sea.

'Yes, it won't be long now,' Maggie agreed.

A little later, I spotted an ice cream van. 'Can I have an ice lolly?' I asked.

'Fancy licking something long and wet, do you?' Fred joked.

I laughed, not really understanding. His tone of voice made me feel uncomfortable. Maggie was having a swim. Something told me that he wouldn't have spoken like that while she was in earshot.

'Teresa wants to get her lips around something. How about you, Emma? Are you dying for a suck?' he went on.

Emma blushed and mumbled something. 'What?' Fred said, cupping his ear.

Emma said that she would prefer a cone to a lolly. 'I bet you would,' he laughed. 'You'd rather have something white and soft and creamy in your mouth. But Teresa wants something hard, don't you, girl?'

Bile rose up the back of my throat. 'I don't want anything,' I said, wrapping a towel around me to shield my body from his greedy gaze. 'You're just an ugly pervert and I wish you'd shut up.'

When Maggie came out of the sea, she announced that it was time for teatime medication. She took various bottles of pills out of her bag and sorted them into two batches, one for me and one for Emma. As usual, we complained that we didn't want them.

'If you do what you're told, you can have some money for the ice cream van,' she said. She couldn't understand it when we said we didn't feel like eating any ice cream today.

Back at Kendall House, Bridget was in a foul mood, picking on anybody who came within her field of vision – except her darling Nicole, of course. First in the line of fire was Jules, whose new haircut was not to her taste. 'No one would have called you pretty before, but now you look bloody ugly!' she shouted at Jules across the sitting room.

'She does not,' I said.

'How would you know, you ugly bitch?'

'Jules, your hair looks great,' I said.

Bridget's dark eyes burned with rage. 'You think that straggly mop of rats' tails looks good? You stupid crazy cow! You definitely deserve the beating I'm going to give you later. I'm going to stamp on your pathetic head and watch your brains ooze out all over the floor.'

She said it with such conviction, and the expression on her face was so vicious and brutal, that I felt compelled to back down. She was a hulking mass of muscle, fat and malice, truly frightening, the stuff of nightmares. I was absolutely petrified of her.

'Let's go, Jules. We don't need this,' I said. The sound of Bridget's terrifying cackle trailed after us as we left the room.

CHAPTER NINE

I was terrified of being injected again, so for a short while I took my pills without arguing. I thought that perhaps if I toed the line and made them think I was happy at Kendall House, they would treat me better, maybe even reduce the amount of tablets they were giving me. It didn't work, though. Nothing I did made a difference.

I tried to endure the mood swings and sleepy patches in silence, but it was hard. I just couldn't understand why I was being so heavily drugged, and none of the staff would give me a straight answer. I spent my days shuffling around the house trying to make sense out of chaos. All I knew was that what they were doing to me was very, very wrong.

The only time my life felt like it had any meaning was when I was tending Dynamutt, or playing with Buttercup in the laundry. I had some nice times with Jules too. But things were getting more difficult with the other girls every day.

Bridget always seemed to be behind me, whispering threats in my ear, enjoying the sound of her own sadistic fantasies. She made a real effort to turn the others against me, not just during an argument, or for an afternoon, but for good. Day in day out she drummed into them that I was unhygienic, mad, stupid and ugly, and the constant repetition seemed to work a spell on them. I probably was quite annoying at times, because I was half off my head and didn't know what I was doing, but I didn't deserve the treatment Bridget dished out. She went on and on about how I had no tits or bum and nicknamed me Titsalina Bumsquirt, which the others found hilarious. I felt increasingly isolated from the group.

Everyone was frightened of Bridget so they did as they were told, except Tina, who had a lot of fight in her. Tina was probably harder than all of us. You could not turn your back on that girl. Sophie K had a vicious streak. Zara was nice at times but weak at others.

Emma and Sophie C sometimes tried to protect me from Bridget, but it was hard for them. The only person I could really trust was Jules. Although her fear of Bridget meant that sometimes she ganged up against me with the others, when we were on our own it felt like we were soul mates – best friends for life – so I always forgave her.

My dad had made several requests to have me home for the weekend, but so far the answer had been no. So I was glad to hear Jules had a new escape plan. There was a trip scheduled to Oaklands Park, near Clacton-on-Sea, the following Thursday and she knew the area well. 'We'll get away quick and easy, through the woods,' she assured me.

Our only problem was to make sure we earned the privilege of going out that day, and that was never going to be a straightforward process. The privilege system, for all its supposed rules and regulations, often seemed to depend on the moods and whims of the staff. I never saw Bridget get carted off to the detention room, for instance, and hardly any of the staff told her off for doing things that would get me put in my nightclothes immediately. She wasn't on any drugs either, nor was Nicole. I did not once see them in the queue for medication.

I wondered whether Nicole got preferential treatment because she was so pretty, or because she was Bridget's best friend. It couldn't have been because she was well behaved, because she wasn't. She talked back to the staff, mucked around in lessons and joined in with Bridget's bullying. But like Bridget, she could also be a sneak, informing on the other girls to the staff, so maybe that's why she had it easy. I didn't trust her an inch.

Thursday arrived and by some miracle Jules and I were both allowed on the trip to Oaklands Park. Before we left, Jules told me to slip into the laundry when Dot wasn't looking. 'Grab some clothes. We'll want to change out of our track suits when we get away,' she whispered.

I had just finished stuffing a couple of clean skirts under my sweatshirt when Nicole came in. I dropped to my knees and pretended to be looking for Buttercup.

'You and that cat!' she sneered. 'It don't surprise me that the only friends you've got are dumb animals. They're the only ones that can stand you.'

'Go away, Nicole. Buttercup won't come out if you're around. She hates bad smells.'

'Cheeky bitch,' Nicole said.

Still on my knees, I rammed my head into her stomach. Leaving her doubled up in pain and winded, I went off to find Jules.

Nicole reappeared while we were queuing up at the shoe cupboard, waiting for Janice to come along and open it. She whispered something to Bridget, who pushed up behind me and kicked me twice, and then jerked her knee forcefully into my side. I drew in a sharp breath and tried to swallow the pain, not wanting to attract the attention of the staff. I regretted reacting to Nicole's taunt in the laundry and was determined not to do anything else that could come in the way of our escape plan.

Bridget clasped my shoulders with her fat fingers. I tried to shake her off. 'If you ever go near Nicole again I will come into your dorm while you are sleeping and suffocate you with a pillow,' she hissed at me. Her mouth was so close to my ear that she sprayed it with spittle. Suddenly she gave a terrifying roar.

I jumped. A violent shiver went through me. 'I won't go near her,' I whimpered.

The shoe cupboard stank when Janice finally opened it. Our coats and jackets were in there too, and they reeked of sweaty feet and leather. It was disgusting. By now my slippers were badly smelly as well. It didn't make any difference how often I washed my feet, they smelt horrible after five minutes in those slippers.

Oaklands Park consisted of a large open field area surrounded by thick woods. Jules and I played ball games with the others, biding our time until the right moment came to slip away. Although I was hot from jumping around, I said I was cold and put on my jacket. Jules did the same. 'You can't be cold!' Dot said. We assured her that we were.

'Can we explore the rest of the park?' Jules asked Janice.

'Only if you stay within sight. Don't go into the woods, will you?'

'No,' we chorused.

We sauntered off towards the end of the field, followed by Sophie C, and then Bridget and Nicole. 'Fuck off, Bridget,' I called behind me.

'Turn round and say that again!' she shouted.

'Come on, run for it,' Jules said as we reached the edge of the copse. We slipped in between a couple of trees and broke into a sprint.

'Wait for me!' Sophie called from way behind, but there was no time to lose. We went on running until we were out the other side of the trees and onto an adjoining road, where we made our way to the nearest bus stop. A couple of agonisingly long minutes later, a bus came along. We flagged it down and got on it, not caring where it was headed.

Two bus trips later we arrived at the nearest train station, where we took the first train to London. It was a cramped journey. Because we had spent the last of our money on the bus, we had to lock ourselves in the toilet to avoid the ticket inspector. In London, we jumped over the barrier on the underground and took the tube to Putney Bridge. From there we walked to my dad's flat in Raynors Road.

Dad was chuffed to see us. 'What a surprise! Come on in!' he said.

Jules's face fell when we got inside. Even I was horrified. The flat was an absolute tip, the worst I'd seen it, and that was saying a lot. Everywhere you looked there were fag ends, empty cans and bottles, dirty plates, glasses and clothes. I peeped into my old bedroom. It looked like a bomb had gone off.

I asked where Bernadette was. Dad said she was staying with friends. I wasn't surprised. How anybody could live like this was beyond me. Bernadette would have hated it. I felt really embarrassed in front of Jules.

'Sorry about the mess,' Dad said, coughing nervously. 'I was just about to give it a good old clear out. But let's get out of here and go and celebrate, eh? They'll be glad to see you at the Fox and Hounds.'

As if sensing my discomfort, Jules nudged me. 'We don't care about the mess. It's just great to be away from Kendall House,' she said, grinning.

She was right. We were free. This was our time to enjoy ourselves and, as it turned out, Mary the landlady at the Fox and Hounds let us sleep in a little box room at the top of the stairs. We spent the evening drinking Fanta and playing cards and snooker. It was really nice to see Dad outside of Kendall House. He got pissed, as usual, but he was in a good mood all night and we had a happy singsong round the piano.

Jules and I got up early and went to see him in the morning, taking tea bags and a pint of milk. It took ages to wake him up, but finally he answered the door. We washed up some mouldy cups and boiled the kettle. I told Dad about all the drugs they were giving me at Kendall House, and recounted the horror of being pinned down and injected. Jules described what it was like to be locked in the detention room. Her eyes filled with tears as she recalled the nights she had spent in that dreadful, tiny room.

Dad looked really upset. 'I'd like to have you back home, but you can't stay here,' he said. His future was very uncertain. Work was patchy and he had no idea when he was going to be evicted from the flat. 'It could be any day,' he sighed.

I suppose we had known all along that we would have to go back to Kendall House, unless we wanted to go on the run and sleep rough. It just wouldn't have worked out at Dad's, even if Wandsworth Social Services had allowed me to stay there, and Jules's family couldn't have us. We tried phoning my mum, but she was living with a man called Peter who wouldn't let me speak to her. I hated how he sounded. I could tell he was violent and controlling.

In the end Dad gave us the money to get the train to Gravesend. I felt suicidal at the thought of going back to

Kendall House, but there was no alternative. The police would have picked us up later that day anyway. Dad's flat wasn't exactly a subtle hiding place.

We found an empty carriage on the train. 'Look what I've got,' Jules said, giggling and taking a tube of Evo Stick and a plastic bag out of her pocket.

I had never sniffed glue before. Although I'd seen other kids do it at Westdean and Long Grove, I had never wanted to join in.

'It numbs everything. It will help you forget that we're going back,' Jules said.

At that moment I would have done anything to block out where we were headed, if only for a few minutes. 'Go on then,' I said.

We sniffed it in our seats. A low humming sound started up in my ears. Opposite me, Jules was laughing hysterically. Her eyes were red and she kept coughing. 'Isn't it great?' she said.

It definitely wasn't great for me. My head felt like it was caving in and the weird humming noise grew louder. Feeling sick, I crossed my arms over my belly and began to rock backwards and forwards. I vowed never to touch glue again.

We got off the train and wandered down to the banks of the River Thames, to a little wooden jetty next to a disused warehouse. It was cold and windy. The sky was grey and swollen with rain clouds. My ears were still buzzing. I felt unbelievably depressed, and my mood kept swooping lower and lower. Crying miserably, I told Jules that I'd rather die than go back to Kendall House. I took off my coat. 'I've had enough,' I said. 'I'm sorry! I can't take it anymore.' I ran to the end of the jetty.

'No!' Jules screamed. She grabbed hold of me just in time to pull me back from the edge. I tried to shake her off, but she clung on to me and pushed me onto the ground. Straddling me, she shook me by the shoulders and yelled, 'You can't die! You're my only friend.'

'I can't live either, not in that place!' I moaned. 'Let me go. I can't go on.'

She started crying too. 'It's the glue making you feel like this. Pull yourself together. One day we'll be free, Teresa. We've got to hang on until we are. You've got to get through this! We've both got to get through it, and the only way to do it is together.'

She begged me not to do anything stupid, but it was at least half an hour before she trusted me not to throw myself in the river. Finally, cold and exhausted, we walked slowly back through the drizzle in the direction of Kendall House.

A man with a dog was walking behind us. I jumped every time the dog barked. It was a scary-looking German Shepherd-mix, dark and ferocious, like something out of a horror movie. 'Don't look now. There's a bloody big mutt following behind us,' I whispered to Jules.

She peeped over her shoulder. 'You must be seeing things. It's a tiny little pooch!' she giggled. I looked again. Sure enough, it was only a yapping little lapdog.

Half an hour later we were back in our nightclothes, back in hell, and the next day Dr Peri changed my medication. There were more pills than ever in the brown envelopes Harriet doled out morning, noon and night, and I was even more zombified than before. I experienced a lot of giddy spells and numbness in my limbs. My stomach pains became more intense and frequent. Most mornings I wondered whether it was worth getting out of bed and trying to face the day. Something always laid me low, whether it was dizziness, a throbbing headache, tummy ache, nausea or faintness. I had a lot of trouble passing urine, which left me with horrible aches in my back.

I really was like the living dead. My reactions slowed. I couldn't keep up with what people were saying. My vision kept blurring and my coordination got worse and worse. I spilled my food down me when I was eating and couldn't keep it in my mouth while I was chewing.

Bridget had every excuse to taunt me now. 'You're turning into bloody Georgie!' she crowed. And to some degree she was right. I was becoming mentally and physically disabled. I just had to hope it was only temporary.

Jules tried to keep my spirits up. A few weeks after we got back from our latest escape, we were finally allowed a walk to Woodlands Park with Janice. As we made our way there, Jules started chanting, 'Kendall House is hell on earth', thrusting her fist into the air repeatedly. I tried to join in, but my arm wouldn't move properly and my tongue kept tripping on the words. I sounded like someone with a severe speech impediment.

On our way back I stepped out into a road without looking. A car screeched to a halt in front of me, missing me by inches, at which point I collapsed on to the ground. Jules dragged me out of the road and Janice slapped my cheeks to bring me round.

Back at Kendall House I was told off for attention-seeking and made to wear my nightclothes day and night for a week. 'Why did you do it, you stupid girl?' Dot asked.

'I don't know. I must have wanted to kill myself.'

'Don't be silly, Teresa. We all know how much you love a drama. And what would your hamster have done without you? You're always saying how much you love that little ball of fur.'

She was clever in that way, Dot. She knew how much I loved animals; her words gave me an instant guilt trip. I vowed to myself then that I would never leave Dynamutt. Along with Jules and Buttercup, he was part of my reason for living, and it wasn't his fault that I was having such a bad time.

If anything happened to me, I knew that Tina would claim Dynamutt. She was always bugging me to hold and feed him. She hadn't been at Kendall House long enough to have her own hamster, and sometimes I let her help with cleaning out his cage.

Every time I took him into the sitting room, Tina asked if she could put him away later. Normally I refused, but one night she looked so eager that I said she could hold him while I opened his cage.

She sat down next to me and watched as I played with him on my lap. 'Where are you going for Christmas?' she asked.

'I don't know. It seems a bit early to worry about it.' It was the middle of October.

'Most of the girls are going home, but I'm going to Miss Woods's house,' she said.

I wondered why Miss Woods hadn't asked me, and where I would go instead. It seemed unlikely they would let me go home.

'Come on, Dynamutt, time for bed,' I said, handing him to Tina. She cupped her hands around him.

As I leant down to unclasp the wire door, I heard her gasp, 'Oh no!'

'What is it?' I said, with a sudden sense of fear.

'There's something wrong with him.' She held out her hands. Dynamutt was lying floppy and lifeless across her palms.

Aghast, I took him from her. 'He was fine just now. What have you done to him?' I said. I sat down and laid him on my lap, tenderly trying to tickle him back to life. 'Someone get help!' I called. Sophie K ran off to find a staff member.

'I didn't do anything!' Tina screeched.

I glanced up at her. There was the barest hint of a smile beneath her apparent anguish. It dawned on me that she had deliberately tried to kill Dynamutt. I turned him over. His neck rolled at an unnatural angle. It was broken. I didn't want to believe it, but he was too obviously dead for me to delude myself that he wasn't.

Pulling my knees up towards my chin and wrapping my arms around them, I gently began to rock my darling hamster in my lap. Tears streamed silently down my cheeks.

'Why did you do it, Tina?' I asked. 'Surely you don't hate me that much.' But Tina was no longer there.

Janice bustled into the room, tutting. I told her what had happened. 'Tina loved your hamster, so why would she kill it?' she said. 'No, no, Teresa, these little creatures can die any time. It probably had a heart attack. Never mind, we'll get you a new one.'

I was hurt and angry at Janice's suggestion that you could replace something you loved so easily. I didn't want a new hamster; I wanted Dynamutt back. I cried all night and in the morning Zara told me she hated me for keeping her up.

I tried to get out of bed, but I had severe pains in my right side. Harriet came to see me. 'Stop messing around,' she ordered. 'This is nothing but attention-seeking.'

I tried to sit up straight, but the pain was overwhelming. 'I can't,' I gasped.

Harriet put her arm around me and pulled me roughly to my feet. 'You see? You can,' she said. She walked me to the detention room. 'Feeling better? If not, I'll have to leave you in there for the day.'

'OK, I feel better,' I said. Even though I was sure I was going to collapse at any minute, I couldn't bear the thought of being locked in that tiny room again.

'I told you it was all in your head.'

She took her arm away, leaving me unsupported. I dropped to my knees, creasing up in pain. My hands were shaking. Huge great shivers coursed through my body like crashing waves.

'You are being really pathetic. Stop faking. Get up.'

Mustering every ounce of energy I had, I staggered to my feet. 'I'll go to school now,' I mumbled, before falling into a dead faint. I spent the next two days in the detention room, in a state of tortured delirium, sweating and constantly thirsty. No one called in a doctor. I lay there having nightmares about Dynamutt's broken neck, wishing I were dead too.

When I got out, Jules introduced me to Danielle, the latest new girl. Like Jules, Danielle was in the morning and teatime queue for medication. Jules thought she was really nice. I reminded her that almost everyone was nice when they first arrived, until the drugs changed them.

As predicted, Danielle's personality began to alter as the days wore on. She went from being a normal, quiet girl to being hyper and rebellious. She slept in Sophie K's dorm along with Jules, and there were loads more fights at bedtime than there had been before she arrived. She and Jules used to spit at each other from their beds.

Danielle could be funny too. I was in their dorm the night she drew a huge red mouth on her face with lipstick, just before Benita came in to turn out the lights.

Benita screamed when she saw her. 'Wipe that off now! You look evil!'

'I am evil, bitch,' Danielle crowed. Benita dragged her off to the detention room.

When Benita came back, Sophie K told her to fuck off, so Sophie K spent the night locked in Sick Bay. It was a bad night for them, but a good night for me because for once I got to sleep in Jules's dorm. We chatted for hours through the darkness about our dreams of life after Kendall House. Jules said she wanted to get married and have children. I said I wanted to run a cat shelter and breed hamsters.

'Don't you want a boyfriend?' she asked.

'No, just lots of baby hamsters.'

Benita came in and snapped on the light. 'If you two don't stop talking right now you will lose all your privileges for a month!' she shouted. Finally we drifted off.

It was around this time that I started having trouble getting to sleep at night. It was crazy – I felt dopey all day and then when it came to the evening I'd get hyped up with nervous energy. Thoughts whirled through my head like leaves in an autumn storm, and I could never quite catch hold of them. A lot of the time I felt utterly confused. Nothing made sense, except my desire to end the misery and turmoil. More and more I focused on finding ways to self-harm, scouring the floor for bits of glass and plastic, drawing pins, safety pins – basically anything with a sharp edge. If I couldn't find anything, I'd smash a light bulb. When someone deliberately left a pile of broken glass on my bed, I didn't question it. I just cut myself with it.

The patterns I made on my arms fascinated me. I spent whole days picking and probing the cuts, grazes and scabs on my skin. Walled in and locked up in Kendall House, with nothing to do and nowhere to go, my arms became my exploring ground, and I hacked out paths from elbow to wrist, creating new routes for the rivulets of blood to flow down.

Cutting myself became an important mode of expressing how I was feeling. When Bridget or one of the others was nasty to me, I took my fears and frustrations out on my arms. It went the other way too. One evening I carved Jules's name halfway up my forearm. The 'J' is still visible today, even after all these years. When Bridget saw what I'd done she accused me of being a lesbian, which was strange coming from her, considering how close she was to Janice. I protested that I loved Jules like a sister, but nobody seemed to believe me.

Sometimes Bridget was all right with me, but it never seemed to end well between us. When I got my new hamster, Vampire, she suggested mating it with her hamster Charlie. Of course I was thrilled at the idea of having some babies to play with.

Miss Woods was often warning us about putting the hamsters in the same cage. I think she was worried that they would breed out of control and overrun Kendall House. So we had to do it in secret. Every evening we let Charlie go in with Vampire for a few minutes. Charlie appeared to be very attached to Vampire. We watched him run up behind her, mount her and jiggle around. Never having seen anything mate before, I thought it was hilarious. Bridget was sure that there would be babies soon and so was I.

I noticed that Vampire was getting fatter. It was time to confess. I went up to Miss Woods's office and told her that Vampire was pregnant. She wasn't happy about it.

'What were you thinking? It will mean more vet's expenses, more trouble.'

'I'm sorry,' I said, but I didn't care that she was cross. The thought of looking after tiny, baby hamsters was just too exciting for words. We took Vampire to the vet's and when I got back I bragged about how I was going to be a grandmother.

The next day Miss Woods called me up to her office again. 'I've seen the vet. Your hamster is back, safe and sound.'

'When are the babies due?' I asked eagerly.

'Teresa, I don't know how to tell you this, so I'll just come out with it. Your hamster is a boy. It's never going to have any babies.'

I went downstairs to the girls' sitting room and shouted, 'Vampire is a boy!'

'That means your Charlie must be gay,' Jules said to Bridget.

Bridget glowered at her. She strode over to me and slapped me round the head. 'Shut up about your fucking hamster,' she said.

'But I saw what Charlie was doing. He was having sex with him!' I laughed.

Some of the other girls made jokes about selling a story about the first ever pregnant boy hamster! Bridget's face was as black as thunder.

She punched me twice in the shoulder and once in the stomach, winding me. Then she grabbed me by the throat and pushed me up against the wall. 'I said shut up! Unless you want to die, that is.'

'Sorry,' I said, but inside I was laughing my head off.

After that, she was worse to me than ever. She and Nicole took to passing me nasty notes in class. They said things like 'We're going to get you' and 'Teresa must die!' At first I tried to ignore them, but after a while they began to scare me. Because I was so befuddled mentally, I became convinced that they really were planning to kill me. Bridget, particularly, looked at me with such hate and spite in her eyes that it was easy to believe that she wanted me dead.

Sometimes I couldn't get to sleep for worrying about whether I would survive the night. Although a huge part of me wanted to die, I was terrified of being murdered by Bridget while I slept. She was constantly telling me about all the ways she planned to kill me. I was sure that eventually she would be driven to act out her violent desires.

One evening as she passed me in the corridor she handed me a scrunched-up note that said, 'YOU ARE GOING TO DIE TONIGHT!' It was signed by several of the girls, including the Sophies, Nicole and Danielle. Scared stiff, I ran into my dorm and shut the door, wedging a chair up against the handle so that no one could come in. A few minutes later, Zara tried the handle. She called to me to let her in, but I shouted at her to go away, or I'd hurt her.

I sat down on my bed. I read the poison note again and started having trouble breathing. I began shaking and twitching as I gasped for air. My head was pounding. It felt as if it would burst. I tried to stand up, but I was too dizzy. I had the strangest sensation that my blood was freezing up in my veins. My skin became cold as ice. A massive pain spread through my chest and my breaths grew shorter and shallower. Panic consumed me. I was beside myself with fear. I clutched hold of the St Christopher's chain that Mum had given me. I must have gripped it too hard because the chain broke and it fell onto the floor.

Kate managed to push the door open. She made me put my head between my knees. Harriet brought me up one of her hot vitamin drinks. 'You are totally doolally, aren't you? Nothing but bloody trouble!' Harriet said.

'What does doolally mean?' I asked Shirley later.

She shrugged. 'Bonkers, barmy ... why?'

'Mad, you mean?'

She frowned. 'Yes, mad.'

'Do you think I'm mad?' She smiled and said nothing.

Again, my blood ran cold. It was like they were brain-washing me, trying to make me believe that there was something wrong with my mental health, forcing pills down my throat, turning me into someone I wasn't.

'*I am not mad!*' I shouted.

'Calm down, or we'll have to put you back in the detention room,' she said.

CHAPTER TEN

I woke up with throbbing temples. Every tiny noise sounded like a deafening crash. When Zara said good morning it felt like she was shouting inside my head. Searing pains shot through my stomach. My mouth was so dry that my lips kept sticking to my teeth.

'You are trying my patience severely,' Harriet said when I told her I needed to stay in bed. 'Get up and go to school now!'

After threatening me with the detention room again, she dragged me into Mrs Connolly's needlework class. But Mrs Connolly soon ushered me outside into the corridor. I heard her whispering to Harriet that I shouldn't be allowed around pins, needles or scissors.

I stumbled into the girls' sitting room, feeling lost and unwanted. Slumping onto a chair, I was overcome by despair. Why didn't Harriet believe me when I said I was ill? I had never felt worse in my life.

Frustration welled up inside me. Enough was enough. I was living in a crazy world where nothing made sense. In desperation, I looked around the room for something to slash my wrists with, but there was nothing. Suddenly I changed my mind and decided to go back into Mrs Connolly's class. I stood up, but my knees started trembling and I had to sit down again. I shook my head angrily. My mind felt so heavy and doped. I was sick of living in a haze. It was driving me mad. I couldn't stand it any more.

I hauled myself up onto a chair and tried to reach up to the ceiling light, hoping to take out the light bulb and smash it, then use it on my arms. One minute I was stretching upwards and the next I had lost my balance and toppled to the floor. I landed on my hip bone. The pain woke my brain up. Rage flooded through me. I started attacking the furniture, throwing chairs against the wall and screaming with fury.

Jules heard my screams. She rushed out of needlework into the sitting room. Stepping in front of me, she raised her hand. 'It's me, Teresa! Shhhh! Calm down, or they'll get nasty,' she warned.

Mrs Ryfield was right behind her. 'Go back to school this instant,' she told Jules. 'I will see to Teresa.'

I whirled round to face her. 'Don't talk to my friend like that!' I shouted. 'You fuck off right now!' I felt as if I might explode at any moment. Moving to the window, I banged my fists on the glass. 'Let me out of here!' I shrieked. 'Let me out before I die!'

By now I was frantic with fear, anger and confusion. My thoughts veered alarmingly from one extreme to the other, from feeling driven to harm myself to wanting to fight ferociously for survival. Either way, death seemed inevitable. I was emaciated and practically starving. I was being forced to take high doses of powerful drugs. I was getting weird, terrifying impulses telling me to kill myself. The other girls were always threatening me with violence. The staff had attacked me. Kendall House was having a hugely detrimental effect on my mental and physical wellbeing. I knew I had to get out, even if I died trying.

Jules tried again. 'Teresa . . .'

'It's no good, Jules! I don't want to live if I have to live here in hell. I can't go on anymore.' I threw myself at the window. The pane of glass vibrated in its frame. One more try and it would break, I reckoned. I stood back and prepared to launch myself at it again.

I heard a shout. Harriet was behind me. Kate was also there, and Shirley. A pair of long arms encircled me, strait-jacketing me. Someone wrestled me to the ground. I kicked out as hard as I could, jabbing randomly with my elbows and knees, struggling against three or four pairs of arms. A hand covered my face, squashing my nose. I tried to bite it. The hand pressed harder. I thought my nose would break. My cheek hit the floor. I heard my jaw crack. Another hand was up my skirt, fumbling with my knickers. I writhed and wriggled to stay out of its grasp, fuelled by panic and desperation.

Sensing a sudden prick at the top of my leg, I knew I'd lost the fight. 'You bastards,' I said just before the drugs took hold.

I woke up in Sick Bay. Someone was knocking at the door. It had to be one of the girls because when it was the staff they just barged in. 'Is that you, Jules?' I called out.

'No, it's Sophie C. Jules is in the detention room. She went mad after they carted you off. She overturned three tables at dinner! You've never seen anything like it: food and smashed plates all over the floor. Harriet and Miss Woods were furious. They injected her too. She told me to say, "Don't give up." OK? Bang on the door and she'll try to bang on the detention room door.'

'Thanks, Sophie,' I whispered.

Somehow it helped knowing Jules was in the same situation

as I was. Although it was upsetting to hear that they had injected her as well, I was touched that she had protested against what they'd done to me. She was a brave, loyal friend.

Her courage gave me courage. I got up from the narrow wooden bed and started banging on the door. Energy surged through me. I felt as if I'd been asleep for a hundred years and now had a century's worth of strength on tap. 'Jules! Jules! Don't let those bastards get you down,' I shouted. I heard a faint knocking from the floor below. She had heard me! I jumped up and down and kicked the door, shouting and yelling. Soon I could hear her banging away as well.

Some time later I went into a bit of a trance. My eyes felt glassy. I couldn't drag my eyes away from a biro mark on one of the walls. Harriet unlocked the door. In her hand was a small tray with a hypodermic needle resting on it. She sat me down on the bed. 'Make it easier on yourself. Lie back and think of England.'

'No!' I tried to push her away, but my strength was gone. I gave up resisting. In the past I had struggled and she'd missed my buttock and injected me in the small of my back or my leg, but she finally got me where she wanted in my bum, which was every bit as painful. However, this time I didn't keel over immediately. Either the drugs weren't strong enough to knock me out or I'd already slept so much that my body refused to sleep anymore.

She sat with me for another five minutes. 'After that much Valium and Sparine, you should be out by now,' she said, looking at her watch.

'Where am I going for Christmas?' I asked. 'Tina is going to Miss Woods. Can I go with Shirley?'

The question seemed to annoy her. 'Who told you that

Tina would be staying with Miss Woods? I know nothing about this.'

'I just heard,' I said. 'I want to know where I'm going.'

'Why aren't you asleep?'

'I don't know. Why aren't I dead? I should be after all the crap you've given me.'

I didn't fall asleep for another hour and a half. Two hours later, Harriet injected me again. Four hours after that, Janice injected me. In the evening they dragged me up to my dorm and put me to bed there. I didn't struggle. I had no reserves of energy left. The next day I was supposed to get up and return to school as normal, but I didn't make it downstairs until lunchtime.

'Morning, lazybones!' Shirley said as I wandered into the dining room on shaky legs.

'Morning,' I said, and immediately sank to the floor.

I came to with Harriet and Shirley bending over me. '. . . the biggest hypochondriac I've ever come across, and such a drama queen!' Harriet was saying.

'Are you . . .' I croaked. My head was spinning.

'Ah, Madam's awake,' she interrupted. 'Let's get her up to Sick Bay.'

I clutched at Shirley's arm. 'No, please, not Sick Bay again! I hate it in there. Just give me a few minutes to get myself together. I'll be fine, I promise.'

Although I didn't have much of an appetite, I ate as much lunch as I could in an effort to build my strength up. I mashed together the hot baked potato and crisps on my plate and added a load of salad cream, until it was one big soggy mix. I took tiny mouthfuls. It went down like baby food. I couldn't remember the last time I had eaten anything substantial. My legs were stick thin. My ribs showed through my skin. My collarbone was sharply pronounced. I was becoming weaker by the day.

My brain was in a constant whirl of conflicting thoughts and feelings. Part of me wanted to get stronger and fight to survive, but another part couldn't see the point in going on living. When I had eaten as much as I could, I pushed my plate off the table. It smashed into little pieces. 'I'm sorry! It was an accident,' I said, leaning down to clear it up.

'Don't touch it!' Trinny screeched. 'I'll get a broom.'

Too late! I had already slipped a couple of jagged pieces into my dressing gown pocket. Five minutes later, I excused myself to go to the toilet. Shirley escorted me. While I was in the cubicle, someone called her away and she left me alone.

I locked the door behind me and cut myself in the darkness. I did it without thinking – I couldn't have explained what was driving me. It was as if I had a destruct button and somebody else had pushed it.

Shirley came back and knocked on the door. 'Teresa?' she called.

I held my breath and said nothing, hoping she would think I'd left. Hearing her footsteps retreat along the corridor, I breathed a sigh of relief and went back to cutting my arm.

The footsteps returned – there was more than one person this time. I heard a scratching sound on the other side of the door, and then the lock turned. Janice, Harriet and Kate burst in. They injected me and dragged me up to the detention room, where I had another energy surge and banged on the door for three straight hours before collapsing in a heap on the floor.

I remember offering up a desperate prayer to God just before I passed out. 'Help me,' I whispered, my palms pressed together, my teeth chattering feverishly. 'Please God, save me from this place and the evil people here. I'm so scared, God! Please get me out of here before I die.' I fell asleep wondering if He had heard me. It was hard to believe that the loving god I had learned about as a child actually existed, but anything was worth a try.

When I woke up, I saw things another way. My zonked brain had gone into reverse and I realised that nothing could get me out of this hell, apart from dying. Death is my only escape, I thought, as I unwound the bandage on my arm and wrapped it around my neck. I pulled it tight. Choking and dizzy through lack of oxygen, I kept tugging it tighter and tighter, until I was on the verge of losing consciousness. Suddenly there was a commotion at the door. Kate and Miss Woods rushed in and caught me as I fell. 'Leave me to die,' I mumbled.

Kate tried to loosen the bandage, but pulled it tighter by mistake and I felt my eyes roll and my eyelids flutter. The next thing I knew I was being thumped on the back, causing me to cough and draw in long, deep breaths. In the distance I heard Harriet's voice saying, 'We'll have to cancel her father's visit tomorrow. He can't see her like this.' I felt the sharp pain of another injection and was asleep within seconds.

When I came to, it was morning. I knew this because Dot and Shirley brought me some tea and toast and referred to it as breakfast. My hand was shaking so much as I raised the mug to my lips that I spilt tea all down my front and over the bedclothes. I couldn't eat the toast. My appetite had gone again. They changed the sheets and I went back to sleep.

The next time I awoke, Dot was standing over me. 'Time

to get up,' she said. She hauled me out of bed and walked me upstairs to Sick Bay.

'Why am I changing rooms?' I asked.

'In case your father visits,' she said.

I didn't get it. The detention room and Sick Bay were almost identical, so what difference would it make where Dad saw me? It was only later that I worked out that because I was so thin and weak, they would have to tell Dad I was ill and confined to Sick Bay. Of course, the irony was that I really wasn't well, but it was their 'medicines' rather than nature that were making me ill.

The rest of the day went by in a blur. Janice brought me a glass of milk and some pills. Harriet brought me two roast potatoes, which I wolfed down greedily even though they were cold. A little later I vomited them back up. Ivy gave me more milk to drink. Harriet brought more pills. 'Is Dad here yet?' I kept asking. But Dad didn't come that day. Or if he did, I don't remember seeing him.

Sometime during the evening, Dot led me downstairs to the girls' sitting room, where I was greeted by a chorus of groans and catcalls. 'Titsalina Bumsquirt!' Bridget exclaimed. 'We were hoping you were dead.'

'You're not the only one,' I said, collapsing into a chair in front of the television. 'I'd rather be dead than sat here with you.'

'You look half dead, so with any luck it won't be long,' she fired back.

I caught Jules's eye. She was staring at me as if she hardly knew me. 'What is it?' I asked.

'Are you OK? You really do look ill,' she said. I was too tired to answer. I fell asleep in my chair a few seconds later.

Dot woke me. She wiped my face with a tissue. 'You were

dribbling,' she explained. 'Let's get you up to bed.'

'Yeah, get her out of here, the drooling spaz!' Bridget shouted. 'She's a fucking weirdo. We don't want her in here dribbling and mumbling rubbish.' I felt like punching her, but didn't have the energy.

Dot led me upstairs to the dorm. I got into bed and then got out again. 'Get into bed,' Dot said.

I got into bed and got out again. 'Let's not have any nonsense. Get back into bed now,' she said.

I got into bed and got out again. Then I did it again. 'What's going on? I don't understand,' I asked wearily. Every time I lay down, my brain signalled to me to get up. Then, when I was up, it told me to get back into bed. I struggled to keep my body from obeying the messages my brain was sending it, but I was like a puppet, a remote-controlled toy.

And so it continued. Against my will, I just kept on getting in and out of bed. It was scary and infuriating. Dot nagged at me to stop it. Harriet came in and shouted at me. I started to cry. I surveyed the room, looking to find a way out of my frustration. Why was this happening to me? Bridget's insults echoed in my head. I was mad. I was ugly. I was a weirdo.

I thought about my dad, David and Bernadette, and remembered a day earlier in the year when we had visited my nan. My mind lit up with flashes of the girl I had once been, not so many months before. A massive surge of anger rose inside me. '*What are you doing to me?*' I screamed at Harriet and Dot. Beside each bed was a locker containing each girl's personal things. I picked mine up and threw it across the room. Then I chucked Zara's locker after it.

'Stop this now or I will have to give you an injection,' Harriet said.

I whirled around and yelled at her, 'Why are you giving me drugs? Are you trying to kill me? Am I some kind of guinea pig in a weird scientific experiment?'

Harriet left the room without responding. In the meantime, Dot did not try to restrain me. It was obvious that it was going to take more than one person to keep me down.

When Harriet came back, I was waiting for her, senses alert. I pushed her away every time she tried to get near me with the syringe, jabbing out like a boxer. Dot made a few clumsy attempts to come closer; it was easy to dodge her. Neither of them were a match for me in my present mood; I could have fought off half a rugby team.

After a while they started calling for back-up. Soon a mix of staff and girls streamed into the room, maybe ten or twelve of them. Bridget was among them, of course. She loved to help out in a situation like this. They formed a semicircle and drove me into a corner of the dorm. In that moment I knew how a hunted fox must feel as the dogs close in.

'Ready; *now*!' Harriet shouted.

They leapt forward, shouting and screaming with savage ferocity. A mass of hands reached out and touched me all over, grabbing, pinching and slapping different parts of me. I struggled furiously while they pinned me down on my front and Harriet injected me – in the back of the neck this time – and I continued to struggle, kicking and punching, as they dragged me upstairs to Sick Bay. But the sheer number of attackers overwhelmed me. There was no way I could escape their clutches.

At one point I heard Harriet cry out. Her cry was followed by a clattering sound.

'You bitch!' Bridget yelled. 'You've knocked Harriet downstairs. I'll get you for that, you fucking cow.' She started slapping me around the face, really hard. The blows left my cheeks stinging with pain. I lunged and tried to bite her hand, but she was too quick for me and began to pummel the top of my head. Dot unlocked the Sick Bay door and I was thrown inside. I landed in a heap on the floor, like an old broken doll. I passed out.

I was vaguely aware of people coming in and out of the room during the night. I woke up around dawn to see Miss Woods standing over me. She seemed on edge and jumped when she saw that I was awake.

'What are you doing here?' I asked.

She held out a packed of biscuits. 'I brought you these. I thought you might be a little bit peckish.'

At the time I didn't question how truly odd this was. With an effort, I raised my arm and took them from her. 'Thank you. I'm not hungry now, but I might be later.' I tucked the packet under my pillow.

'Well, I'll leave you to rest. You've been sleeping like a log, haven't you?' She seemed to be seeking reassurance. 'No disturbances?'

'No,' I said.

'Good.' She left me in peace.

The next day the pains in my back returned with a vengeance. It felt like my lower back was on fire. I'd never experienced anything so agonising. I begged Harriet for some painkillers and she gave me some pills that I'd never seen before, but they didn't give any relief. So, despite my hatred of medication, I pleaded with her to give me some Normison sleeping pills, or some Valium to knock me out. By now I was getting to know the names of some of the medicines I was being given, although I still didn't know why I was taking them, or what most of them were supposed to do.

Finally she brought me a handful of pills. Normally I would have wanted to throw them back at her, but all I cared about was escaping from the pain, even if it meant losing myself in unconsciousness. I swallowed them down quickly and waited for oblivion to hit.

For the next two days I lay doubled up on the bed in Sick Bay. I began to have trouble urinating again. I kept thinking that I wanted to go to the toilet, but then when I got there I only managed to force out a small, agonising dribble. I was allowed to have the Sick Bay door open most of the time, so that I could go to the toilet without having to call a member of staff, but it reached the point where I was in too much pain to walk unaided.

Miss Woods came to see me on the third day. She looked alarmed when I told her I had not been to the toilet for at least twenty-four hours and said that she would call a doctor instantly. By now my bladder was obviously distended, pushing out my belly and giving me a malnourished appearance. My back felt sore and my kidney area hurt so much that my fists were constantly clenched. I found myself speaking through gritted teeth a lot of the time. I also started feeling very sore in my groin area, especially when I woke up.

The pain came in waves and I kept getting a feverish sensation in different parts of my body, as though there was a patch of hot blood chasing around my veins. One moment my cheeks would be burning, the next moment it would be my thighs, and the next my upper arms and shoulders were on fire. It was a really strange feeling. I told Miss Woods I would go mad unless it went away soon.

The doctor prescribed antibiotics, which began to work the next morning. The relief was incredible. I realised just how much energy I'd been using up simply coping with the pain of the previous few days. Finally I was able to urinate. I still felt very delicate, though, and slept the rest of the day away. When I woke up, Harriet forced me to take a handful of pills. Again I slept, still and dreamlessly, for a long stretch.

When I asked if I could start sleeping in the dorm again, Harriet told me no. Miss Woods also said it would be better if I stayed in Sick Bay for a while longer. I pleaded with her to change her mind, but she remained firm, without giving me a proper explanation.

With every day that passed in that horrible room, I felt my mood drop lower and lower. I couldn't understand why I was being kept in there, isolated from the other girls and dosed up to the eyeballs with injections and pills of every colour. I began to feel suicidal again and confessed as much to Shirley. As usual, she offered to brush my hair, something she knew I liked having done. She said that she could do me a home perm if I wanted. 'Yes, please!' I said. I was grateful for anything that would break the monotony of those long, boring days in the claustrophobic hell that was Sick Bay, even if I did look like a fright when she had finished with me.

Kate told me that both Harriet and Shirley had invited me for Christmas. I knew I would much rather go to Shirley's house, but was worried what Harriet would think if I chose Shirley over her. Harriet wielded much more power in Kendall House than Shirley did, especially when it came to the medication I was being given. I was terrified of her. On the other hand, I was desperate for a stable mother figure and Shirley was the nearest to maternal that I'd been able to find so far. I wanted to nurture our relationship and sensed that spending Christmas together would be an important landmark for us, a bonding event. I kept turning the pros and cons over in my mind, but found it impossible to make a decision.

Then suddenly Christmas wasn't important anymore. Just a week after I'd got rid of my waterworks infection, I woke up with a very sore groin, both inside and out. 'It's rebound pain,' Harriet said. 'It won't last.'

I assumed that she meant it was something to do with the urine infection, although I couldn't see how the two could be connected. When I asked her, she said, 'Why do you have to question everything? Shut up and it will go away.'

But it didn't go away. In fact, it got worse with each passing day. It always felt most painful during the night and in the mornings. I tried to describe how it felt to Shirley. 'It's like someone has smashed me down there with a hammer,' I said. The whole external area felt bruised, from the top line of my pubic hair right down to my genitals. My pubic bone was incredibly tender. My vagina felt sore and some days the whole area was swollen. I had no idea what could be causing these problems and became very scared that there was something seriously wrong with me.

Harriet and Shirley kept telling me that it was all in my head. When I told Miss Woods about it she said not to worry because I was being monitored by the staff and nurses. But no one actually gave me an examination, so how could they know what was really going on?

I began to fear going to sleep. I no longer had dreams, just nightmares filled with people and monsters. I started to associate them with the pain in my groin. Scary, distorted versions of Harriet and Miss Woods featured heavily – I had visions of them laughing demonically at me, egging on various members of staff to pin me down and inject me. An unfamiliar man kept cropping up. He was half-man, half-monster, with a mouth that opened so wide it could have swallowed me up. I kept waking up bathed in cold sweat, screaming silently, my groin throbbing with pain.

I asked Shirley if dreams could ever be powerful enough to make a person ill. She laughed and began to tease me about having an overactive imagination. 'No, really,' I insisted. I was desperate to be taken seriously. 'It's as if the monsters I'm dreaming about are real. It's as if they are actually doing what they're doing in my dreams in real life.'

'And what are they doing in your dreams?'

'Punching me. Bashing me down there. Hurting me. Pressing on me, and in me.'

She frowned. 'Dreams can be very vivid sometimes. It's probably just a phase you're going through.'

As time went on I became certain that there was a link between the pain in my groin and my recurring nightmares. No one would listen though. I started to wonder if Sick Bay was haunted by a violent poltergeist, or if Bridget had found some way of getting in during the night and hurting me. I begged to be allowed back to the dorm. Finally, after more than a week, Shirley said that I'd been given permission to leave Sick Bay.

I was hoping for a peaceful night's sleep at last, and went to bed early. But at around 9.30 p.m., Bridget, Sophie K, Sophie C, Jules, Danielle and Zara crept into the dorm and sat in a circle on the floor around a tiny keyring torch, whispering and giggling. I heard paper being ripped up and someone reciting the alphabet, then Bridget said, 'Is there anybody there?' Her voice was ghoul-like in the darkness. 'We call on you to speak to us.'

By now I was fully awake. 'Go away, I'm trying to sleep,' I said.

'Fuck off, or we'll set the spirits on you!' she said. The others laughed.

My heart began to pound. It didn't take a genius to work out that they were messing around with a ouija board – Jules had told me that a gang of them had been doing it for several nights in a row. 'Stop it! It's dangerous,' I said. I had always been scared of the supernatural.

'Shut up!' Bridget snapped. She started speaking in a ghostly voice again. 'Is there anybody there? Speak to us.'

After a few moments of silence, Danielle said, 'Look, the glass is moving! It's spelling out a word. D-I . . .'

I listened apprehensively as the next letter was disclosed. '. . . D . . . no, E! D-I-E, die!'

Lying stiffly in bed, frozen with fear, I heard Sophie C say, 'It's not funny like before. I don't like this, it's scary.' There was a muffled laugh, followed by several whispers.

'Shush, it's continuing! D-I-E-T-O-N-I . . .'

Fingering the broken St Christopher that my mother had given me, I tried to remember how the Lord's Prayer went. But it was no good; my mind was fogged with drugs. I could only recall the first few lines, and those only sketchily.

'. . . G-H-T . . . Die tonight!' Bridget said. Zara screamed.

'Stop it!' I shouted, leaping out of bed. I ran across the room and switched on the light.

Bridget jumped up and made as if to run at me, growling. I fled the dorm, calling for help. A member of staff called Paula appeared out of the staff dorm. 'What's wrong? You look like you've seen a ghost,' she said.

'Where's a Bible? I need a Bible to protect me. They're trying to bring dead people to life,' I stuttered, pointing towards the door of the dorm.

Ivy came hurrying up the stairs, her bunch of keys jangling

like ghoulish chains. 'Aaagh!' I shouted. Paula clamped her hands on my shoulders and told me to calm down. I went on insisting that I needed a Bible. I knew from films like *The Omen* and *The Exorcist* that a Bible could protect me from supernatural harm.

Bridget emerged from the dorm and told Ivy that they'd only been having a laugh. 'The glass was moving by itself, though, honest,' she said. 'Someone was trying to get a message to one of us. I wonder who?' She gave me a sideways glance. 'Wouldn't it be creepy if one of us died during the night?'

'Stop it!' I shouted. I couldn't bear it. I'd only just managed to get away from Sick Bay and my demon-filled nightmares. Now Bridget and the others had introduced ghostly spirits into the dorm. Nowhere felt safe. My knees started trembling.

'Stop scaring Teresa and go to bed,' Ivy told Bridget.

It struck me that perhaps the monsters in my Sick Bay dreams had been invoked by Bridget and the others. Maybe they had been sending them to torture me during the night. '*Get me a Bible!*' I yelled, over and over again, until I was nearly hysterical. Finally Paula went through my case and found the red, Revised Standard version that I had been given all those years ago at The Haven. I clutched it against my chest. 'God protect me,' I kept saying. 'Please don't let me die tonight.' I slept with the Bible under my pillow for several months after that.

Two days later, on Halloween night, Miss Woods organised a little party. We played blind man's buff, dunking apples and hunt the thimble. For once I actually enjoyed myself, because Bridget was staying the night at Janice's house, and in her absence the other girls were a lot friendlier than usual.

Even though I was feeling woozy from my daily dose of drugs, it brought back to me how it felt to be a normal fourteen-year-old girl having good old-fashioned fun. I forgot my troubles for a couple of hours and really let myself go. It was a welcome respite, but it was all too brief.

CHAPTER ELEVEN

Assembly was held every morning at 9 a.m. in the front schoolroom. It lasted anything up to an hour. I was usually too tired to register much of it, if I made it downstairs at all.

It was considered a privilege to choose which hymn or song we sang, so it was usually Bridget who got to decide. She always opted for a ridiculous kiddy song about a bear and a butterfly. It was about ugliness and beauty: the bear had fuzzy wuzzy hair; the butterfly grew wings and became beautiful. It was definitely a song to send you doolally and we were far too old to be singing it, but Bridget loved it. The rest of the assembly was taken up with a reading by one of the teachers or staff, followed by a boring lecture.

One morning in early November, while Miss Woods was reading out a particularly dull passage, Nicole yawned in a very loud and exaggerated way. Miss Woods looked up from her book and glared at her. I tried not to laugh, but the teacher's face was such a picture of outrage that I couldn't help letting out a quiet chuckle. On my right, Jules heard me laughing and snorted. Then Danielle giggled and let off a noisy fart. Blushing, she said, 'Whoops!' and the room erupted into muffled laughter.

Miss Woods paused for a few moments to shoot dirty looks at various girls, before continuing with the reading.

'Fuck me, Danielle, you smelly, stinky cow,' Bridget said under her breath, flapping her hand in front of her nose.

'Yeuch!' Nicole exclaimed.

'Don't pick on her. She couldn't help it,' I said.

'Shush!' said Mrs Petsworth.

'Have you got a dead animal stuck up your arse?' Nicole asked Danielle.

'Yeah, your hamster,' Danielle replied.

Jules started laughing.

'That's disgusting,' I said.

'Is that what you do for your kicks, you dirty bitch? Stuff animals up you?' Bridget hissed, her eyes glinting.

'Well it's better than sticking my head up the teachers' bums like you do,' Danielle said.

'If you say that again I'll make sure your head goes so far up your own arse that it comes out of your mouth, you arse-hole.'

Miss Woods stopped reading. 'Right, that's enough. Will Bridget, Nicole, Teresa, Jules and Danielle please leave the room now! I will speak to you later about your disruptive behaviour. All privileges are to be suspended as from this moment. No walks, no television.'

Mrs Petsworth led us to the schoolroom on the first floor. On our way up the stairs, Nicole sang a dirty version of 'What shall we do with the drunken sailor?'. This was apt, because her leg was in plaster after an accident in the garden and she was walking like a peg-legged pirate.

'Will you stop being so immature!' Mrs Petsworth barked.

'You treat us like babies, so why are you surprised that we behave like babies?' Nicole said.

'Goo-goo,' Jules said.

'Ga-ga,' I added, joining in the fun.

Mrs Petsworth handed out paper and crayons to keep us occupied. I scribbled like a child on my piece of paper. 'Look at da pwitty pitcha I drawed,' I said.

'Mine's better than yours,' Jules said, holding up her kiddy scrawl.

Bridget and Nicole started a babyish conversation about tits and fannies. Danielle soon joined in and it wasn't long before the three of them were singing another dirty song. Bridget started writing on the table with her crayons, and Nicole followed suit.

'Stop that now!' Mrs Petsworth shouted.

'Won't!' Bridget said petulantly.

Soon it came to that time of day when my breakfast medication started to kick in. Suddenly I felt tired, so I put my head down for a catnap. When I woke up, Bridget was cleaning off the crayon marks she'd made on the table. Meanwhile Nicole was shaking Ajax powder out of the window. 'Look, it's snowing!' she cooed.

'Shut that window, it's freezing!' Danielle said.

'Shut it yourself,' Nicole said.

Danielle moved towards the window. Bridget stood in front of it to block her. Danielle lunged at the window and pulled it shut. Bridget pushed her out of the way and opened it again. In the scuffle that followed, the handle got broken, which meant that the window could not be closed. The draught that came through it was icy.

Mrs Petsworth tried to settle us and handed out some Maths worksheets. 'No slacking, Teresa! Sit up straight and concentrate.'

'I can't. I'm too tired.'

'I see, we're in that kind of mood, are we? Well, I've just about had enough of your faking for today.' She glanced at her watch. 'I'm expecting you to have worked through at least one side of the page by the end of the lesson and believe me, I will not be happy if you haven't completed it.'

I wanted to please her but it was a struggle to keep my eyelids from closing. 'Please, Mrs Petsworth, just let me have five minutes' rest and I'll try again.' I looked at the sums on the page. They made no sense to me. I was no longer able to function at school, not on a normal wavelength. It was very upsetting.

'On no account will I allow sleeping in my lesson!' she snapped. 'Danielle!'

Danielle was snoring, her head resting in the crook of her elbow on the desk. She jerked awake at the sound of her name. 'Sorry, Miss!'

'Danielle's tired because she's been up all night having sex with hamsters,' Bridget said.

'That's enough, Bridget.'

'It's true! She told me it was,' Bridget whined.

'I said enough!'

Unable to keep my eyes open, I went back to sleep. The next time I awoke Danielle and Bridget were no longer in the room and Sophie K had joined us. Mrs Petsworth was at the door talking to Mrs Ryfield. 'Just keep them downstairs!' she was saying.

I heard Bridget's voice, and Danielle's, and then Mrs Petsworth stepped outside the door. Suddenly Bridget and Danielle stormed into the classroom. They slammed the door behind them and leant against it to keep it shut. 'Quick, help us keep her out!' they said.

In the heat of the moment we all helped to barricade the door. This wasn't difficult because it was a big heavy fire door that opened inwards, so it didn't take more than a couple of old chairs to wedge it shut. Mrs Petsworth and Mrs Ryfield knocked loudly and demanded to be let in, but Nicole told them to go away.

'Finally, some bloody peace and quiet!' she said, when the teachers had gone. 'I'm knackered.'

'Me too,' Danielle drawled sleepily. 'I hate these fucking drugs they keep giving me.'

I didn't care one way or the other what they did. I just wanted to go to sleep, so I pushed two desks together and lay down on top of them. Bridget and Danielle did the same. Nicole sat in a corner and dozed, while Sophie K doodled on a piece of paper.

'I'm going back outside. I don't like the feeling of being locked in,' Jules said. She pushed aside the chairs blocking the door and left. Sophie K replaced them.

About an hour later, Bridget and Nicole woke up and started looking around for something to do. By now I'd recovered from my morning slump and was feeling a lot more energetic. What's more, the rebellious spirit in the air was contagious and I felt like making a bit of mischief. 'Let's break open the art cupboards and do some painting,' I suggested.

Nicole's eyes lit up. She forced the locks on the cupboards and took out a load of paints and brushes. We used them lavishly. It was brilliant having free range of the art materials for once. At first we were constructively creative. I found a plaster bust of Alexander the Great in the cupboard and my artistic side ran riot as I decorated his bald, wreathed head in trippy psychedelic colours. Although I say it myself, Alexander the Great had never looked so good. He was a masterpiece by the time I'd finished with him.

Meanwhile, Sophie had noticed that some spanking new staffroom furniture was being carted outside into the back garden. Soon a load of stylish chairs and tables had been lined outside the back door while the staffroom was being cleaned.

Looking down from the window, I felt intensely irritated. 'Look at that!' I said. 'They get all that lovely fancy furniture while we have to sit on their rickety old cast-offs.' I flicked a glance over at the scruffy plastic chairs stacked up against the door.

'Yeah, it's totally unfair!' Nicole said. She grabbed hold of a squeezy bottle of red poster paint and squirted it out of the window, splattering the chairs and tables below.

'Let's have a go,' Bridget said eagerly, picking up a bottle of blue paint. Five minutes later we had all made an artistic contribution to the appearance of the staffroom furniture. The result was fairly appalling. Miss Woods was going to be hopping mad when she saw it. We went a bit paint-crazy after that, decorating the schoolroom in pretty colours. It looked a million times better than it had before, even though there were paint spills everywhere.

Nicole started skidding and sliding across the wet floor with her weight on her plaster cast, shouting, 'Whee, look at me!'

'Watch it, or you'll hurt yourself,' I warned. Sure enough, she slipped and fell awkwardly on her bad leg. Clutching it, she began to howl in pain. Bridget rushed over to comfort her.

There was more banging on the door. 'What's going on? Let us in!' several of the staff were shouting. For once they were powerless over us.

'No,' I shouted back. 'I'm not going to let you in, not by the hair on my chinny chin chin!'

For some reason this struck us all as hilariously funny and

the others started repeating it, even Nicole, who was still in pain. The more we said it, the funnier it became, and soon we were chanting away like demented little pigs.

When our laughter had died down I heard a man's voice coming from behind the door. He was telling people to get out of the way so that he could get through and force an entry. I froze. The voice belonged to Matthew, who had frequently featured in my Sick Bay nightmares. I began to feel dizzy and scared. It was weird: I really didn't want to see Matthew – the thought made me feel sick – but I didn't exactly know why. I couldn't understand why I kept dreaming about him, or why the dreams were still so vivid in my mind. Sitting down heavily, I held my head in my hands and tried to regulate my panicky breathing.

My energy drained away. I felt as if a huge concrete block had fallen inside my head and crushed my brain. I wondered again why I was being so heavily drugged. It just didn't make sense. Fear and confusion churned inside me. Frustrated, angry and shivering with cold, I picked up a block of hard paint and threw it at the open window. The window broke.

'Christ, you've done it now!' Sophie gasped.

Zombie-like, I stood up and went over to survey the damage. The middle of the pane had fallen out and there were huge long shards of glass sticking out of the frame. Because I'd developed a thing for self-harm, I couldn't help sizing them up for their arm-cutting potential. My eyes lighted on a really nice sliver that had fallen onto the windowsill. That's pretty, I thought, feeling oddly detached.

For some reason, hearing Matthew's voice again triggered the urge to cut myself. My mind was fogging up; I sensed that I had to do something dramatic to avoid whatever was going to happen when Matthew burst through the door. I picked up the sliver of glass and slashed my arms. Blood spurted everywhere.

Bridget screamed. The staff were now clamouring at the door, shouting and pleading with us to let them in.

'She's fucking cut herself!' Bridget shouted. She took off her blouse, soaked it in the sink, wrung it out and tied it around my wrist. I tried not to look at her great pendulous boobs as she tended to me. She was wearing a bra, but Bridget minus her shirt was still a disgusting sight.

'What the fuck did you go and do that for?' Sophie asked me.

'I don't know,' I said, feeling very faint. 'I just don't want to face that lot again.'

'Christ, look!' Bridget said, pointing at my arm. Her shirt was already soaked in my blood and the crimson stain was growing by the minute.

Sophie spotted a policeman in the back garden. 'We're in big trouble,' she said with a nervous giggle.

Soon there were policemen banging on the door. Then the fire brigade turned up.

'We'd better let them in,' Danielle said, gesturing towards the door.

'No!' I protested. I was quite happy to bleed to death. I think I must have been in shock.

But the others were worried not only about my arm, but also about Nicole's leg, which was still hurting from her fall. Bridget was desperate for her to have it seen to. So finally I gave in, mainly because Nicole really did appear to be in severe pain. What's more, I was beginning to feel really weak and didn't have the oomph to debate it any longer.

Bridget moved the chairs away from the door and pulled it open. All hell broke loose as a gang of staff rushed in shouting and yelling.

'I was trying to get us out!' Bridget told them. 'I didn't want to be here, but they wouldn't let me go.'

'That's a lie!' I mumbled.

'Teresa forced us to block the door – and then she hurt Nicole! I was scared to go against her. I didn't know what to do,' Bridget sobbed.

That woke me up. 'What a load of bullshit!' I screamed. 'I just wanted to go to sleep.'

Benita and Harriet dived on me, winding me in the process and smacking my head against the floor. They dragged me into the detention room, where at last I lost consciousness.

I was taken by ambulance to Joyce Green Hospital in Dartford, where I spent the next eight days on a psychiatric ward, as per Dr Peri's phoned instructions. Dr Peri didn't bother to put in a personal appearance, thankfully. I'd seen him a couple of times at Kendall House and that was enough to know that I didn't want him anywhere near me.

The first few days at Joyce Green went by in a haze of pain and medication hangover. Unbeknown to the nurses – because no one had told them – I was withdrawing from an extremely powerful combination of drugs and literally going cold turkey. My skin crawled; I became fluey and feverish. I kept begging for Valium, but was told that Valium was for adults. They would only administer it to someone of my age in an absolute emergency, they said.

'That can't be right!' I protested through chattering teeth. 'At Kendall House they give me at least four Valium a day, and sometimes they inject me with it as well.'

'Impossible,' the staff nurse told me. 'You must be muddling up the names.'

Dad and Bernadette visited a couple of times. Even though I was feeling awful, it was great to see them outside

Kendall House. Bernadette brought me some bubble bath, which was a surprise. She must have been feeling extremely sorry for me, because she'd never given me anything before in her life. I was touched.

I began to perk up. Although I was on a ward with a bunch of fairly unstable-looking characters, none of them tangled with me. Most days I watched telly, read magazines and chatted to the nurses. Physically, I began to feel better than I had in ages. My mind was gradually becoming clearer and, although I developed another uncomfortable urine infection, the pain in my groin had almost entirely disappeared.

Halfway through my stay I was given a gynaecological examination. The nurses seemed very concerned about the puncture marks in my bum and at the tops of my legs. I explained that this was where Harriet had injected me. They looked at me in disbelief when I said that sometimes I'd been injected three or four times in a day.

They took swabs from my vagina and rectum. 'It looks rather sore and inflamed around the anal area,' one of them said. 'I would say that you definitely had an infection. Have you been practising anal sex?'

'What's that?'

She raised an eyebrow. 'Anal penetration.'

'Sorry, I don't know what you mean.'

'Well, let's start with a simpler question then. When was the last time you had sexual intercourse?'

'I don't understand. Are you asking if I'm a virgin?'

'Not in the least! I'm asking when you last had sex.'

'I've never had sex. I'm only fourteen.'

She sighed. 'Are you sure? Well, if you say so. The results will be back from the lab in a few days, so then we'll all have a clearer picture, won't we?'

When the results came through I was informed that I had a Strep B infection, commonly associated with anal sex. The diagnosis confused me. I hardly knew what it meant. No one had ever sat me down and told me the facts of life; everything I knew about sex and procreation had been gleaned in snippets in the playground at school or from the older kids in the different homes I'd been at. As a result I was fairly clueless. I'd fallen for all the classic myths in the past, including the one about getting pregnant if a man put his hand on your knee. Once I'd even rushed off a bus before my stop, convinced I was pregnant after a man accidentally touched my leg with his hand.

The nurse gave me a course of powerful antibiotics, to be taken twice a day for a week. I took them without asking questions. I felt embarrassed, without really knowing why.

On my third or fourth day, a doctor appeared at my bedside. 'Your blood tests show traces of a surprising, if not alarming, variety of prescription drugs,' he said. 'Can you tell me why you're taking all these medicines?'

'You'd better ask Dr Peri. He's the one that prescribes them.'

'Indeed. Well, Dr Peri certainly knows his stuff, so far be it from me to question his methods. But I am amazed all the same.' He went away shaking his head.

When I saw him again a couple of days later, he asked me a lot of questions about my life. I explained that basically I had been sent to Kendall House because my dad was an alcoholic who couldn't get it together to pay the electricity.

'I haven't got a history of mental illness, or crime, so why are they giving me all those drugs? Do you think they should? Can you tell them not to? Can you tell Wandsworth Social Services that Kendall House is the wrong place for me?' Tears rolled down my cheeks. The thought of returning to Harriet's drugs regime horrified me.

'I can't promise anything, but I will certainly look into it,' he said, a look of grave concern on his face.

'Please do something,' I begged. 'Tell the police, tell Social Services! I'd rather die than go back there!'

Later that day he told me that he had contacted Wandsworth Social Services and the police to say that in his opinion it seemed inappropriate for me to return to Kendall House. 'I have written a report on you, and my conclusion is that there is nothing psychologically wrong with you,' he said. I don't know why no one listened to him. He was a doctor, an expert, but for some reason that counted for nothing.

On the day I left, Miss Woods tried to reassure him – and me – that Kendall House was the best place for me. I heard her say, 'It's a therapeutic environment for a disturbed girl like Teresa, and you cannot deny that she is very troubled. Don't overlook the fact that she was admitted here for cutting her wrists.'

'Of course not,' he said politely. 'But it seems to me that her desire to harm herself is a direct consequence of the drugs she is ingesting on a daily basis. I've seen the results of the blood tests. I cannot understand why . . .'

'It's not for us to question Dr Peri, is it?' she cut in. 'He is one of the most respected psychotherapists in the country.'

He tried again. 'All the same . . .'

Miss Woods held up a hand to stop him. 'I'm afraid I haven't time to discuss this any further. Goodbye. Thank you for looking after Teresa.'

'You're taking her straight back to Kendall House?' he asked.

She smiled primly. 'Indeed we are.' She hustled me out of the hospital and into her car, where Kate and Harriet were waiting.

On the drive back, I asked Miss Woods why neither Dr Peri nor Elizabeth Pryde had come to visit me at Joyce Green. She replied that neither of them had felt it necessary.

I pressed her further. 'Did you speak to Mrs Pryde? Is that what she said?'

Miss Woods hesitated. 'I didn't actually speak to her in person, but . . . she's a very busy social worker and it's not always possible to get hold of her at short notice.'

'You mean she doesn't really care about me,' I said.

'Not at all,' she replied brightly. 'But you're not her only responsibility!'

We drew up outside a set of tall buildings. I spotted a sign saying, New Stonehouse Psychiatric Hospital. 'What are we doing here?' I asked.

'Dr Peri felt that it would be helpful if you spent some time on his ward,' she said.

'Oh no,' I said, trying to get out of the car.

'Not so fast, young lady,' Harriet said, jumping out to block my escape. 'If Dr Peri says it's a good idea, then it is.'

My head swirled. What was going on? I was sure I had heard Miss Woods tell the doctor at Joyce Green that she was taking me straight back to Kendall House, but now I was at a mental hospital. Harriet and Kate walked me into the building and down miles of long gloomy corridors to the ward where Dr Peri had assigned me a bed. My heart sank as I took in my surroundings. The ward was filled with truly deranged-looking patients. They had mad eyes, and mouths that opened and closed like the mouths of suffocating fish. I felt as if I had entered a living nightmare.

'Can I have my own room?' I asked the nurse on duty.

'Not unless you want to sleep in a padded cell,' she laughed.

My first night at Stonehouse was incredibly scary. I was the only child on a ward of twelve patients, and the youngest by several decades. I felt like a rabbit that had been thrown to the wolves. Some of the other patients were severely schizophrenic. I was scared of them all, but one woman in particular gave me the creeps. She kept pointing at me and saying something that sounded like, 'I'll get you. I'll get you.'

One of the nurses tried to reassure me. 'No, Teresa, I think she's saying, 'Look at you,' because she thinks you're so pretty.'

I wasn't comforted. The woman had a crazy look in her eyes. There was a cruel curve to the shape of her mouth and she had a strangely flattened nose. I found it almost impossible to go to sleep in the same room as her, and even if she hadn't been there, it would have been hard to get any rest. Most of the other patients looked as if they were capable of violence or some kind of scary behaviour. One woman kept crying out all through the night; another would answer her every cry with a weird cat-like sound that made me shiver with fear. I lay in bed tense and alert, constantly on guard, my eyes darting around the room in search of any sudden movement. I relaxed only when it started to grow light, and finally I managed to snatch a couple of hours of sleep.

The woman with the flat nose continued to show a special interest in me. The next day she tried to sit next to me as I was watching TV and she kept following me around the dim, dingy day room. The more I saw of her, the more I wanted to get away from her, and the more she seemed to want to stick to me. There was something about her that gave me goose bumps and made the hairs at the back of my neck stand up.

In the evening I got talking to a very nice black nurse called Molly. I liked Molly because she treated me like an equal and talked to me as if I were an intelligent being, rather than an idiot, or a nutter. I was so used to being talked down to by the staff at Kendall House that it was quite uplifting to spend time with her, even if I was on a mental ward in a nuthouse. She invited me to sit with her and knit while she was on duty, and I really enjoyed our conversations, which were about everything and nothing.

The next time she was on duty I told her about my unease over the attentions of the flat-nosed madwoman. The woman had been especially troublesome that day, constantly trying to snatch my knitting needles away from me in the day room when the staff on duty weren't looking.

'Yes, I'd try and keep a distance, as much as you can,' Molly advised. 'That one can be dangerous.'

My eyes widened with fear. 'Why is she in here?' I asked, trying to keep my voice steady.

'I'm sure I don't know, but I've seen her in action and she can be difficult to contain. She's a strong one, a fighter.'

'I'm scared to go to sleep with her around,' I said.

'Don't worry, that's what I'm here for. I'll make sure you're safe.'

I found Molly's words reassuring, but didn't want to leave anything to chance, especially after one of the other patients told me that Flat Nose had murdered her entire family. 'Stabbed them in their beds,' the woman whispered. 'Husband, kids, the lot.'

Her words reduced me to a terrified wreck. Whether what she was saying was true or not, I was now even more petrified of sleeping on the ward. I pleaded with the staff to let me spend my nights alone in a padded cell, but it was out of the question. One night, however, Flat Nose got it into her head to jump out at me when I came back from cleaning my teeth. I screamed and ran to the end of the ward, looking wildly about for somewhere to hide. Seeing an open door, I slipped through it – and sure enough I found myself in a square white room with spongy, quilted walls. The door could only be locked from the outside, so I hid behind it, quaking. I stayed there for hours, until one of the male nurses discovered me and led me back to bed. Even then, I wouldn't allow myself to sleep. By morning I was strung out and exhausted.

'Why have I been put in with nutters and murderers?' I asked Molly.

'Dr Peri's orders!' she said. 'He's a very good doctor. I'm sure he must have his reasons.'

I soon discovered what those reasons were – not that I hadn't already suspected that this was some kind of sick punishment. On his one visit to the ward in my two weeks there, Dr Peri told me, 'This is what comes of talking nonsense to the staff at Joyce Green Hospital, Teresa. As usual, you have caused me unnecessary trouble.'

'I told the truth!' I protested.

'When are you going to learn to be obedient?' he snapped.

'Never,' I fired back. 'You will not break me.'

'We shall see about that,' he said with an ominous smirk. 'We shall see, indeed.'

I began to despair of ever getting away from Stonehouse. It wasn't that I wanted to go back to Kendall House, because of course I didn't want a return to the drugs, bullying, isolation and injections that characterised my life there. But the days and nights at Stonehouse were hair-raisingly bad. It was obvious that Dr Peri's intention was to frighten me into compliance to his rules and make an example of me to the other girls.

'I wish you could have me home again,' I said to Dad the next time he visited.

'You know I can't,' he sighed. 'I won't even have a home myself for much longer.'

It was Mum who got me out of there, believe it or not. I don't know how she got to know about it, but one day she just turned up and barged in, much against Miss Woods's wishes, apparently. The staff at Stonehouse had been instructed not to let my mum near me, on any account, but when it came to it they didn't try to stop her. She arrived with her best friend at the time – a big woman called Lisa – and she brought me lots of Avon goodies.

The first I knew about it, I heard shouting in the day room at around midday. The voice was familiar; suddenly I realised whose it was. I hurried towards the day room, my heart racing. Mum was going ape shit at Dr Peri, calling him every name under the sun.

'What the hell are you doing keeping my daughter here?' she yelled. 'You should be struck off for this! I'll see that every newspaper in the country knows what you're doing to that poor defenceless girl before I'm done with you, if you don't let her go *right now*. I'm telling you, and it's no idle threat! How dare you keep her here, you fat bastard? It's criminal to put a young girl in with this bunch of animals!'

For once, Dr Peri seemed not to know what to say. 'Madam, I would ask you to . . .'

'Don't you "madam" me! I know what goes on in these places. I've been locked up myself enough times. But now I'm telling you – and I'm only telling you once, mind – you had better discharge Teresa today, or you will pay the consequences. Are you listening to me? Mark my words, you fat fucker, or I'll bash the living daylights out of you.'

Mum was a champion that day; she really came through for me. Despite her pretty blonde, blue-eyed looks, she was hard as nails and could be very intimidating. Admittedly she didn't sweep me up and take me home – as I used to dream she would one day – but at least she saved me from mad murderous Flat Nose. She did what she could, within her own limitations. Within an hour I had left Stonehouse Hospital and was on my way back to Kendall House in Lisa's car.

CHAPTER TWELVE

Mum stormed into Kendall House like a bloody hurricane. 'My daughter says that you've been drugging her and locking her up. On whose authority, I ask you?' she said, jabbing her index finger at Miss Woods. 'What right have you got to treat a fourteen-year-old girl in such a way? No wonder she hates it here!'

'Mum . . .' I said.

Shirley popped her head around the office door. 'Is that you, Teresa? Good to have you back!'

Miss Woods gave Mum one of her infuriating smiles. 'Please calm down and join me in my office for a cup of tea,' she said.

But Mum wasn't having any of it. 'Don't patronise me with your fake tea and sympathy! I intend to get some answers here today. I'm asking you again, why have you been drugging Teresa? She's just a girl. From what she's told me, you are putting her through total misery. Shame on you, you big bully!'

Harriet sidled up beside Miss Woods. She shot me a look of contempt. 'Is that right, Teresa? Have you been telling people that you hate it here and we treat you badly?'

A bolt of sheer terror went through me as I took in her spiteful expression. 'Er,' I said. It was all very well for Mum to make a fuss, but unless she could get me out of Kendall House, it was me who was going to reap the consequences of her outburst. 'Well, no, I don't hate it. I don't hate it exactly, Mum,' I stuttered.

I could see Mum was riled. 'Is that so? Have you been telling me lies?'

'No, Mum!' I frantically tried to signal my dilemma with my eyes, but she wouldn't look at me. I turned to her friend Lisa. 'Help!' I mouthed at her.

Lisa got the message, thankfully. She took hold of Mum's arm and hustled her towards the door. 'Let's get out of here. You've done what you can for today.'

On her way out, Mum turned around and shook her fist at Miss Woods. 'You keep your dirty hands off my daughter, or I'll smash your fucking face in!' she yelled. 'Stay strong, Teresa. I'll get you out of here by Christmas.'

The moment she had gone, Harriet ordered me into the ground floor office. 'So it seems that you've been telling all kinds of untruths while you've been away,' she said, handing me a brown envelope with my name on it. 'Well, your lies won't get you far at Kendall House. Now, take your medication and join Mrs Connolly's class immediately.'

I pushed the envelope away. 'I don't want it. I don't need it. The doctor at the hospital said so. He said there's nothing wrong with me.'

'Dr Peri, was it?' she said sharply.

'No, another doctor, a nice doctor! He said I shouldn't even be in here.'

Her eyes narrowed and her mouth twisted into an ugly grimace. For a second she looked absolutely evil. 'More lies!

You really are the limit. Now take your medicine!'

Her tone was so aggressive that I swallowed the pills as quickly as I could and left the room, heart thumping. Harriet could be incredibly nasty. Quite often she scared me half to death.

That evening, Charlie, a newer member of staff, made a point of coming to talk to me. Charlie was a nice man, a gentle giant over six feet tall with short ginger hair, glasses and a beard. He was a bit ugly, but he was kind and I liked him. He had been an undertaker in his previous job, which I found fascinating. He was always telling me stories about how dead bodies were prepared for funerals and burials with embalming fluids and the like. I think it was his way of trying to put me off trying to commit suicide, although I was only vaguely aware of it at the time.

I'll never forget one particular incident he told me about, when he went to work on a very old dead woman. He stitched her mouth up so that she was smiling in her coffin, but when her family came to view her, they were outraged. 'She never smiled once in her life!' they told him. He had to unstitch her mouth and redo it before they were satisfied. I loved that story. It made me laugh and laugh.

Charlie put a brotherly arm around me and tried to draw me out about why I had cut my arm in the schoolroom. I told him there was nothing to say. 'You'd want to kill yourself if you were me,' I said. 'Anyone would.'

Despite his best efforts to talk me round, I had already plunged back into what felt like an irreversible depression. The drugs were kicking in again, interfering with my thought patterns and slowing down my body. Once again I had almost zero control over my life, my mind or my physical functions. What's more, I'd been away for more than three weeks and felt isolated from the group. Bridget ignored me completely when she saw me, and Nicole and the Sophies followed her lead.

Jules didn't let me down though. Just before bedtime she gave me a big hug and told me not to lose hope. 'I've got another escape plan!' she said, brimming with excitement. She explained that every day for several weeks she had been gradually unscrewing the metal bar that restricted the opening of the large window in the front schoolroom. She had also been to work on the securing block that held it down, painstakingly unscrewing it with her fingernails when no one was watching.

'They don't call me Houdini for nothing!' she said glee-fully, referring to the nickname she had picked up for her multiple escape attempts. 'We go tomorrow after tea,' she added, sounding like a prisoner out of *Escape From Colditz*. Her enthusiasm cheered me up no end.

The next day was Friday, the day we were allowed one phone call each. Dad called, furious that Mum had been to see me. They were still arch enemies, even after all this time, and Dad couldn't bear it when I saw Mum.

When I came back from speaking to him, Jules gave me a wink, and nodded towards the front schoolroom. 'We're leaving in a minute. Follow me or Bridget,' she whispered.

'Who else is going?'

'Danielle, Zara and Bridget.'

Just then, Jules was called away for a phone call and Janice called Ivy and Charlie into the staffroom, leaving the rest of us momentarily unsupervised.

'Christ, it's now or never! We've got to go right this minute,' Bridget said.

'We can't go without Jules. She did all the work to loosen the window,' I said.

'Suit yourself, Titsalina. The rest of us are going.'

I had to follow. The thought of getting out was too tempting to pass up. We slipped into the front schoolroom, climbed through the window and legged it. When poor Jules came back from her phone call, we were gone.

Less than two hours later, a police car picked us up in Dartford as we tried to hitch a lift to London. We were taken to Dartford police station, put in separate cells and told to wait until a member of staff turned up from Kendall House.

After what seemed like ages, a policeman came into my cell and told me to strip off my clothes, because he needed to check me for drugs and firearms. I refused.

'But I'm on my period!' I said, when I realised that he was deadly serious.

'A likely story, but it makes no difference. You still have to be searched.'

I felt totally sick and embarrassed about having to show him my body. Shakily, I began to take my clothes off.

'Get dressed!' he snapped when the search was over. He turned and left the room. The cell door slammed.

After about an hour, Mrs Tarwin arrived to pick us up. Mrs Tarwin was the biology teacher at Kendall House. She also had a hand in supervising our medication, perhaps because of her science background, or maybe just because she liked to put her oar in everything. By her side was Matthew, the part-time book keeper, dressed in his standard garb of brown suit and graying white shirt. The sight of him made my blood freeze. I hadn't seen him in person for some time, but he was still haunting my dreams, along with Fred, Harriet and Miss Woods.

I heard Mrs Tarwin telling a police officer that we girls were dangerous and mentally ill. 'That's a lie!' I shouted. 'I ran away because you're drugging me. And if you need proof of it, that policeman who strip searched me saw the bruises and injection marks.'

The policeman and Mrs Tarwin exchanged a knowing look. He obviously believed her side of the story. In his eyes we were a bunch of psychos.

'Come along, now,' Mrs Tarwin said, when she noticed that I was lagging behind the others. I felt like bursting into tears. Aside from the horror of having to go back to Kendall House, the thought of getting into a car with Matthew made me feel intensely uncomfortable. I felt sick as he drove us back, and tried not to look at his veiny, sinewy neck rising up from the seat in front of me. By the time we reached Kendall House, I was a nervous wreck. My hands were shaking and I was on the point of throwing up.

Miss Woods let us in and we went through the usual ritual of doors unlocking and locking as we entered the building. Suddenly I was overcome by claustrophobia. The fear of being trapped again, caged in like a helpless animal, appalled me. I hurled myself at the middle door in the hall, which had a glass pane in it. The glass wobbled. I went to punch it with my fist, but Matthew grabbed my arm. His touch made my skin crawl. 'Get your hands off me!' I shrieked. I began to scream hysterically.

Miss Woods scrabbled around with her keys and eventually turned the lock. I burst through the door into the main hall area looking for somewhere to run, but Matthew was too quick for me and clasped me around the waist from behind. He dragged me into the office, where he held me in a tight grip while Janice prepared an injection to 'quieten' me down. As I struggled to get away from Matthew, I heard her measuring out the doses. 'Haloperidol, 20; Valium, 20; Kemadrin, 10.'

Kemadrin was a new one on me. 'What are you giving me now?' I shouted. She ignored me.

Miss Woods came in and between the three of them they held me still for long enough for Janice to inject me. Feeling myself go limp in Matthew's arms, I pushed away from him and he let me fall to the floor. Then he lifted me up and carried me to the detention room, where I was locked up for the night, back in the land of nightmares.

I was in and out of the detention room for the next month, right up until Christmas. I was constantly made to wear my nightclothes and must have been injected at least five times during that period, if not many more, in addition to being given my daily dose of pills. They were using all kinds of drugs on me now. The names were totally meaningless to me, but I heard them so many times that I was able to recite them: Depixol, Disipal, Largactyl, Sernace, Haliperidol, Droleptan, Sparine, Normison, other drugs and lots and lots of Valium. Some came in tablet form, some were injected and some were given both orally and intravenously.

'We never see you in the dorm anymore,' Zara remarked one day over breakfast. 'That room's become your own private bedroom, you poor sod.'

'I've turned into the Kendall House dartboard too,' I said, thinking of the puncture marks on my legs and buttocks.

I developed another round of worrying symptoms, including facial twitches, persistent trembling in my left arm, pains in my back and sides, a tendency to go hot and cold, and horrific, brain-splitting headaches. I pleaded with the staff to let me see a doctor, but all they said was, 'You're not ill! It's all in your head.'

Although I knew that it was about as likely as snow in summer, I longed for a phone call from Mum to say that she had found a nice place for us both to live. I kept recalling how she had promised to get me out of Kendall House by Christmas. I wondered if she even remembered saying as much.

As it turned out, she did. But, as she explained on the phone one day in the middle of December, her situation was still too precarious to make room for me. She was now living with yet another bloke, somewhere near Petersfield in Hampshire, I think, and working as a housekeeper again. 'Just give me a few more months, Teresa,' she said.

'Yes, Mum,' I said dolefully.

All the other girls were getting excited about going to stay with their families over the Christmas break, but I had to make do with a visit from Dad and Bernadette on 23 December. It was great to see them though. My sister and I had a much closer relationship than we had done as children and I appreciated her regular visits. We went into Gravesend and wandered around the shops.

Before we left, Harriet had a word with Dad. 'I must emphasise that Teresa is not allowed cigarettes inside Kendall House. So please do not give her any to bring back here.'

Dad bought me a packet of Embassy just before we left Gravesend. 'Whatever you do, hide them from that miserable bint,' he laughed.

Christmas Eve arrived. The other girls left Kendall House – all except Bridget, that is. Like me, she had nowhere to go, and we were stuck with each other over the holiday. I had been dreading being left alone with her, but she was surprisingly friendly to me. I suppose she was just being pragmatic. Without me, she wouldn't have anyone to talk to apart from the staff. So for once she called a truce.

She was usually such a dark and scary figure in my life

that it was a relief to be on her good side for a change. I went along with whatever she wanted, just to keep her happy. On Christmas Eve, we played records and danced around the sitting room. The rest of the time we tended to the hamsters and rabbits. I now had two hamsters, Vampire and Nipper, and I loved them dearly.

On Christmas Day, we played a bit of a trick on Brenda, one of the members of staff. Brenda was okay, I suppose. She wasn't particularly sharp, so she was easy prey for hard types like Bridget.

Bridget's idea was to wrap up our Christmas dinner in pretty Christmas wrapping paper and give it to Brenda, as if it were a proper present. It sounds stupid, but it was actually such a silly trick that I couldn't help laughing. We wrapped up a couple of slices of turkey, roast potatoes, sprouts and gravy in some tin foil, wrapped that in another layer of tin foil, and then Sellotaped it up with a sheet of paper decorated with festive holly and ivy.

Brenda's face lit up when Bridget handed her our gift. 'Girls, how very kind of you!' she exclaimed.

'Well it's not much, but we really hope you like it,' Bridget said meekly. My stomach muscles ached from trying to hold in the laughter that was bubbling up inside me.

'Never mind, it's the thought that counts,' Brenda happily assured her, taking pains not to tear the paper as she unwrapped it. 'Ooh, shiny!' she said when she spied the tin foil. She started to finger it gently, evidently trying to guess its contents. By now I was rocking with suppressed laughter, and yet at the same time half-regretting what we'd done.

Brenda looked completely deflated when she finally got through the foil to the cold food and gravy, which dripped messily over her fingers. I felt a bit sorry for her, but the situation was so ridiculous that I had to laugh out loud. 'That's not very nice, is it?' she said crossly.

'Sorry, Brenda, it was just a joke,' we told her. She stalked off to wash her hands and we doubled up in hysterical giggles.

Later in the day, I went to Shirley's house and Bridget went off to Janice's. Shirley lived in a modern farmhouse building on a quiet lane. There was a big garden and a shed out the back, where Shirley tried to teach me to pluck a chicken. I couldn't do it. It made me feel sick. I was a lot happier playing with the poodle and the Labrador, or having a ride on Stan's tractor.

A couple of days later I went to Harriet's for the day. Hers was a fairly bog standard house, perhaps even a council house, on some kind of estate. Harriet's husband was white and very tall. She had two mixed race children. I don't remember much else about my time there because Harriet gave me a port and lemonade shortly after I arrived. This was not a very good idea, to say the least. Considering the cocktail of medication I was on, it's not surprising that I reacted badly to alcohol on top. I felt sick and woozy all afternoon and vomited twice when I got back to Kendall House.

New Year's Eve came and went, and the other girls returned to the house. Zara was one of the first back and we became quite close. I had hoped that Bridget might go on being nice to me beyond the holiday time, but it was not to be. Once Nicole and the Sophies were back, she reverted to her old ways. She seemed to get a lot of enjoyment out of manipulating the others, and I was always her target, whether directly or indirectly.

Bridget beat me up countless times, but she was scariest when she was playing mind games with me. When everything went quiet, I knew for sure that she was plotting some new torture. She totally controlled the others. If she told them to ignore me, no one would speak to me until she lifted the ban. If she told one of them to attack me, they did. It often got to the point where I'd be scared to walk from one room to another for fear of what or who was waiting around the corner. The not knowing used to terrify me. My life was dominated by fear.

I complained to the staff, but they seemed to think that it was my fault that the others treated me badly. Miss Woods used to lecture me about the compromises we needed to make to live harmoniously with each other. She called it, 'Living Together Syndrome'.

'If you're not pleasant to others, how can others be pleasant to you?' she'd say.

She was blind to the reality of the situation. How could I be pleasant when I was being beaten up every other minute and ignored the rest of the time – not to mention being drugged to high heaven?

The only chance I had to be pleasant was on the rare days when Bridget decided to be nice to me, usually after she'd had an argument with her darling Nicole. Suddenly, she would want to go out on a walk with me, or sit next to me in class or in the dining room. It always took me by surprise, but I never questioned it. Although I couldn't stand Bridget and had no real desire to be friends with her, when I was in her good books it simply meant that I had one less thing to worry about.

Towards the end of January, I started experiencing extreme stomach discomfort and sharp pains in my right side. I was also sick a lot. Harriet and Janice made the usual complaints about me being a hypochondriac and doled out extra Valium and sleeping pills. I tried not to swallow them – or any of the other medication they were giving me – because I was convinced that all the different tablets were making me worse, but Harriet caught on. 'Open your mouth!' she'd say after every dose, to check that I wasn't holding any pills on my tongue or in my cheeks.

I was certain I needed a doctor, but after two days of really bad stomach ache, Harriet still held the opinion that I was faking. 'I've heard it all before a thousand times, and you're not even a very good actor,' she sighed.

By the afternoon of the third day, I could barely walk. My stomach was distended and so sensitive to touch that I cried out in agony at the slightest brush of fingers or clothing. I began to feel feverish and extremely nauseous. My vision blurred. I couldn't focus on anything apart from the pain. Harriet told me to go and lie down in the detention room for an hour. 'I'll bring you something to help you sleep.'

'I don't want to sleep. I need a doctor,' I said.

'Of course you don't. It'll pass. It always does.'

Zara was allowed to come and see me. 'I brought you a Mars bar,' she said.

I was really touched, but I couldn't even look at it, let alone eat it. She tried tempting me to take a small bite, but I retched. 'I think I'll save it for later,' I said, slipping it under my pillow.

A little later, Shirley popped by to see how I was doing. 'Harriet says you've got your usual aches and pains,' she said.

Harriet had obviously made light of my symptoms, but I didn't have the energy to complain. Practically unconscious now, I pointed to my stomach. 'Don't touch it!' I croaked.

Shirley's face fell. 'Have you eaten anything?' She propped me up so that she could plump up my pillow. 'What's this doing here?' She pointed at the Mars bar. Knowing how much

I liked sweet things, she was surprised to hear that I didn't want it. 'I think Harriet ought to see you again,' she said anxiously.

Eventually Harriet took my temperature. She looked mildly perturbed as she read the results. Putting one hand on my forehead, she told me to show her where my stomach hurt. I screamed when she pressed it. The pain was horrific. I was sure I was dying.

'Shut up, you big baby.' She shook her head. 'If this turns out to be one of your attention-seeking exercises, I will be very angry.'

'I think we'd better call an ambulance,' Shirley said.

'That will not be necessary,' Harriet said firmly.

'This time she looks really ill,' Shirley insisted.

'She'll recover.'

In the end, Shirley dialled 999 against Harriet's wishes. I kept passing out in the ambulance, but at one point I heard Harriet say, 'If this girl is acting, then she deserves an Oscar.'

At West Hill Hospital I was given an emergency appendectomy. Four days later, when I got back to Kendall House, Harriet was the first person I saw.

'I've got a new name for you, Teresa, and it's Moaney. Because I have never known anyone moan as much as you do. So, are you feeling better now, Moaney? Or are you going to go on living up to your new name?'

'Well, I'm not dying of a burst appendix anymore,' I said. 'But if you go on drugging me, I expect I'll go on being ill – and complaining about it.'

Dad's next visit was in early February. While he was waiting to see me, he got talking to Nicole's dad. They got on so well that they decided to start coordinating their visits to Kendall House and take the train to Gravesend together. I was glad that they'd made friends, because Nicole was a bit nicer to me as a result – although only when Bridget allowed it, obviously.

Bernadette came to see me as often as she could and we began to get a lot closer. I didn't see Mum, but she rang quite regularly. One day I suggested that she come and see me with Dad. It was still my fantasy that they would get back together and make the family whole again. But Mum said that she had been told by various staff on the phone that she was no longer allowed to visit me.

I couldn't believe that they would try to stop me from seeing my own mother. Half-suspecting that she was making it up because she couldn't be bothered to make the trip, I asked Janice whether it was true.

'Yes, your mother's visiting rights have been suspended for now. Your father is adamant that she is a bad influence on you and has requested that she doesn't see you. What's more, she was very rude to Miss Woods the last time she was here. Such behaviour from visitors is unacceptable, I'm afraid. So she's only got herself to blame.'

My world was shrinking and I felt myself diminishing with it. I began to focus obsessively on trying to be good and earn the privilege of walks outside Kendall House. Walks were precious because we weren't allowed many, and they were our only little bit of freedom. Sometimes we were permitted fifteen minutes and sometimes half an hour; every second outside the house was a treat. But often we'd be promised a walk later, only to be told when the time came that the staff were too busy to bother with getting our shoes from the coat cupboard. It was incredibly frustrating. There was no consistency.

One day in early March, I was allowed to go out for a

walk at 3 p.m. – with Bridget, of all people. I sometimes wondered if the staff paired me up with her deliberately, because they knew how nasty she could be to me. Anyway, this particular day, Bridget decided to be nice, and Kate said that we could go out for a whole hour. For once, things felt like they were going my way, even though I had a streaming cold and the usual fluey symptoms that were a recurrent side effect of my medication.

As soon as we were out of the house, Bridget told me that she had stashed a bottle of wine behind a bush in the local park. 'I brought it back from my weekend away!' she said excitedly.

I'd had very little experience of drinking. Seeing Dad on the piss had put me off it, and after months on drugs at Kendall House I didn't like the idea of clouding up my brain any more than necessary. But this was a chance to bond with my deadly enemy and perhaps even disarm her by making friends, so I wasn't going to pass it up. When it came to Bridget, I lived in hope – pointlessly, as it turned out.

We rushed to the park and found the bottle in its hiding place next to the public toilets. Bridget was so happy that it was still there. But then her face dropped. 'I forgot to bring a bottle opener!' she said.

Fifteen long minutes passed as we tried to work out how to open the bottle. In vain we tried to dig the cork out using a twig. Extreme measures were called for. Finally I said, 'I've got an idea!' and whacked the neck of the bottle against the toilet wall. The bottle neck shattered and the cork flew out. Bingo! We had an open bottle of wine, albeit a lethally jagged one.

Bridget wasn't too keen on the idea of drinking from a broken bottle, but I tipped it up and poured wine in my mouth without the glass touching my lips. After a few moments, she did the same. We had to be really careful, because some of the jagged pieces had fallen into the wine, but we still managed to down about a quarter of the bottle each. Happily drunk, we strolled back to Kendall House.

As usual, Harriet was waiting to frisk us for hidden fags and matches on our return. However, she was so distracted by the smell of booze on our breath that she wasn't as thorough as she would have been normally, and I managed to smuggle in a fag, a match, and a strip of matchbox to strike it on.

'What have you been up to? I can tell you've been drinking!' Harriet said.

Bridget concocted some story about a man calling us into the pub and buying us a drink. I didn't dare speak, because I was so off my head. Harriet made us drink black coffee to sober us up, but it didn't really do the trick because I was on a wide variety of drugs as well as the booze, and no amount of coffee could counter their effects. My memory of what happened next is very patchy, but I do know that somehow I made my way upstairs and started chasing poor Georgie around, yelling abuse at her. A member of staff called Denise grabbed me and locked me in the detention room.

While I was banging on the detention room door shouting to be let out, Tina kicked off outside, yelling her head off like a mad woman and threatening Denise. What with Georgie running around like a headless chicken, Tina screaming and me banging, Denise certainly had her hands full.

I fell asleep, but it can't have been for long because when I came to, I still felt drunk. Remembering my hidden cigarette, I used my one match to light it. But it dropped out of my mouth, and the next thing I knew the covers on the bed had caught fire. I tried to get out of the room, but of course the door was locked, so there was nothing for it but to smoke the rest of my fag and go down with a smile on my face. Or that's how I saw it in my drunken state.

Suddenly, the door flew open and Denise pulled me outside. 'Quick! Where's a fire extinguisher?' she shouted.

I heard Sophie C say, 'I think there's one in Miss Woods's office, but the door is locked.'

'Well, find a member of staff to unlock it! This is an emergency!'

Feeling extremely lightheaded, I ran into the bathroom to finish my cigarette. Denise caught up with me a few minutes later, once the fire in the detention room was out. 'It's time for your teatime medication,' she said crossly.

'What? You've got to be joking! Considering all the wine I've drunk, more medication would probably kill me,' I protested. In a foul mood, I made my way to the downstairs toilet, which had been left open after someone else had used it. I locked myself in. I wanted to be alone.

Kate turned up and ordered me out of there. She fiddled with the lock and managed to get it undone from the outside, but I sat against the door so that she couldn't get in. To my surprise, it wasn't long before Bridget and Jules joined the quest to get me out of there. 'Go away,' I shouted. I was in floods of tears by now, convinced that the staff were waiting on the other side of the door to inject me – as a punishment for drinking wine and refusing my medication. 'You'll have to kill me before you get me out of here,' I said.

'Come on, Teresa,' Bridget coaxed. 'No one's going to hurt you. We're just worried about you.'

Although she had been nice to me earlier, I knew Bridget for the traitor she was and didn't trust her. She could turn against you quicker than you could say knife, so I wasn't taking any chances.

'If everyone else goes outside, I'm sure I can talk her round,' Jules said. I heard the sound of footsteps receding. 'Hey, it's just you and me now,' she added. 'What's wrong?'

I poured my heart out to her. I told her I wanted to die, and that I didn't think I could hold out much longer in this hell.

In a calming voice, she told me that she felt the same way. 'But I know I couldn't survive without you here, so please don't even think about dying. I couldn't bear it if anything happened to you.' She kept her voice to a whisper. Bridget was standing by the bathroom door and Jules didn't want her to hear what we were saying.

'Just imagine how great life will be when we get out of here,' she went on. 'We'll be free to do whatever we want. We can go to concerts together and . . .'

All of a sudden Kate rushed into the bathroom and ordered me out of the toilet. 'The house is on fire! Everyone needs to get out right this minute.'

'No way,' I replied, thinking it was just a ploy to get me out and inject me. I was staying firmly put. The fire in the detention room had already been extinguished, I hadn't heard the fire alarm and I couldn't smell any smoke. The big red alarm bells were situated right outside the office door, next to the bathroom, so I figured I would have been able to hear them if they'd gone off.

Just then, there was a lot of commotion outside the door and the next thing I knew a fireman's head had appeared over the toilet door. 'Teresa, is it? We need you to come out of the toilet because there is a fire. If you don't come out I will have to kick the door in and I don't want to do that because you might get hurt,' he said calmly.

Standing up took a lot of effort. My legs were like jelly and I was trembling all over. I opened the toilet door and fell into the fireman's arms. He led me through thick smoke in the direction of the back garden. I could see the smoke but still I couldn't smell it, because of my blocked nose.

Passing the sitting room, I saw huge flames licking the doorway. 'The hamsters!' I shrieked. Pulling away from the fireman, I dashed into the burning room and tried to grab at least one cage. But the metal bars had heated up and burnt my fingers as I touched them.

The fireman caught up with me and dragged me out of the room into the back garden. 'Please don't let my hamsters die,' I begged him.

'I'll do my best to get them out for you,' he replied, before running back to help the other firemen get control of the fire.

Meanwhile, there was another drama going on in the back garden. Bridget lunged at Tina like a lunatic and started to punch her. Then the other girls set upon her too. Everyone was shouting about the fire and the hamsters, and in my muddle-headed state it took me a few seconds to realise that Tina had started the blaze by holding a match to the curtains. I slapped my forehead. What an idiot she was! We had all joked about how great it would be if Kendall House burned down, but I'd never imagined anyone would actually try it.

A fireman walked into the back garden carrying Bridget's hamster cage. Panic surged through me. What if Nipper and Vampire hadn't made it? 'I will kill you if my hamsters are dead!' I shouted at Tina.

The fireman came back with another cage, this time containing Georgie's hamster. I was certain that my hamsters were dead now. In my rage and sadness, I went for Tina, but Jules held me back.

Then out of the blue – or out of the smoke, I should say – the fireman who had saved me appeared with my hamsters' cages.

'They were saved by the bedding in their little houses,' he said with a smile.

I had my babies back! I was so happy, even though the bottoms of their cages had melted.

Now the fire was out, we could breathe a sigh of relief. Or could we? A thought struck me. 'Why didn't the fire alarm go off?' I asked Miss Woods. 'What if one of us had been locked in the detention room, or Sick Bay, or we'd all been locked upstairs in our dorms at night?'

Miss Woods said nothing. She and the rest of the staff on duty stood apart from us, staring at the embers that continued to smoulder in the burnt-out sitting room.

CHAPTER THIRTEEN

I don't know whether they increased the dosage of my medication, or dramatically changed the combination of drugs they were giving me, but two days after the fire in the sitting room I woke up feeling very, very angry. My hackles were up. I was itching with rage.

Even Tina decided to give me a wide berth. I heard her telling Nicole, 'Teresa is in a really weird mood. Something's eating her. Stay away! She's a bit scary today.'

In class, I was rude to Mrs Petsworth, who wouldn't allow me to bring Vampire into the lesson. When she told me off for being a loudmouth I threatened to throw my books at her. Since I usually spent my time feeling doped up and sorry for myself, my new-found aggression was as much a mystery to me as it was to the others. It was strange and totally uncharacteristic behaviour.

Mrs Petsworth called for Harriet. Fearful of being injected, I agreed to settle down to work. But later in the day, the surges of rage returned. Heat kept rising up inside me like volcanic lava, threatening to erupt.

What happened next seemed such a relatively small incident – compared to some of the other stuff that went on – that in the months that followed I struggled to understand its significance, or why it might have triggered the unhappiest period of my life.

We were in the sitting room playing records after school and Bridget was dictating the playlist, as usual. Since I wasn't enjoying her choice in music, I got out my favourite Aswad twelve inch. When the track she had chosen came to an end, I went to put on my record.

'Hey! What do you think you're doing?' she asked.

'What does it look like?' I kept my voice light.

'I'm putting on the next one,' she said, swaggering over to the record player.

'Sorry, but this comes first.' I pressed my disc firmly down on the deck.

She looked around the group for support. 'I don't think so!' she sneered. 'Does anyone else here want to listen to Teresa's crappy reggae?'

The other girls said nothing. They were waiting for me to react. I didn't disappoint them. For once I wasn't going to give in to Bridget.

I placed the needle on the record and the Aswad song began to play. 'Come over here if you've got a problem with it.' I met her eye and held her gaze steadily.

A tiny hint of uncertainty flitted across her face. I had never challenged her so directly. In fact, since Maya had left, no one had. She seemed to hesitate, but there was no way she could let it go. Her position as queen bee of Kendall House was in jeopardy and she knew it. We all knew it.

She flew at me like a demon, spitting venom and abuse. I fought back angrily. Although she was a solid lump of lard and muscle, I had a feeling that I might be able to beat her just this one time. But the next moment someone was forcing us apart. I heard Harriet's voice, then Benita's, and felt the prick of a needle in my bum. I remember falling to the floor, face down, and then I blacked out.

I woke up in Sick Bay feeling woozy and disorientated. Whatever Harriet had put in the injection had totally cancelled out every last ounce of energy I had. I tried to get up, but could barely raise my head from the pillow. It felt floppy on my neck. My body was bruised and achy. I tried to call for help, but all that came out of my mouth was saliva. Instead of speaking, I was dribbling. My eyelids kept closing against my will. I had often thought I was dying before, but this time it had to be true. I couldn't even lift my arm up from the bed.

I'm paralysed, I thought. My heart raced in panic, but I found that I still couldn't move, not even with adrenalin pumping around my body. I tried to call out again. 'Help!' I mouthed the word but no sound came out. My head felt dizzy, as if I'd come to a sudden halt after spinning round and round in a circle.

My mouth filled up with saliva again, before overflowing with sour, creamy vomit. I turned my head and spewed it onto the pillow, coughing as it caught in my throat. Despite its acrid smell, I didn't bother trying to brush it away, or turn the pillow over. My eyelids started flickering; a muscle in my cheek twitched uncontrollably. I had an involuntary spasm in my leg. My foot flew towards the ceiling and fell heavily onto the bed again. So perhaps I wasn't paralysed after all? Thick waves of tiredness overcame me and I passed out.

The next thing I remember is that Janice was in the room. She made me take some pills. Finding that I could speak at last, albeit in slow, slurred tones, I asked what they were. 'Sparine and Valium,' she said matter-of-factly.

'What will it do?'

'Keep you sedated.'

'Why?'

'Dr Peri's orders.'

I inhaled a disgusting whiff of dried vomit. 'I've been sick.'

She smirked. 'You don't have to tell me. I can smell it.'

Tears welled up in my eyes. 'Can you change my pillow-case?'

She bristled. 'Let's make sure this medication goes down first.'

'When can I go back to the dorm?'

She took my pulse. 'Not yet. You stay here with the door locked and no visits from anyone, apart from staff.'

My heart sank. 'How long for?'

'However long it takes.'

'Why?'

'I think you know why.'

'I don't! What have I done wrong?'

'Well, for one, you deliberately started a fight with poor Bridget. She was very upset afterwards.'

'Poor Bridget? But she's the bully …' It was incredible. I felt sure that Bridget hadn't been locked up for fighting with me. I didn't even bother to ask.

'Miss Woods has decided that you should be isolated from the group for the time being. Hence you stay here until such a time as she decides to reintroduce you to everyday life.'

'How long will it be?'

She pursed her lips. 'That's not for me to say.'

I slept a little after she had gone and woke up in a cold sweat, with red blotches all over my skin. My vision was blurry. The ceiling kept zoning in and out of focus. My stomach started cramping up. My groin was painful and I needed to go to the toilet, but I was locked in and didn't have the strength to get up and bang on the door. I called for help but my pronunciation was skewed and it came out sounding like 'Howrp'. I tried again to get my tongue around this simple word. This time it emerged in a throaty, unintelligible rasp.

Lying on the bed, repeatedly trying to call for help, I realised that the sounds I was making seemed barely human. I had no idea what was happening to me, or what I was becoming. It was terrifying.

Shirley came into the room. There were two of her. Both Shirleys enquired if I wanted a drink. I slowly shook my head. 'Tor-lay,' I said.

The Shirleys merged into one and then divided again. They cocked their heads. 'What's that, Teresa?'

With effort, I raised my voice. '*Tor-lay!*'

'Do you mean the toilet?'

I nodded as vigorously as I could.

'Can you get up?' she asked. There was only one of her again.

I tried to sit up, but instead my arm flew upwards and fell across my face. My legs played dead. It felt as if I had no control over my physical movements. I tried to explain. 'Can't, can't . . .'

She drew back my sheets and dragged my legs around until my feet fell to the floor. After helping me to sit up, she put her arms around me and heaved me into a standing position. My legs gave at the knee, but she managed to hold me up. Almost in slow motion, we shuffled out of Sick Bay to the toilet. Once there, she helped me to pull up my nightdress and sit down on the toilet seat. My head flopped forwards. I almost lost my balance and rolled off the seat.

I thought it would make me feel better to urinate, but at first nothing came out. Suddenly I felt a tremor of a contraction down there, followed by a needle-sharp pain. 'Aaah!' I screamed. A flush of intense heat swept through me and I collapsed onto the cool bathroom floor, where I lay half in relief and half in agony until Shirley hauled me up.

'Goodness me, you're like a dead weight!' she exclaimed. 'Have you finished with the toilet?'

Although my bladder still felt full, I was terrified of trying to urinate again. 'Infection,' I said, but my clumsy tongue and slurry voice made it sound like 'invasion'.

'Say again?' I pointed to my waterworks and repeated my attempt to say 'infection' about ten times.

Finally she got it. 'I'll ask Harriet to have a look,' she said in a reassuring voice.

'No!' I cried out. I had no confidence in Harriet after the burst appendix episode, which might have killed me had she continued to ignore my pleas for medical attention for very much longer.

I think Shirley understood my fears, because she said, 'I'll ask her to sort out some antibiotics immediately.'

Some time later, Harriet came in with a load of pills. Haltingly, I asked what they were. She wouldn't say. 'I haven't got time to sit around and chat with you. You're not the only girl in Kendall House!' she snapped.

Anger welled up inside me. I felt it flood into my brain like water gushing through the walls of a burst dam. 'I hate you!' I yelled.

'I can't understand what you're saying, nor do I much care to,' she said briskly.

She thrust a tumbler of water at me. The rim banged against my mouth. I went to drink, but couldn't coordinate my lips and the glass and liquid flew everywhere. 'I want my dad!' I wailed.

This she did appear to understand. 'You're getting no visits, oh no. You're staying in here until we can be sure you're not a threat to the staff.'

I didn't understand what she meant and asked her to explain. A threat to the staff? This was a new one. But she either didn't want to expand on her comment or couldn't make out what I was saying. Soon she was gone.

I lay back and tried to work out why I was being drugged and held in Sick Bay. It had to be a punishment for something, but surely it couldn't be the argument with Bridget. Most of the time that big bully never even got told off for beating me up, so it would be totally unfair of them to lock me up for starting an argument. It hadn't even been an argument. It was just a case of standing up for myself.

Hot tears dripped out of my eyes. Why was I even trying to think things through logically? Nothing made sense at Kendall House. Bridget had received preferential treatment from Day One, despite her vindictive ways. The staff knew she was malicious and ruthless, but instead of punishing her for it, they actively encouraged it. In return, I strongly suspected that she collaborated with them and their vicious regime, informing on the girls and stirring things up. Certainly, they seemed to like her. She was the one they invited into the staffroom for tea and the occasional cigarette, and she rarely – if ever – lost her privileges.

On the other hand, I was punished for the slightest wrongdoing. I was constantly being ordered into my night-clothes. I was more familiar with the detention room and Sick Bay than I was with the dorm. Apart from Shirley, the staff appeared to despise me. And I was being drugged to death. It was all so unfair, so wrong. Why didn't the staff like me? OK, I complained about being at Kendall House, but so did everyone else, including Bridget. So why was I the scapegoat? Overcome with self-pity, I sobbed myself to sleep.

The days and nights merged into one continuous long lonely torment punctuated by tea, pieces of toast and doses of medication. I was now being drugged more than four times a day. Sometimes I'd be given six envelopes – or more – within a twenty-four-hour period, and be forced to swallow their contents. If I kicked up a fuss, Harriet would inject me forcefully, leaving me with large black bruises.

For some reason I was still not permitted visits from any of the girls. I missed Jules the most, but would have made do with seeing any of them, apart from Bridget. Perhaps even Bridget; I felt so desperately isolated. I tried to make the staff stay and talk to me when they came to take me to the toilet, or give me medication, but they usually said something like, 'I've got work to get on with!' or 'Attention-seeking, as usual.' Most of them were so hard, so heartless. Couldn't they see how desolate I felt? Didn't they understand how cruel it was to place a fourteen-year old girl in solitary confinement for days on end?

'Please let me see the others. Please let me go back to the group,' I begged Harriet.

'I'm not sure that would be a good idea, even if Miss Woods allowed it,' she replied. 'Understandably, the girls aren't feeling very well disposed towards you at the moment.'

'What do you mean? Why?'

Harriet sighed. 'They weren't happy about your uncalled-for attack on Bridget – or the way you treated Mrs Petsworth.'

'But Bridget attacked me!' I didn't remember treating Mrs

Petsworth badly and so felt I couldn't answer that particular accusation.

I had often longed to get away from Kendall House, but all I cared about now was getting out of Sick Bay and down to the other girls. Of course I still wanted to escape entirely, but it was a case of one step at a time. I was in a prison within a prison. If I could only get out of my own private cell, I felt I could almost bear life in the main house. In reality, I would have felt suicidal either way, but being locked in a tiny cramped room for so long had shifted and warped my horizons. First and foremost my priority was to get the hell out of my tiny claustrophobic dungeon. I pleaded with every member of staff I saw, but they all said the same: in a word, no.

Shirley was the only one who was even a little bit kind to me. It was usually Shirley who took me to the bathroom and helped me wash. Depending on how drugged up I was, she had to guide, support or sometimes even half-carry me there. Although I was still extremely shy about showing anyone my body, I had to lose my inhibitions when it came to staying clean during this time. Sometimes I couldn't even get up, in which case Shirley gave me a bed bath. She was always very gentle and caring with me. When I was able to sit up, she'd brush my hair with soothing strokes and listen to my stories about life before Kendall House.

One day as she was helping me along to the bathroom, we passed the upstairs classroom while a lesson was going on. This was unusual, as my toilet and bathroom visits were normally timed so that I didn't have any contact with the other girls. The classroom door was open and I could just about make out a few faces through my fog of blurred vision and muzziness.

Suddenly I heard a shout. 'There's that fucking bitch! I'll fucking get her. Die, bitch, die! Don't even show your face around here no more.'

I recognised Bridget's voice. Her aggression was palpable, even to my confused mind. Shivers of fear ran through me like electric currents. I began to shake uncontrollably. Tears streamed down my cheeks.

Another shout went up. This time it was Zara, of all people. I thought we'd made friends, but apparently the connection had been severed by my absence from the group. 'Yer fucking uglier than ever, you scraggy cow,' she yelled. A burst of laughter followed this comment.

'Yeah, Titsalina Bumsquirt, you're wasting away!' Bridget added gleefully. 'You'd better hurry up and die, or we'll do it for you. How'd you like to be murdered in your bed tonight? Suffocated, or stabbed? Cos we're coming for you, bitch face! See ya later.'

'That's enough, girls!' Shirley said. She turned to me. 'Don't take any notice, Teresa. They don't mean it.'

I knew better. 'They do mean it. They hate me. Harriet told me so.'

Back in Sick Bay, I couldn't help dwelling on what Bridget had said. After all, I had nothing else to think about. 'They're going to kill me,' I told Janice when she came to give me my pills around 7.30 p.m.

'Nonsense! They can't get in here,' she said.

Just then there was a battering at the door. 'Are you in there, Titsalina?' Bridget shouted. 'We've come for you, just like we said we would. Are you ready to die? Are you? Have you made your peace with God? You'd better start praying, you bitch. You're going to need a guardian angel if you don't want to get killed tonight.'

There was more shouting from some of the other girls, along with various hissing and growling sounds. They sounded like a pack of wild animals. Bridget was obviously having a field day as the leader of the gang. I heard Zara's voice, and Nicole's. Tina was there too, and Sophie K. They banged and kicked the door some more. I started to tremble again. My mind felt like it was exploding with fear.

Janice stepped outside the door and tried to calm the group down. 'Go away! This is very silly behaviour,' she said.

There were gasps and a few muffled giggles. They had expected me to be alone. 'It's not you we're after, Janice, it's that titless squirt you've got locked up in there. I'm just itching to put a fist in her face,' Bridget said. Janice stood her ground and saw them off.

I burst into tears and began crying hysterically. 'Why are they like that? What have I done to them to deserve it?'

Janice seemed unsympathetic. 'I have no idea. You will just have to sort it out when you get up and rejoin the group.'

'When will that be?' Having been desperate to get out of Sick Bay and be with the others again, I was now feeling extremely apprehensive about what might happen when I did.

Janice seemed to have no idea of when I might be allowed out. She told me that Miss Woods was on holiday for the week – and obviously nothing would change until she was back.

'Why not?' I screamed.

Janice shrugged. 'Stop acting up. You really can be a pain, can't you?' Her words hit me like a slap in the face. Why didn't she care about me? Why couldn't she just have shown me a bit of sympathy?

'I'll stop forever if you want,' I said, clutching her arm. 'Just get a piece of glass and you won't have any more problems with me.'

She shook me off. 'Don't be silly.'

After she had gone, I worked myself up into a frenzy of worry. I was petrified that Bridget would return and somehow find a way in through the Sick Bay door. I had visions of her standing over me with a knife, laughing maniacally before she repeatedly stabbed me in the chest. I imagined her hands around my neck, pressing hard on my throat, strangling the life out of me.

There was a loud bang outside the room. I heard laughter and a scraping sound. A note slowly edged its way under the door. I reached out and grabbed it, hoping it was from Jules. To my dismay, it was signed by Zara.

'I DON'T WANT TO BE YOUR FRIEND ANYMORE. I HATE YOU. I'M GOING TO GET YOU KILLED. YOU DESERVE TO DIE. FROM Zara'

Ten minutes later, another note came through, expressing similar spiteful thoughts and threats. This time it was signed by all the girls. 'Stop it!' I shouted, suspecting that some of them were on the other side of the door, listening for a reaction.

I was right. I heard scuffling and whispering very nearby, and then Benita's voice rang out. 'You two! Get to bed this instant!' The sound of girlish giggles and running footsteps trailed away into the distance.

In a trance of fear and despair, I searched the room for something to cut myself with. But Janice had taken everything away, even the book that Mrs Connolly had brought me earlier in the day. My eyes lighted on Zara's note. Perhaps she had done me a favour by pushing it under the door, after all. I folded it into a point and dug the point into my arm. The skin of my forearm was still delicate from previous cutting; it wasn't long before I broke through it and released several drops of blood. I worked the paper edge into the cut, gently expanding it until a tiny stream of blood ran down to my elbow. I started to make another incision, but my weapon became soggy and I had to fold up the other note.

When Janice came back to give me a final dose of medication, she found me with scratches and small cuts all over my arms. 'And you wonder why you're in here!' she said with raised eyebrows, as if I were some kind of halfwit. 'I don't suppose it has occurred to you that you're just a little bit sick in the head?'

Her words made me snap back to reality. I looked down at my arms, aghast. 'I don't know why I do this! It's the pills. For some reason they make me want to cut myself.'

'What rubbish. Quite the opposite is true, in fact. Without the pills, things would be a good deal worse for you.'

She was wrong, but she wouldn't listen. The next day I took the light bulb out of its socket, smashed it and used the pieces to continue cutting myself. When Harriet came up with a tea tray in the late afternoon, she found me in darkness, my arms covered in blood. The sheets on the bed were also spattered. She was furious. Dragging me out of the room, she marched me down to the detention room and locked me in. She and Brenda complained heartily about having to change the Sick Bay sheets and hoover the floor.

Brenda escorted me back to Sick Bay. 'You've shot yourself in the foot with this latest escapade,' she said smugly. 'Miss Woods says that from now on you can do without a light bulb.'

I pretended that I didn't care. I told myself that the darkness in my room now matched the darkness in my soul. But in truth, those black hours of night terrified me. There was hissing and whispering outside the door at frequent intervals, along with banging fists. But at least I couldn't see to read the nasty notes the girls kept pushing through. Although what they wrote was still horribly mean, it definitely wasn't as scary in the light of day as it would have been in the dead of night.

As the days passed, my appetite diminished, until I stopped wanting to eat altogether. On the other hand, I was constantly thirsty and drank as much water and milk as I could persuade the staff to bring me. Often they left me dry-mouthed for hours, gasping for liquid like a dying man in the desert. They didn't care. 'You never stop, do you? No wonder they call you the moaner,' Trinny used to say when I complained about not having enough liquid.

Some days I slept fairly constantly, only managing to wake up for long enough to take the next batch of medication. Other days I would fidget for hours on end, unable to sit still. I had an invisible itch in my legs that drove me mad. I felt compelled to keep moving, because there was no way of scratching it. It wasn't on my skin, it was deep under the skin.

I had been suffering from rashes and dry patches of skin from the very beginning of my time at Kendall House, but these worsened considerably during my time in Sick Bay. I would flush hot and cold with fever or the sweats, and pink blush flames would appear on my legs, arms and stomach. The patches of dry skin on my arms and legs became red and inflamed, shedding flaky, silvery scales. They itched like crazy, and bled easily when scratched. Sometimes they cracked and bled without even being touched. Harriet said she thought it was psoriasis.

As time went on, the patches grew and spread and merged into each other, until my ears, arms and legs were thick with it, and my head was encrusted. On bad days, the pain was unbelievable. On better days it was merely a constant irritant.

Sometimes I had trouble breathing. I had no idea whether this was down to the stale Sick Bay air or my sense of claustrophobia or whether it was a side effect of one of the drugs they were giving me. I asked if I could go out for a walk every now and then, or even just spend some time in the garden.

'It would be nice, but Miss Woods says you can't be trusted quite yet,' Shirley told me.

'Does she think I'm going to steal the flowers?'

I hadn't talked to Miss Woods once since I had been locked up. She was either on holiday, on her day off, or 'out at a meeting' when I asked to see her. It was hugely frustrating. I needed her to explain why I was being isolated and sedated – and I was desperate for the chance to defend myself against whatever accusations she could throw at me.

Finally she agreed to see me. I was feeling really listless, so Brenda washed my hair for me and helped me clean myself up. As I was leaving the bathroom, I took a good look at my reflection in the mirror. My eyes were sunken and there were deep shadows under them. My face was thin and drawn. My hair was dull and lank, even though it had just been washed.

I shuffled into Miss Woods's office. 'I hear you wanted to speak to me, Well, speak away,' she said.

Earlier, in a rare moment of clarity, I had decided that it probably wouldn't be a good idea to go into this meeting with all guns blazing. Instead I told Miss Woods that all I wanted was to be liked by the staff and girls. From now on, I promised, I would do my best to get on with everyone. If she would let me out of Sick Bay, I would never be bolshy or answer back to the staff again.

She began to ask probing questions about what it was like to spend time in solitary confinement. It wasn't long before I broke down and told her how miserable and lonely my days and nights were. 'No one loves me. No one even likes me,' I went on weepily.

She guffawed. 'We all like you! We all love you, in fact. It's just that we don't like what you do – and we don't love the way you behave. Here at Kendall House we know you can grow into a nice person, Teresa, but you have to learn where you're going wrong. That is all that's going on here. We're teaching you right from wrong.'

'But I know right from wrong! I've never stolen anything or broken the law. I've never been violent . . .'

'Never been violent?' she said archly. 'Why do you think you're in Sick Bay at the moment?'

'But Bridget attacked me first!' I protested.

She frowned. 'Bridget? I'm not talking about Bridget. I'm referring to your unbridled attack on Mrs Petsworth.'

My head spun. Someone else had mentioned it, as I recalled, but I had no idea what she was talking about and said so.

Her lip curled in disbelief. 'Do you mean to say that you don't remember flying at Mrs Petsworth in a rage? Or that she tripped and fell as a result, bringing the blackboard down with her?'

I racked my brain, but had no recollection of anything like the scene she was describing, which seemed strange considering I could clearly recall the argument with Bridget. 'I don't remember it at all,' I said.

'Well, you are confined to Sick Bay as a result of the incident with Mrs Petsworth. And in Sick Bay you will stay until I'm fully convinced that you have learned right from wrong.' She waved a hand, as if the situation had started to bore her. 'That will be all now. Brenda will take you back upstairs.'

CHAPTER FOURTEEN

The days and nights in solitary confinement were long, lonely and desperate. There was nothing to do, no one to talk to, nowhere to look and no fresh air to breathe. Physically weak and getting weaker by the day, mentally confused and disorientated, I lay in bed, barely existing, as the hours, days and weeks of nothingness drifted by. Often the only sounds I heard were hissed insults and abuse through the Sick Bay door. Not a day went past when I didn't wish myself dead.

In the mornings I woke up wondering what would be wrong with me next. My nightdress always seemed to be stuck to me, glued to my skin with clammy sweat. I had headaches that mushroomed inside my head until I was sure that my brain would explode. Often I felt angry, agitated or nervous. Other times I was so sleepy and listless that my mind was a total blank.

My skin felt either cool and sweaty or hot and dry. The slightest irritation would cause it to flare up into a rash, and it was easily bruised. I suffered from tremors, twitches, shaking and convulsions. I had a lot of sore throats and it was often painful to swallow. Bitter flavours permeated my mouth, and I would spend whole days plagued by the taste of liquorice or mould or clay. My breathing went from rapid and shallow to scarily slow and deep. Sometimes there was a rattle in my chest. Walking was often a struggle. My sense of balance was all over the place, my coordination askew. My heartbeat would race or pound for no reason. I had frequent bowel problems, both constipation and diarrhoea.

I was still being forced to take medication at least four times a day. The number of pills they were giving me varied wildly, and for no apparent reason. Sometimes my night-time dose comprised up to nine or ten tablets, but no one would explain why. Whenever I had a crying fit, became angry or was rude to one of the staff, they'd give me 'crisis medication', which was just a bunch of extra pills, sometimes accompanied by something called Phenergan Syrup, which Harriet said would help with my waterworks, and also my rashes. The different tablets sent me from high to low and then knocked me sideways. As time went on, I could feel the various chemicals kicking in, usually within half an hour of being given my medication. I'd be swept away on one wave or another – to a place of drowsiness or restlessness, deepest sleep or tension and jitters.

One morning Shirley came up to Sick Bay with a cup of tea to find me cowering in the corner of the room, shaking with fear.

'What's wrong? What is it?' she asked.

I pointed at the bed. 'Can't you see them? Look at them all! They're revolting! Get rid of them now! Please, please get rid of them!'

She frowned. 'I don't see anything. There's nothing there apart from sheets and a bed.'

'No, look!' I screeched, leaping to my feet. 'Bugs, millions of them, pouring out from under the sheets, look at them, where are they going? Argh! Don't let them come near me, please, Shirley – stop them, save me, please, help me!'

'I'll go and call Harriet,' she said, hurriedly leaving the room.

'*Don't leave me!*' I called after her, hysterical with panic. 'They'll get me and kill me and crawl into my mouth!'

It seemed ages before she and Harriet appeared. Harriet was carrying a hypodermic syringe on a small tray. Filled with terror, I cried out, 'Don't inject me, please don't inject me! I need to stay awake, or they'll get me.'

Harriet's lip curled. 'You know what I always say, Teresa. This will be a lot easier for both of us if you lie back and think of England.'

Since the bed – to my eyes – was currently a seething mass of repellent creepy-crawlies, the last thing I intended to do was lie down. I pressed myself flat against one of the walls and resisted all attempts to pull me towards the bed.

'Go and get Janice and Benita,' Harriet told Shirley, who immediately scurried away. When Janice and Benita had been rounded up, the four of them held me face down on the bed – face down in imaginary wriggling bugs – and Harriet rammed the syringe into my buttock. I went out like a light.

The hallucinations got worse. There always seemed to be something creeping in or out of the bed. I started seeing little triangles with wings. They floated around the room. They followed me as I was accompanied to the toilet and they danced in front of my eyes, swooping over my head and fluttering in my peripheral vision. They were maddening, like nasty little faceless fairies sent from hell to tease and torment me.

I had one urine infection after another and was constantly uncomfortable. The old familiar pains returned to my groin area, which started to feel battered and bruised again. I experienced a burning sensation down there, as well as a sharp, prickly feeling that made me curl up in agony. My genitals were often sore, as if they had been rubbed raw.

I complained to the staff, but as usual they dismissed my worries as make-believe. Nothing made a difference. I could be howling in agonised torment, my face hot with fever, my body slippery with sweat, my hand tucked between my legs as if to shield my groin from further pain, and Harriet would simply say, 'Snap out of it, Teresa. I've had enough of your shenanigans today.'

'Help me, Harriet!' I would say through clenched teeth. But no matter how graphically I described what was going on down there, not one of the staff took me seriously or bothered to give me an examination.

Even Shirley, who was a lot more sympathetic than the rest of them, used to say, 'I expect it's hormones. You're at that age.' Or, 'It could be female growing pains.' Or, 'Perhaps it's a touch of thrush – don't worry, it's perfectly normal.'

I was ignorant, but not stupid. Was she trying to tell me that every teenage girl went through a phase of writhing in bed with her groin on fire, suffering from racking pain? It was just a part of growing up, was it? No need to call in a doctor? I couldn't believe it. I knew about periods, but no one had ever mentioned anything like this to me. It just couldn't be normal. Pain was your brain's way of telling you that you were ill – I knew that much.

My terrible nightmares returned. I was haunted by visions of scary men. A couple of their faces were familiar, but most of them were unrecognisable. They did unspeakable things to me. They hurt me. They enjoyed hurting me. They laughed as they hurt me. In the dreams I screamed for help, but my voice had no power and the screams came out silent.

I became intensely agitated during my waking moments. Harriet's way of dealing with this was to prick and pierce and puncture and stab my body with needle after needle, not caring if she left me covered in bruises. I was unconscious for most of the day and night, but the nightmares continued. The pain in my groin grew worse. Urination was often excruciating. I began to experience extreme discomfort when it came to my bowel movements. My back passage itched and ached and felt tender and sore. But still no one listened to me when I complained.

Then one evening I realised just how real my nightmares were. I woke up in a panicked haze. My brain was swirling; I couldn't see very well; everything felt dreamlike. There were two men in the room. One of them was pushing between my legs; the other was forcing himself in and out of my mouth. There was a belt tied around my neck. When they noticed that I was conscious, one of them tightened the belt. I fought for breath and passed out again.

The next time I woke up, they were gone. As I recalled what had happened, I vomited violently over the side of the bed. There were red marks on my neck. My lips were bruised and sore. My groin was tender and swollen. An unpleasant odour lingered in the air. It was familiar; I had smelled it before. In the past I had associated it with waking up from long stretches of drugged stupor. Thinking about it now, I realised that there was a link between the smell and my genital discomfort and pain.

In that moment I knew that this had happened before. Not once, but many times. Over and over again, these men and other men had violated my body while I slept, semi-comatose, under the influence of multiple prescription drugs, while I was oblivious to what they were doing to me.

My body started to convulse with shock at this realisation. My teeth chattered; my arms and legs shook uncontrollably. I threw up again and then dry-retched repeatedly. I searched my mind desperately for some way to contradict what I knew to be true. I didn't want to believe that these unspeakable things were being done to me. Surely it couldn't be possible. The Sick Bay door was locked day and night, so how could anyone get in?

I tried to reject the sickening knowledge that, for the men who worked in and around Kendall House, getting hold of a key to Sick Bay was probably kid's play.

But how did they get up the stairs without being seen? How did they do what they did to me without being heard? If my nightmares were in any way representative of reality, in the past they had laughed and joked as they abused me. So why had nobody heard them? Could I possibly have imagined the whole thing? Could it have been an hallucination?

By now my heart was pounding furiously. I was finding it increasingly difficult to breathe. Staring ahead into space, my eyes wide as saucers, my brain overloading with information I didn't want to absorb, I went into a full-blown panic attack. Triangles with wings crowded my vision. Bugs crawled all over my skin. As I tried to brush them off, I went into a frenzied bout of scratching.

I fell to the ground, shuddering. I rammed my head against the floor, frantically trying to smash the truth inside it to smithereens, desperate for this to be another dream or nightmare, just another hallucination. I yelled for help. I cried out to God. I begged the ground to swallow me up.

I couldn't cry enough. I couldn't scream enough. My mouth wouldn't open wide enough to express the enormity of my anguish. How could they do this to me? How! Why! The bastards! I felt my brain folding in on itself. Hate and fury surged through me. Self-pity flooded my mind. I pulled at my hair. I pummelled my fists into the floor.

I heard the clink of keys at the door. Harriet came into the room. 'Oh, look who's creating! Well, what a surprise. Having another one of your turns, are you? Dear oh dear.' Her voice dripped with disdain.

Her heartlessness blew me away. Lying on the floor in front of her, red-eyed, tear-stained, shaking, crying, and in obvious physical and emotional pain, was a fourteen-year-old girl. And yet all she could do was mock.

I pulled myself into a sitting position and tried to marshal my thoughts. 'I'm hurt, Harriet,' I said eventually, in a low, faltering voice. 'There were two men in here last night. They . . .' I couldn't go on. I began to retch again.

'Two men? In here? Oh, Teresa, really . . .' Her voice trailed off into a deep sigh of disbelief.

'It's true, Harriet. They hurt me down there. One of them, he, he, he . . .' I just couldn't say it.

'More nightmares,' she said matter-of-factly, passing me a handful of pills and a glass of water.

I shook my head. 'No, Harriet, it was real. They really hurt me. Two men. They were in here. In Sick Bay. On the bed. They shouldn't have been here.'

'Take your medication,' she said in her usual dictatorial way.

I looked down at the tablets in my hand. Orange. White. Blue. Yellow. Pills. Although I longed for oblivion, for an escape from the pain of what I now knew to be true, I was scared of going to sleep because of what might happen while I was unconscious. I threw the pills onto the floor and chucked the glass at the wall. 'I've been attacked!' I yelled at Harriet. 'Why won't you listen to me?'

Fifteen minutes later I was out cold again, and there was another great big pinprick hole in my bum.

I confided in the other members of staff. I pleaded with Shirley to believe me. I told Benita, Trinny and Ivy. No one took a blind bit of notice apart from Shirley, who tried to calm me down as she brushed my hair for me.

'I feel very sorry for you having such awful dreams, but you really don't have to worry. It's just not possible for anyone to get in here unauthorised,' she said soothingly.

I wanted to believe her. I wished it had been a dream. I started to question my sanity. Perhaps I'd gone mad. Maybe it had all just been an hallucination.

Fear overwhelmed me. Fear became my way of life. I was like a hunted animal, frightened all the time. I was scared to go to sleep, but it took so much energy to keep myself alert all the time that I was always dropping off, despite myself. I tried to stay awake, but it was so hard. I suspected that someone – Dr Peri, or even perhaps Harriet – had upped my nightly doses of sleeping pills. Such was my sensitivity to the different effects of drugs that I could feel them shutting me down more powerfully than before. It was like being hit on the head with an iron bar.

I became weaker and sleepier by the day. It felt as if the essence of life was draining out of me. Convinced that I was slowly dying, I dreaded the times when Shirley wasn't on duty. She was the only member of staff who showed any concern for me. She fed me when I was so out of it that I was physically unable to lift a knife or a fork to my mouth. She led me patiently to and from the bathroom, and never told me off for being slow, even when I could only shuffle at a snail's pace.

Eventually I was so frail that I didn't have the strength to chew my food. I couldn't hold it in my mouth. It would drop out and spill down my front. I was literally starving to death, so I was given soup for every meal. Shirley spooned it into my mouth. I wasn't eating much, but when she wasn't around I ate even less, because no one else could be bothered to take so much time and care over feeding me.

By now I was scarily thin. My ribcage was visible under my skin. My hip bones stuck out and my cheekbones were very prominent. When I looked in the mirror, I appeared to have aged dramatically. I looked like an old woman. My eyes were blank and empty. I was beginning to resemble a half-starved concentration camp victim.

The drugs profoundly affected my speech. A lot of the time I spoke so slowly that I sounded like I had severe learning difficulties, or a permanent disability. I began to forget how I normally spoke and became unsure about my accent. I tried to copy other people, but since there was a mix of regional and national accents among the staff at Kendall House, I found it hard to be consistent in my pronunciation. My mode of speech sounded very odd – I know it did, because people scrunched up their faces as if they couldn't make out what I was saying, or simply didn't like the way I was saying it. Communication was suddenly a lot harder. My identity was slipping away from me and I was helpless to do anything about it.

Who was I anyway? It was hard to recall that I was just a child whose parents had been unable to look after her, whose mother had persuaded her to make a suicide attempt and whose father couldn't get it together to pay the electricity bill. I could still just about remember the chatty, cheeky, card-playing schoolgirl who went to meet her dad in the Fox and Hounds, but I couldn't see how I could ever get back to being that person again. I was someone else now, a girl full of fear and rage, a child drowning in drugs and loneliness.

I started presenting symptoms of lockjaw, possibly caused by an infection picked up when cutting myself with something grubby. It began with stiffness in my muscles, and spasms in my jaw and neck. My speech deteriorated even more. I developed a high fever and suffered from convulsions and a persistent sore throat.

My psoriasis was horrific. Large areas of my body were disgustingly scabbed up. I only hoped that this would put off the men who had hurt me. Why anyone would want to touch someone with huge dry scabby patches all over their skin was beyond me. On the other hand, it didn't take a genius to realise that men who got their kicks raping an unconscious underage girl had to be totally sick in the head, and so couldn't be judged by normal standards.

The second time I was consciously aware of them in the room, I woke up to find myself being anally and orally assaulted. In the morning there was an agonising tenderness in my back passage area and blood on the sheets.

Benita was on duty that day. Now Benita was as hard as nails and not particularly nice, but although she might not take bullying or fighting very seriously, she was definitely not the kind of person to find sexual abuse acceptable. To her, it was a different matter altogether. She insisted that I be given a thorough medical examination.

She and Ivy were present when Harriet finally investigated my symptoms. Harriet took several swabs and cultures. It was an unpleasant, painful experience because the whole area was extremely tender. Benita looked shocked when Harriet said that there were tears in the fold of my rectum. I didn't know what this meant. Benita told me later that it was probably the result of a rash, or an infection.

Harriet sent the cultures off to a clinic for analysis. I was found to have thrush, a urine infection and a genital strep infection front and back. Harriet treated me with antibiotics and creams, but otherwise the symptoms – and my claims of being attacked – went uninvestigated. No one called in a doctor, or the police.

The staff were totally unsupportive. Benita wouldn't meet my eye for a long while afterwards, and didn't want to discuss my allegations. Harriet just tutted when I brought them up. Miss Woods told me I had an overactive imagination. Trinny rolled her eyes. Janice said it was all in my head. Most insulting of all, Dr Peri dismissed my claims as 'typical teenage fantasies'.

After that I had a long series of consecutive urine infections, each one worse than the last. The soreness in my rectal region healed and recurred, and healed and recurred, never fully going away. Antibiotics became a part of my daily dosages. As a result, I almost always had thrush. My discharge was foul-smelling, discoloured, and sometimes bloody. I had always suffered from bad period pains, but during my months in Sick Bay they became even more severe.

I began bleeding in my back passage. It became so bad that eventually Harriet took me to hospital, where the doctors treated me for rectal fissures. I also had a bowel stretch under anaesthetic, probably because they made the wrong assumptions about why I had anal tears. Unfortunately I was just too confused and out of it to question what was going on. All I knew was that I was a total mess physically.

Mentally, I was a paranoid wreck. I felt I could trust no one, not even Shirley. Although Shirley was becoming like a mother figure to me, and I was genuinely fond of her, I could not be a hundred per cent sure even of her. After all, if she couldn't put two and two together when the evidence was staring her in the face, how could she genuinely be on my side? A real mother would have believed her daughter. A real mother would have moved heaven and earth to save her child from further suffering. Or even forgetting the maternal side of things, a real friend would have felt compelled to speak up on my behalf. But Shirley did nothing apart from brush my hair and tell me nice stories. Perhaps she also felt helpless.

I felt so alone. I wasn't allowed to see the other girls. As spring became summer, they started going out for more trips to the beach and the park. I knew this because I was only allowed to come out of Sick Bay while they were out. 'They've all gone to Camber Sands,' Shirley would tell me. I longed for the chance to go with them, to see the sea and the horizon again.

Most of all, I missed Jules. I felt desperately lonely without her to talk to. I knew she would be worried about me. The feeling was mutual. I dearly hoped that she was taking care of herself, and that the staff weren't treating her badly.

As the weeks went by, enormous anger welled up inside me. It grew and grew out of all proportion until I was hardly able to contain it. I shouted at the staff, biting off their heads at the slightest incitement, growling, screaming and yelling at them, my mouth a cesspit of swear words and abuse. I self-harmed at every opportunity, taking my fury out on myself, slashing at my arms, scratching my scabs, drawing blood wherever I could, wanting to drown in my own blood.

I became incredibly sensitive to noise. My nights were tense and full of terror. I woke up at the slightest sound outside the Sick Bay door, convinced that it was the sound of the men returning to hurt me. It was like living through my own personal horror film. I badly needed rest, relaxation and proper sleep, but they were as far out of reach as Australia. Peace of mind was an alien concept. I longed for death, because I figured that dying was the only way to sleep without fear. No one could hurt me if I was dead. Finally I would be safe.

CHAPTER FIFTEEN

Time had very little meaning in Sick Bay. The days drifted and merged, the weeks stretched and contracted. An hour could last a week. A week felt like a year. The minutes dragged. The months bled into one another. There were moments when I even wondered if time had gone into reverse.

But then I would find that the days had suddenly zipped forwards. One morning I asked Harriet the date. She checked her watch. 'June the twentieth, why?'

'Oh,' I said. 'I've been fifteen for more than a week without knowing it.'

I had heard from the other girls that we were supposed to get a cake and a gift of fifteen pounds on our birthdays. But I got nothing. No one had even acknowledged the day, or thought to point it out to me. I asked if I could have the cake and money now.

'You should have mentioned it before. It's too late now,' Harriet said dismissively.

The summer months wore on. Locked in a tiny, airless room, stifled by its stale, unhealthy atmosphere, I lay slumped on the bed in a slick of sweat, motionless for hours on end. My days were a blur. I felt like a slug in slime. But at night, I took on a different incarnation. After sleeping all day, I'd be restless and agitated, banging on the door like a hyped up maniac, screaming to be set free.

Mrs Tarwin kept lecturing me about restoring normal sleeping patterns. 'How do you expect to get to sleep at night if you laze around all day?' she scolded.

'But what else is there to do, locked up in here?'

'Read, write, draw, knit, no end of constructive activities,' she said. 'You just have to be more disciplined with yourself.'

My muscles, unused, began to waste away. My legs trembled during visits to the bathroom. My skinny calves and thighs were barely able to hold me up. I developed bedsores, which were hardly distinguishable from my psoriasis scabs. It hurt to urinate. I had constant thrush. I begged Harriet to give me an overdose and kill me. She accused me of being melodramatic.

I pleaded with Mrs Tarwin to get a gun and shoot me.

'Oh dearie me,' she said absently. 'You really are in a bad way, aren't you?'

'I can't go on living in this hell. I want to die,' I told her, in floods of tears.

She turned to look at me, a frown on her face. For once she actually appeared to be seeing me for the person I was, rather than just a nuisance that had to be dealt with. I saw a flash of something in her eyes. 'Poor Teresa,' she said with what sounded like genuine compassion.

Whenever Bridget walked past the door she kicked it. She encouraged the others to do the same, so the door was constantly being thumped. She would whisper, 'We're going to kill you tonight. We've planned everything. First we're going to beat up the staff and steal the keys off them. Then we'll come in there and kill you.'

Lying in bed, drugged out of my head, I trembled at her

words. It got to the point where I stopped wanting to come out of Sick Bay because I couldn't face the thought of being bullied again. On the other hand, I was desperate to leave because of the men who came in to hurt me.

I hallucinated on and off, day in, day out, and it was truly scary to be seeing bugs and winged triangles that weren't there. I was petrified of being injected again. One way or another, I was terrified all of the time.

I was aware of very little that went on in the rest of the house, but the staff would give me snippets every now and then. I heard that Emma had left and a new girl called Estelle had arrived. I rejoiced for Emma and felt sorry for Estelle. Whoever she was and whatever she'd done, she didn't deserve to come to Kendall House.

Meanwhile, I watched the blue sky through the tiny window high up on the wall and imagined a world beyond my cell, where people lazed on park benches and kids splashed in fountains, where families packed picnics and towels into their cars and drove off to the seaside.

Teenage girls all over the country were falling in love for the first time. They were going to their first pop concerts, experimenting with make-up and jewellery, lying their way into nightclubs and sneaking into over-18's films. But these simple pleasures were denied me. I was trapped in a vacuum, learning nothing, experiencing nothing – except the dire consequences of mixing endless prescription drugs.

I cried for hours on end, unable to make sense of what was happening to me. I still hadn't been given a real explanation of what I was doing in Sick Bay, day in day out, or why I had been separated from the other girls. I still had no idea what the drugs were for – what they were or why I was being given them.

And what of the future? It was a huge black hole. I was given no incentives or goals, nothing to work towards or look forward to. No one seemed to know how long I was staying in Sick Bay, or what I had to do to get out. As usual, they trotted out that catch-all reason for everything – 'It's for your own good'. It was almost laughable, in a sick, dark, bleak way.

I had arrived at Kendall House healthy, lively and relatively happy. Yes, I'd had problems, but I had also been described as 'pleasant and charming' by a psychiatrist, and I'd always been able to see the brighter side of things. Well, most of the time, anyway. But now I was thin, ill and depressed. I was half dead. You only had to look at me to see how much I was suffering. So how could anyone say that anything good was being achieved during my time at Kendall House? They were either stupid, blind as bats – or consciously evil.

Mrs Tarwin started coming to see me more frequently. Tall, with blonde roller-curled hair, she was probably in her late forties or early fifties. She really seemed to feel sorry for me. Out of the blue, she said, 'I've got some friends who are interested in meeting you. I'm going to take you to their house. You'll like it there. They've got a swimming pool.'

I was only half-interested. Some days I didn't much care about anything except praying to God to let me die. Anyway, I was so out of my head that I wasn't sure if she was telling me a story, or talking directly to me. With all those drugs in my system, it was often hard to concentrate. 'That sounds nice,' I said, my eyelids closing. I drifted off to sleep.

A couple of hours later, she came back into the room holding an armful of clothes. 'Put these on, we're going out to tea,' she said, laying them on the bed.

It felt strange to change out of my nightdress, and even stranger when I put my shoes on downstairs. It was a long time since my feet had been out of slippers, and ages since I'd been down to the ground floor of Kendall House. The hall was eerily empty, because the other girls were all out at the local swimming baths. The staff were too afraid for my safety to risk another meeting. Bridget had turned the entire group against me. She was still furious with me for standing up to her and nothing could halt her bitter vengefulness towards me.

Outside the front door of Kendall House, I took a deep breath of fresh air and went into sensory overload. Fresh sights, sounds and smells assailed me: the sun on my face; a summer breeze in my hair; birds singing; a lorry passing by; my clumpy winter shoes crunching across the gravel drive; Mrs Tarwin's car starting up. It was hard to take it all in after so long inside.

I watched curiously out of the car window as Mrs Tarwin drove us along. I felt incredibly detached, as if the glass between me and the world was an extension of my body rather than the car's. I saw a young girl of about my age walking purposefully along the pavement, a large holdall slung over her shoulder. There was something buoyant in the way she walked that suggested confidence, happiness and freedom. I couldn't imagine strolling along like that, without a care in the world. I stared down at the contours of my bony legs, thin as broom handles beneath the dreadful flowery skirt that Mrs Tarwin had brought into Sick Bay for me. It struck me that I probably wouldn't be physically able to move like that girl moved, even if I wanted to.

We passed along several country lanes and through a village, before turning off a hill into a drive. At the end of the drive were two bungalows, one on each side, with a garage connecting them. We drew up next to the bungalow on the left, where there was a nice pond in the front garden.

A plump older lady with white hair and glasses answered the front door. She had a lovely smile. Mrs Tarwin introduced her as Mrs Whattler. 'Come in!' she said in a very friendly voice.

She led us into the sitting room, on the left of the hall. I noticed that she walked with a limp and her arm was disabled. I later found out that she had been paralysed down one side of her body as the result of a stroke she had suffered after the birth of one of her children. She motioned to a comfortable armchair and I sat down, eyeing the delicious spread that had been set on the coffee table in the middle of the room. My tummy rumbled at the sight of plates laid out with sandwiches, rolls and cakes.

A very tall older man with kindly eyes joined us. He had greying hair and striking dark eyelashes. He introduced himself as Mr Whattler. 'Nice to meet you, Teresa,' he said warmly. 'Are you hungry? Mrs Whattler's done a lovely tea for us.'

I instantly felt comfortable with Mr and Mrs Whattler. They were such nice people. Their kindness shone out of them. After tea they showed me around the house and out into the garden, where there was a porch with a swinging chair. There was also a shed and a swimming pool. The garden was blooming with flowers and there was a vegetable patch at the back, near the pool. To me, it looked like paradise after the dull, blank walls of Sick Bay.

Mr Whattler told me how much he loved gardening. Although I was dopey with drugs and didn't take in everything he or his wife said, I showed as much enthusiasm as I could muster and replied slowly and politely to every question they asked. I really wanted these wonderful people to like me.

They had a lovely kitchen. In one corner there was a basket for Henry, their dog. He was a gorgeous golden Labrador, a really gentle, soppy mutt. I loved him from the start.

When we left, Mrs Whattler said, 'It's been very nice meeting you, Teresa. We hope we'll see you soon. We'd very much like you to come and visit us again. Maybe you'd even like to come and stay the night in the spare bedroom?'

Her words touched me deeply, as did the soft, gentle way she spoke them. 'Yes, I would. I'd like that a lot,' I said, tears pricking my eyes.

She went on to suggest that I might like to go for a swim in the pool sometime. Hoping that she didn't detect the panic in my eyes, I made an excuse about not being a good swimmer. In actual fact, I was mortified by the thought of revealing my psoriasis. I felt like a leper under my clothes and was convinced that the sight of my legs, back or belly would repel her.

She must have sensed that my hesitation went beyond a fear of drowning, because she said, 'We'll just see how it goes next time, shall we? I just thought you might fancy a dip.'

As we left, she and Mr Whattler stood in the drive and waved us off. I waved back until long after they were out of sight. That night in Sick Bay I dreamed of Arctic Rolls and roses.

A few days later, I was summoned to Miss Woods's office by Dr Peri. 'How is life?' he asked. What a stupid question that was.

My words came out in a torrent. I told him how unhappy I was in Sick Bay. I asked why I was there, and what he was hoping to achieve by locking me up and isolating me. I demanded an explanation. I begged to be let out. I accused him and the other staff of cruelty.

He gave me the smug, superior smile that seemed to be reserved just for me. 'When we first met I knew it would only be a matter of time before you showed your true colours,' he said, his blubbery chin wobbling as he spoke. 'Hey presto, you went on to reveal yourself as disruptive, disturbed and aggressive.'

'That's not true! I'm not a troublemaker and I never have been,' I protested. 'I was fine before I came here. I was well behaved.'

'You may have thought you were fine, but I could tell that you were not. You have deep-seated problems and, as I say, it did not take long for you to reveal your true colours.

'It is a fact that you are known to bang on the door of Sick Bay for hours on end, to the extent that the staff are wary of entering for fear of being attacked. What's more, you have fought with the other girls and threatened violence towards a teacher. This is what I expected of you right from the start, and during these past months I have been treating you for your personality disorders.'

Hearing this, I was momentarily speechless. The thought of the staff being scared of me was ridiculous – and everybody knew that Bridget was a hundred times more aggressive than I could ever be. Tina, too. As usual, he was distorting everything.

'Your behaviour is erratic and you suffer from violent mood swings,' he continued. 'So what do you . . .'

'That's what your drugs have done to me!' I interrupted. 'I was never like that before.'

'So you admit that you are difficult and unpredictable,' he said, his eyes glinting.

'Not before I came to Kendall House, I wasn't. But what

do you expect when you're giving me all these pills? They make me feel weird! I'm not myself anymore.'

'My aim has always been to get to the root of your problems, in the hopes of calming your aggression and turning you into a normal, healthy girl. I feel that we have made some headway in this area. There is evidence to suggest that you are improving.'

Again, I had nothing to say. My physical and mental health had deteriorated to such an extent that no one could possibly call it an improvement. 'Are you going to keep me locked up?' I asked, finally.

'Well, the good news is that it will not be long before we reintroduce you to the group. After that, we will see about rehousing you in the dorms at night, but we will take it one step at a time.'

He pulled himself out of his comfortable chair with some effort, before stepping towards me. Taking my head in his hands, he planted a kiss on my forehead. I nearly puked on the spot. 'Get away from me!' I said, pushing him away.

He laughed. 'You are a tough girl, that is for sure. Almost too tough,' he said. He waved an arm. 'Take her to her room,' he told Harriet. For once I was almost relieved to get back to Sick Bay.

Later I thought long and hard about what he had said, and what his words actually meant. None of it made sense. What on earth could his motive be for turning a happy, healthy girl into a nervous wreck – and then smilingly pronouncing that she was getting better? The only explanation I could think of was that he had deliberately set out to mess with my brain so that he could treat me and then announce that he had 'cured' me. But why would anyone – especially a doctor – want to do that? It was crazy.

It wasn't long after that meeting that the number of pills in my daily doses began to be reduced. Very gradually my brain began to wake up. I felt like a patient coming out of a coma, slowly and agonisingly. But physically I felt no better. I started suffering from the worst itching I had ever experienced, along with the same kind of flu symptoms I remembered from my time at Joyce Green Hospital, when I was coming off the Kendall House drugs.

'It's perfectly normal,' Mrs Tarwin told me when I complained to her.

'In what way?' I asked miserably.

'Dr Peri is rebalancing your medication. You are bound to take some time getting used to the new doses,' she said.

One night as I was mercilessly scratching my skin from head to toe I heard the sound of a girl screaming. I strained to listen, wondering who it could be. The screams went on and on. They were unbearable. I wanted to cover my ears, but I was powerless over my hands, which wouldn't stop scratching. I heard shouting too. Who was it? I didn't recognise the voice. 'Stop! Stop!' she was crying. 'Help me!'

Are the men hurting her too? I thought. The noise went on for hours. I lay in bed and sobbed, sharing the girl's pain with every scream she let out. It was heartbreaking.

Mrs Tarwin took me to see the Whattlers again. On the way there, I asked her about the screaming girl. 'Oh, don't worry about Annie. She's just taking some time to settle in,' she said.

'What are you doing to her? She sounded like she was being attacked.'

'It's none of your business, is it? Don't put your nose in where it's not wanted. Annie is fine. She is getting the treatment she needs.'

'How can she be fine? She doesn't stop screaming.'

Mrs Tarwin clicked her tongue. 'If you go on with this, I will simply turn the car around and take you back to Kendall House.'

I didn't dare say any more. There was no way I was going to jeopardise my trip to the Whattlers' house. I couldn't wait to see them again.

This time, Mrs Tarwin left me with them for the whole day. I sat in the garden for most of the time, soaking up the lovely sunshine and talking to Mrs Whattler while Mr Whattler pottered around the garden. Again they suggested a swim. I refused. I was so conscious of my psoriasis and the self-harm scars on my arm that I wouldn't even roll my sleeves up in the heat, let alone change into a swimming costume.

We had cold meat and salad for lunch. I still didn't have much of an appetite, but I tried to eat as much as I could, so as not to seem rude. About five minutes into the meal, I became aware of Mr and Mrs Whattler watching me. 'Don't worry, Teresa, your food's already dead. You don't need to kill it all over again,' Mr Whattler said jokily. Mrs Whattler laughed softly.

No one had ever taught me how to use a knife and fork properly. I just used to hack my food to pieces, stab it and stuff it in my mouth. I didn't have the slightest idea about table etiquette or manners and so it didn't occur to me not to speak with my mouth full. No wonder they looked slightly alarmed during that first meal. I must have seemed completely primitive to them, especially as I was out of the habit of eating solids. But they were kind enough not to scold me. Instead they showed me how to eat properly and, conscious of my ignorance, I accepted the lesson gratefully.

Later on, when they began to show me how to do other basic things, I was eager to learn. I hadn't a clue about how to look after my appearance. My hair was in a terrible condition and it didn't help that I never brushed it. I didn't clean my teeth on a regular basis, so they were really yellow. When I did clean them, I gave them a five-second brush and that was it. 'You won't keep your teeth healthy if you do it that quickly,' Mrs Whattler told me, before showing me how to brush properly.

My nails were severely bitten, chewed down to the cuticles, and I chomped into the skin around them until it was ragged. Mrs Whattler put Stop 'n Grow on my nails to stop me biting them. I loved her for it but it didn't work. I just got used to the taste and went on chewing nervously.

After a few visits, I was allowed to spend the night at the Whattlers' house. Mrs Tarwin would drop me off there with an overnight bag and several envelopes of pills. Sometimes there were four or five tablets in each envelope, but other times there were as many as nine. Mrs Whattler used to pour them into my hand four times a day. She was shocked by how many there were.

'I don't want them. They make me feel weird. Can't we just throw them away?' I used to say.

'If we don't give them to you, they won't let us see you anymore,' she'd sigh.

So, of course, I took them because I loved Mr and Mrs Whattler and couldn't bear the thought of not seeing them. All I lived for were those visits.

Back at Kendall House, my days and nights continued to be disturbed by the tortured screams of the new girl Annie. Once when I was going to the bathroom, I caught a glimpse of her. She was a really pretty girl with glossy hair and a nice open face. I hated to think of what the staff were doing to her. Another time, I passed her in the corridor. She was being dragged along the landing by Harriet and Trinny. 'Don't let them break you,' I whispered, but I doubt she heard. Her eyes were half-closed and her body was limp.

I really began to worry about her after that, and with good reason, because it turned out that they were injecting her left, right and centre. A few weeks after I had first seen her, there was a huge kerfuffle just outside Sick Bay. I'd just come from the bathroom and Janice was about to lock me in when the sound of Annie's screams pierced the air. Janice rushed out of the room without locking the door, so I was able to take a peep at what was going on.

What I saw shocked me, even though I saw it through an anaesthetic film of drugs. While Annie struggled and yelled for help, Mrs Tarwin, Harriet, Janice and two other members of staff wrestled her to the ground with extreme force, grabbing, slapping and punching her. They pulled down her knickers and held her down while Mrs Tarwin injected her. Seconds later, she became motionless and utterly, eerily silent, as if dead. They dragged her into the room next to mine. I heard her body being dumped on the floor like a sack of garbage.

A few minutes later she woke up and began to vomit violently. I could hear her retching over and over again. Bleary as I was, I could tell that there was something seriously wrong with her.

The staff took her into the staffroom, which was almost opposite Sick Bay. She couldn't support herself or walk at all. There was vomit all over her and she continued to heave. She looked terrible, so bad that I really thought she might be dying. Judging by the expressions on some of the staff's faces, they were worried too. Someone rushed off for a bucket, someone else for a blanket. I heard Janice say that it was time to call a doctor. Meanwhile Annie just went on vomiting.

'What's going on? What's wrong with her?' I asked Janice.

'Get back to your room! She's got a tummy bug,' she replied.

'I don't think it's just a tummy bug,' I said. 'She's really ill. You'd better get an ambulance.'

'Who's got the Sick Bay key?' Janice shouted. Moments later, I was a prisoner again.

Was Annie lucky that she didn't die that night? I thought so at the time. I pleaded with the staff to let me spend some time with her and eventually we were allowed a few minutes together. She came into Sick Bay out of her head on drugs and sat on the bed, dribbling and jerking as she spoke. Her hair had lost its gloss. There seemed to be nothing shining within her, not even the tiniest flame of life.

'I want to die,' she said starkly.

'I know the feeling, but you must try not to give up,' I told her.

'I've already given up. I will kill myself. I promise I will. Even if I get out of here, I'll do it. I'm already dead anyway. My heart may be beating, but they've killed me. I hate them for it. I hate Mrs Tarwin. She has destroyed me. I'm a dead person in a living body.'

She slumped sideways on the bed and passed out. I sat beside her and gently stroked her hair, tears streaming down my face. I believed her when she said that she felt dead. She looked it.

I never found out why Annie was sent to Kendall House, or why she was being so heavily medicated. If her case bore any resemblance to mine, then there probably wasn't any logic behind the way she was being treated. Equally, was there any reason why I was being weaned off the heaviest drugs I had been taking while she was being knocked out? Who knows? Nothing made any sense at Kendall House. There were never any answers, only questions.

Around this time I was reintroduced to the group, which was a nightmare experience all of its own. The girls were like vultures and I was their prey. Bridget had brainwashed them into thinking I was bad, mad, odd, weird and dirty. No one apart from Jules had the least sympathy for what I had been through, and Bridget had become so powerful and intimidating that even Jules was reluctant to have anything to do with me now. When I was injected or sent to the detention room, Bridget would tell everyone that I deserved it. She said that I had been locked in Sick Bay all these months to protect the group from me, because I was wild and dangerous. I couldn't understand why she took so much pleasure in hurting me.

I was continually shunned. At mealtimes I'd sit on a table on my own while the girls made nasty remarks about me from across the room. The staff did nothing, not even when I had things thrown at me, and I was too scared to retaliate in case I was injected again. Whole days went past without one single girl saying a word to me. It was hell.

I was weak, a softie, a sucker for a kind word or gesture, and the girls took advantage of this, drawing me in by pretending to be nice only to reject me again and again. Ever hopeful and desperate to be liked, I fell for it every single time.

'I saved this sweet for you,' one of them would say and I would take it gratefully, only to find that it was a pebble wrapped in sweet paper.

'You look pretty,' someone else might say, before following up with, 'Pretty fucking ugly, I mean.'

When they suddenly said that they wanted me back in the dorms, I wanted to believe them so much that I went along with it. It was Nicole who went to see Miss Woods to ask if I could come out of Sick Bay. She told Miss Woods that the girls felt very sorry for being mean to me and wanted to make it up to me now. Miss Woods beamed as she related their conversation to me. 'Isn't it good news?' she said.

It was. I was thrilled, especially when the girls started to argue over whose dorm I would sleep in. By now I had been in Sick Bay so long that my old bed had been given to someone else, so I had the choice of sleeping in Bridget and Nicole's dorm with Sophie K, Zara and Tina, or in with Jules, Danielle, Estelle and a couple of others. To no one's surprise, I chose Jules's dorm. All the same, Nicole spat at me for turning down the bed next to hers.

My first night in the dorm felt really strange. I was so used to the isolation of Sick Bay that I couldn't get used to the sound of other people breathing in the same room as me. I lay there with my eyes closed, but sleep wouldn't come. I couldn't stop thinking about Annie. Images of her twitching, dribbling and telling me she wanted to die kept revisiting my mind.

The next thing I knew there was a pillow over my head and I was struggling to breathe. I kicked and thrashed, but the pillow stayed over my face. I could feel myself choking airlessly. Whoever was holding the pillow pressed it down. It felt like they were sitting on it. I began to panic. The fear of God ran through me. I was being asphyxiated. I am going to die, I thought.

A heavy weight fell onto my legs. Unable to kick out, I

lashed around with my arms and struck something or some-one. I heard a yelp, and then the words, 'You bitch!' The pillow moved, the pressure momentarily lifted, and with one final effort, I pushed upwards and threw it off. I gasped, desperately gulping in air, then leapt from my bed and ran screaming out of the room – past Zara, Bridget and Tina. The pillow lay on the floor at Tina's feet.

I ran downstairs to the staffroom, where Ivy and Mrs Kale were nursing cups of tea. 'They've just tried to suffocate me!' I yelled.

Ivy sighed. She was very obviously unconcerned. 'Who has?' she said wearily.

Still finding it hard to breathe, I sobbed out a brief account of what had happened. But neither Ivy nor Mrs Kale wanted to know. 'I knew there would be trouble tonight,' Ivy said. 'Why they let you out of Sick Bay I just do not know.'

They sent me back to bed. I collapsed on the way upstairs, but neither of them came to help me. When I came to, I made my way back to the dorm on unsteady legs. Terrified that Zara, Bridget and Tina would come back for another go, I didn't sleep a wink that night. Too scared even to lie down, I spent the entire night sitting up.

CHAPTER SIXTEEN

'Teresa and that bloody cat!'

Everybody said it, from Mrs Tarwin to Bridget. I don't know why it annoyed people that I spent every spare moment in the laundry with Buttercup, but I ignored their comments and taunts just the same. Nothing would stop me visiting her. I loved her dearly and she was wonderful and loving back to me.

I felt that Buttercup was me in cat form. I identified with her because she was as lonely and scared as I was. It took months to win her over. I sat and talked to her endlessly until she got up the courage to poke her head through the hole in the wall. I was thrilled when eventually she ventured into the room. The biggest breakthrough came the first time I stroked her. She trembled with fear, but my patience had paid off. After a while she began to purr and rub her head against my face.

It meant a lot to me that she trusted me. She came when I called her, but no one else could tempt her out of hiding – apart from her owner Dot, of course. I'd make a really high-pitched squeal and she'd leap out of the hole in the wall and onto my lap. But if somebody else came into the laundry while I was stroking her gorgeous tabby and white fur, she'd run away and hide until the person had gone. She was extremely timid.

Buttercup was therapy and therapist to me. When I wanted to die I'd go to her and tell her all about it, safe in the knowledge that she wouldn't look down on me for crying or expressing how sad I was. No matter how drugged up I was, she didn't judge me. By loving me and making me feel wanted and needed, she was everything that the staff at Kendall House weren't. What's more, being with her and stroking her had a truly calming effect on me.

Once Bridget went into the laundry and mimicked my call. When Buttercup jumped through the hole in the wall, Bridget lobbed a heavy book at her. She boasted about it afterwards. I wanted to kill her so much that I cut my arms to shreds with a sliver of glass – turning my anger and frustration inwards, as usual.

Bridget was cruel and violent, but Tina was worse in many ways. She was a nutter. I was always having to defend myself against her. Although she was tiny and really quite pretty, she was scarily disturbed. After a petty argument over feeding the hamsters, she attacked me in the kitchen and stabbed me in the chest with a knife, causing a superficial but nasty wound. Another time she jumped on me in the upstairs schoolroom, because apparently I'd 'looked at her funny'. Ginger-haired Charlie managed to pull her off. He was constantly putting a stop to Tina's assaults.

I suppose that the difference between Bridget and Tina was that you just didn't have a chance with Bridget. If you punched Bridget, your fist made no impact. It would just disappear into her considerable muscle and fat. But I was able to defend myself against Tina, even though she was the dirtiest fighter you could come across. She was always attacking me from behind when I wasn't expecting it. Once I sat down to dinner and the next thing I knew she was hanging off my hair.

Tina was Mrs Tarwin's pet. She worshipped the ground Mrs Tarwin walked on, even though Mrs Tarwin used to inject her 'to calm her down'. If anyone said anything bad about Mrs Tarwin, or to her face, Tina would attack them. It was an odd kind of loyalty. I didn't understand it.

I resented Bridget, and to a lesser extent Tina, because life was already so awful at Kendall House that it was mean of them to make it even worse. How much better things could have been if the girls had stuck together. We could have supported each other through the hard times, instead of constantly being at each other's throats. Our stay in hell would have been so much more bearable if we had formed some kind of sisterhood. Perhaps it wasn't our fault. It was probably staff policy to divide and conquer, and it worked very well. But surely everyone – even the staff – would have been happier if there hadn't been so much squabbling.

As it was, practically every girl inside Kendall House was a miserable wreck. We bitched, scrapped, fought, self-harmed and regularly attempted suicide. Why the Council of Social Responsibility (who ran the place) or the local council (who helped fund it) didn't realise that there was something seriously wrong there during the early 1980s is anybody's guess.

Jules was having a very unhappy time. Her wrists were constantly bandaged. I tried my best to help her through, even though she wasn't supposed to have anything to do with me. When Bridget wasn't around we would exchange a few stolen words of mutual comfort, hoping that no one would grass us up later. And we still paired up for the ballroom dancing classes, taking care not to hurt each other's slashed wrists and arms as we bumped around the dance floor.

'Hey,' she said after class one day, 'let's try to get out again.'

We went to the toilets and sat in adjoining cubicles. Jules unscrewed a light bulb, smashed it on the floor and gathered up the glass pieces. After dividing the pieces in half, we set about eating a handful of glass each. I remember that it made a really weird crunching sound between my teeth. Strangely, it wasn't hard to swallow, and didn't hurt at all.

I hate to think what kind of damage it could have done to our insides, but we appeared none the worse for it afterwards. We were incredibly lucky; it could easily have ripped us to shreds internally. We told Harriet what we had done, but she didn't bother to call a doctor, as we'd hoped she would. Our plan had been to get to the local hospital – and run for it.

'Any more good ideas, Houdini?' I asked Jules.

'Give me time,' she said with a determined glint in her eyes. 'I'll come up with the perfect plan in the end.'

At least I had a form of escape in Mr and Mrs Whattler. I don't know what I would have done without them. By now I trusted them enough to know that they wouldn't peep as I changed into my swimming costume in the shed in the back garden, so I took up their offer of a swim in the pool. They understood my paranoia about my psoriasis scabs and swore that they wouldn't even come near the garden until I'd changed. Around this time they told me that I could call them Uncle Don and Aunt Betty.

They respected me every step of the way, which restored my confidence, and in the end it didn't matter to me if they saw my scars and scabs. While I swam and sunbathed, Uncle Don happily did his own thing, pottering around the garden.

Every now and then he'd call me over to look at a flower or an insect, never once remarking on my psoriasis. He taught me a lot about flowers and gardening, and as time went on, my skin began to clear up in the sun.

Occasionally I exposed it to the UV rays for too long. 'Oh my God, you're burnt!' Uncle Don said when I went to the kitchen for a glass of water one August evening.

Aunt Betty gasped. 'Go into the sitting room!'

They followed me into the sitting room with a great big bowl full of vinegar and water, which Aunt Betty gently dabbed all over my skin. It felt good to be tended to by someone who so obviously cared about me. Although my skin was on fire, I felt incredibly happy. What's more, the vinegar took away the stinging and I cooled down. It really did make a difference.

The Whattlers' kindness knew no bounds. To give me an incentive to keep my hair and nails nice, Aunt Betty took me to her local village beauty shop in Higham, Kent, where they permed my hair properly and gave my nails a manicure. She bought me my own nail file, clear nail varnish and two hair-brushes, and taught me to rinse my hair with cold water after washing it, to give it a shine. The perm was fine but it wasn't exactly modern in style. I was pleased with it, even though it made me look a bit old-fashioned.

I had my own box of muesli in the kitchen cupboard. Aunt Betty always made sure to buy the particular brand I liked at the Co-op. She showered me with little gifts that helped me to take pride in myself. I had my own personal products and sanitary towels, which meant that I didn't have to ask for them. My periods were often painful and she would rub my tummy and back. She constantly refilled my hot water bottle because the heat eased the pain.

She taught me a lot of basic things, like the value of money, how much a loaf of bread cost, how to shop sensibly, budget and work out the bill, how to make toffee and bake a cake. Uncle Don gave me lessons in wiring plugs and basic DIY. He even showed me how to gut a fish, which I didn't much like. All in all, they taught me how to look after myself.

Going back to Kendall House from the Whattlers' was always hard. I could never get to sleep the night before, whether I had been there for a week or just a night. A horrible fear would creep over me at the thought of what lay in store for me at the hands of people like Bridget, Harriet, Dr Peri and the men who hurt me while I was confined to Sick Bay. It wasn't like the fear of a spider or even of knowing a murderer was coming to get you. It was pure fear, fear in its largest form, sheer fear. I don't think anything could compare to that fear.

One night as I lay in bed contemplating my return to Kendall House, I became very distressed. I started panicking severely and it was a struggle to breathe. Aunt Betty came in with some kind of Vick's product, which she sprayed around the room. 'I don't very often use this,' she said. 'They don't sell it any more.' Somehow she calmed me down and talked me into breathing properly again, but I could tell that I'd really worried her.

Another night, Uncle Don came into my room while I was crying, concern written all over his face. 'Teresa, you've got to tell us what's going on at Kendall House,' he said. 'We know about the medication, but there's something else, isn't there?'

I couldn't bring myself to open up. I was scared that I'd be stopped from seeing them.

They hated having to administer my medication. On many

occasions they watched me vomit because of a bad reaction to the pills, and it worried them that I had such a small appetite as a result.

Since I never knew how many tablets I was supposed to be taking because the amounts varied so much, I unwittingly took a double dose one day. Someone back at Kendall House had made a big mistake, but we didn't realise it at first. It was lunchtime. I took my pills and went onto the back porch to lie in the swinging chair. All of a sudden I felt paralysed. I couldn't even move a finger. By the time Aunt Betty and Uncle Don called me for dinner, I was drifting in and out of consciousness and dribbling.

Uncle Don picked me up and carried me into the house. I heard Aunt Betty shouting into the phone. 'What the hell is it? What has happened?'

On the other end of the line, Mrs Tarwin told her to open up the other envelopes and tell her what was in them. She then phoned her son for advice. He was a doctor at one of the big London hospitals. When she rang back, she told Aunt Betty, 'She's been overdosed. We're going to come and pick her up.'

'We'll take her to hospital,' Uncle Don said, but Mrs Tarwin wouldn't hear of it. She insisted it wouldn't be necessary. She picked me up, took me back to Kendall House, injected me and stuck me in Sick Bay. Aunt Betty rang up to complain, but she was ignored.

The next time I went to visit, Aunt Betty told me that they had put in an application to adopt me. I was over the moon. The only time I felt anything close to happiness was when I was with them. 'But don't get your hopes up too high,' she said. 'We won't know for several months if we'll be allowed to.'

In early October, Dad came for a visit. It felt like I hadn't seen him for months and months, but because the drugs made it so hard for me to gauge time, it was impossible to know for sure. Unbeknown to me, the staff had been trying to keep him away with every excuse under the sun, no doubt because they were worried how he would react to my appearance. In the end, he turned up without an appointment and threatened to force his way in.

I met up with him in the dining room. He had a fit when he saw me. 'Oh my God! What have they done to you? You were in a bad way before but now you look forty years older, like an old woman,' he said.

I was shocked to see that he was crying. He took me in his arms and cuddled me, rocking and weeping and trying to comfort me while I sobbed out an account of what had been going on. He had never been emotional towards me in this way before. I felt so close to him.

Harriet came into the room. 'Mr Cooper, I'm afraid it's time to end the visit. Teresa has lessons to attend.' Her tone was brisk.

Dad gave her a withering look. 'You stop giving my daughter drugs *right now*, or I will take serious measures against you,' he said. 'What the hell do you think you are doing to her? I am going straight to the council, the Social Services and my MP to report you.'

Harriet bristled. 'I can assure you that Kendall House has Teresa's best interests at heart. Given her background and her mother's history of mental illness, you will understand that there are special concerns at play here. Of course, it's very difficult for a non-professional to understand . . .'

'Don't give me that!' Dad retorted, getting to his feet. His face was hot with anger. Harriet took a step backwards.

When Dad was in a rage, he could be pretty frightening.

'Teresa, leave us now,' she snapped. I had little choice but to obey if I didn't want an injection after Dad had left.

Poor old Dad didn't get anywhere with his complaints. Unbelievably, Wandsworth Social Services totally denied that I was being given drugs. He didn't get any further than their lies even when he and Nicole's dad got together to make their voices heard. Nicole's dad had already aired his grievances to the council and been ignored. He knew all about the drugs we were being given. He'd done a lot of research and was more than happy to share the information. Dad was outraged. He could see what they were doing to me was totally wrong, but he was helpless to do anything about it.

I dwelt a lot on Dad's comments about my looks. When I passed a window or a mirror and caught a flash of my reflection, I barely recognised myself. My self-image was poor anyway. I was constantly teased about being ugly. But things reached an all-time low when Shirley's daughter Mandy chose Nicole to be her bridesmaid at her upcoming wedding.

It was a massive humiliation for me, because Nicole rarely had anything to do with Shirley, whereas I was supposed to be close to her. Clearly she didn't love me as much as I had thought. I was gutted. I felt betrayed and angry. Nicole had only met Mandy once, whereas I had been to Shirley's house several times. OK, I didn't know Mandy at all well, but it was obvious that I had been passed over because I wouldn't look good in the photographs. I was the butt of everyone's jokes after that.

The taunting was constant: 'Your ugly mug would break the camera. You're too fucking hideous to put on a bridesmaid's dress. Mandy doesn't want her guests to run screaming out of the church!' On and on it went.

It was awful watching Nicole get all excited about her dress fittings. Shirley gave her a lot of attention in the run-up to the wedding, which made me feel that all the love and trust we had built up over my months in Sick Bay counted for nothing. At the actual wedding, I was shoved to the back while Nicole paraded around in her lovely dress. I felt so small and unloved that day.

Life dragged on. Christmas came and went. Easter came and went. I was devastated to hear that the Whattlers' application to adopt me had been turned down on the grounds of Aunt Betty's disability. Uncle Don and Aunt Betty seemed equally upset. We all felt that it was unfair. The staff went on injecting me. They'd jump on me, drag me onto the floor, grab my arms and legs and hair, hold me down on the floor – face down or on my back – kneel on me, with all their weight on me, hold my arms down, turn me on my side, pull my knickers down, exposing everything, and jab me with a huge needle.

When they put their knees into my back and neck, my jaw would click to the side, and I developed an unstable mandible, or loose, damaged jaw. I often vomited in reaction to the drugs. I was always covered in bruises. They went on locking me in the detention room and Sick Bay. I don't have any clear memories of further abuse while I was locked up, but I was treated for countless urine and genital infections.

Bridget and the others continued to scorn me. The torture just went on and on, and I wasn't the only one suffering. Jules attempted suicide again. Annie drank bleach and ate razor blades. A pretty, plump girl called Amanda arrived and screamed the house down for days. There was deep pain and sadness everywhere you turned.

One day it all kicked off when Mrs Tarwin and three other members of staff dragged a screaming Annie up the stairs after she refused to be quiet in assembly. It was a nasty scene and it upset us all. By now Amanda was very close to Annie and it hurt her to see her friend being treated so roughly. She complained loudly about the drugs we were being given. The remaining staff on duty started on her, telling her to shut up or she was next.

We could all hear Annie screaming, all the way from the ground floor. It was horrible to hear her in such distress. We didn't know what was going on upstairs but from my own experience I knew it wasn't good. The next thing I knew the staff were pulling Amanda up the stairs by her hair. She wasn't a small girl, either. At first Amanda laughed hysterically, like a mad woman, but the staff became more aggressive – yanking her hair, pulling her neck out of joint – and she began to shriek with pain.

Another girl called Shelley was so distraught at what was happening to Amanda that she started banging her head repeatedly against the wall. Her forehead split open and blood went everywhere. Now there were three girls shouting and screaming, one of them badly injured. The staff were obviously finding it hard to cope.

'Bridget!' Janice shouted as she struggled with Amanda. 'Come and help.' Bridget leapt to the aid of her pet member of staff. You could see that she relished dragging Amanda upstairs by her long black hair.

I don't know where they took Shelley, but Amanda was locked in the detention room and they stuck Annie in Sick Bay. A sudden hush descended over the house. It was almost scarier than the girls' screams of distress, because we all knew what had befallen them. That silence was deafening.

I hated Bridget for the way she treated me, but I hated her even more for helping the staff to control the girls. As time went on, I became so sick of being bullied that it became inevitable I would boil over with rage.

The moment finally came when Kate summoned me into the office for a phone call. I knew it had to be big news, because it wasn't a Friday, which was the only day we were allowed to take calls. I picked up the receiver. Bernadette was on the other end. She gently broke it to me that our nan had died. I was very upset, especially when Kate said that I wouldn't be allowed out to go to Nan's funeral. I left the office in tears.

At bath time, a girl called Ally came up to me in the bathroom with a big smile on her face. Ally was the tallest of all of us, even though she was only twelve. She was a very attractive girl who had been sent to Kendall House because she was highly sexually promiscuous, to the point that her mother couldn't control her.

'Your nana dead, is she? Is your nana dead?' she taunted.

I stared at her in shock. How did she know? I had asked Kate not to tell anyone, wanting time to grieve quietly on my own first.

'Ya boo diddums, your nana's dead as a doornail,' she went on.

A white hot rage shot through me. As she was running her bath, I flew at her furiously and ducked her head under the water. 'I'll give you bloody dead, you scumbag!' I howled, holding her head down. One of the staff had to pull me away before I drowned her. I broke free and lunged at her again.

Bridget came into the bathroom. Big mistake. I let go of Ally and went for Bridget instead.

Finally Bridget got a taste of her own medicine. All the rage that I'd built up towards her during my time in Sick Bay surged to the fore. It made me stronger than I had ever been in my life, giving me the power to beat her up.

'Stop!' she whimpered, finally. 'Please, you're hurting me.'

At last Bridget was scared of me, instead of the other way around! It was a sweet, sweet victory. Now it was me who was passing her in the corridor, saying, 'I'm going to get you later.' Not that I followed up on my threats – I was simply concerned with keeping her at bay. It worked too. She pretty much left me alone after that, which was a huge relief.

One day I woke up and Jules was gone. That was that – they hadn't even let her say goodbye. 'But where is she?' I kept asking.

'Forget about Jules. She's gone back to her family,' Mrs Tarwin told me.

Her absence created a huge hole in my life. I missed her terribly. But since I had no way of contacting her, there was nothing to do except continue with my miserable existence, without her. It seemed that there was nothing but loss in my life. One way or another I'd lost my mum, my dad, my brother and sister, my nan, my friend, my freedom, my peace of mind . . . the list was endless. So the last thing I expected was to find a long lost relative. It was one of the biggest surprises of my life.

It all began with an amazing coincidence. Nicole went home one weekend and while she was sitting on the toilet reading the newspaper, she noticed my mum and dad's names in a personal ad.

She brought the paper back to Kendall House and gave it

to the staff to follow up. I didn't actually see the ad, but it was a little notice that said something like, 'I'm looking for Georgina Cooper, married to Derek Cooper. If you have any information on their whereabouts, please call this number.'

My first thought was that they had been left some money in somebody's will. I wondered if I would get a reward for calling the number. My heart leapt. However, Kate wouldn't let me make the call. She made it for me instead.

She called me into the office. 'Good news,' she said, smiling. 'You've got a relative who wants to meet you.'

I didn't know what she was on about. 'What do you mean?'

She explained that a distant relation on my mum's side, Karen, had put the notice in the paper. Apparently Karen had played with us as kids and, even though she was a few years older, she still had fond memories of the family. An only child whose parents were now dead, she was looking to renew the connection.

I was thrilled. The idea of having a long lost relative definitely appealed. It was like something out of a fairytale and I couldn't help but fantasise about Karen in a fairy godmother role. I was impatient to meet her, but it took weeks for Kendall House to arrange a meeting. She and her husband Trevor finally came to see me one Saturday. I was very nervous as I walked into the dining room, desperately hoping she would like me. Karen and her husband got up to greet me. She was around thirty and very pretty, with auburn hair in ringlets and large hazel eyes. I was disappointed that she wasn't very well spoken but she seemed nice and I decided I liked her. I was a little bit wary of Trevor though. He was tall and big set, with ice blue eyes and a skinhead haircut.

They didn't stay long, just long enough for Karen to

explain who she was and that she had been trying to find Mum for a couple of years. She asked me if I'd like to visit her at her house. 'Yes, I'd like that,' I said, but in my heart I wasn't so sure. Something in her attitude and way of speaking suggested to me that she wasn't the most desirable addition to the family. She did a lot of casual effing and blinding and came across as quite hard, as did Trevor.

Kendall House took girls up to the age of sixteen, so I was getting too old to stay there. Yes, I'd had another birthday, and no, I didn't get a cake or fifteen pounds that time either. My future seemed very uncertain. Wandsworth Social Services had care of me until I was eighteen, so I wouldn't be entirely free for another two years. In the meantime, I had to find somewhere to live, but there was nowhere for me to go. Dad couldn't have me, neither could Mum or Bernadette. My job prospects weren't exactly good either. I had no qualifications. I wasn't exactly unemployable, but the kind of work that would pay me enough to support myself was definitely out of reach for the time being.

Miss Woods called me into her office late in 1983. 'We've found you some foster parents to go to. They are wonderful people! You are going to be very happy with them.'

'What are they like?' I asked suspiciously. Obviously I didn't trust her. Not only was she in cahoots with Dr Peri, but as the head of Kendall House, I held her largely responsible for its cruel regime.

'Well, I haven't met them yet, but I've heard nothing but good reports of them.' She went on to tell me about the wonderful Novicks. The dad was called Doug. The mum was called Pam. There were three children, two girls and a boy. One was a baby. She blabbed on for a bit longer. She obviously knew very little about them apart from their names.

Typical, I thought. As usual there's a gloss on things, and it's bound to be a fake one.

I was desperate to leave Kendall House though. I was more than desperate. I was dying to leave, almost literally. So I agreed to have my photos taken for the forms, and I agreed to meet the Novicks. What choice did I have?

The first time we met, they came to Kendall House. They seemed OK. Pam was plump and a bit blousy. She wore bright flamboyant clothes and spoke in a low, husky voice with a slight lisp. Doug had a rugby player's build and was bald apart from a few brown tufty wisps. I noticed that he kept looking me up and down, as if I were an item in a shop. This made me feel slightly uncomfortable, but it was nothing serious. I hoped that I'd feel less nervous around him when I got to know him better.

The second time I met the Novicks I went to visit them at their house in Broadstairs. It was a big bungalow, big enough to accommodate two lodgers as well as the family. I liked it there. The children were really sweet and the appeal of having my own bedroom overcame any anxiety I had about living with strangers.

Doug Novick drove me back to Kendall House. In the car he told me that he was a keen golfer and he'd teach me how to play if I was interested. I said that I thought golf was a game for retired men, but he laughed and informed me that lots of young people were taking it up these days. I was aware of trying to like him, but not really managing to like him at all.

We stopped off at a McDonald's. I found that I couldn't eat in front of him. By now I knew that there was something about him I really didn't like. He kept looking me up and down and staring at me in the wrong places. But I continued making an effort to get on with him. I didn't want him and his wife to say no to having me. I was prepared to tolerate anything if it meant getting away from Kendall House. Or so I thought.

CHAPTER SEVENTEEN

Everything was arranged. After two overnight visits to the Novicks and a couple of sessions with my new social worker, Kerry Parker, and various members of Kendall House staff, it was agreed that I would move into the house in Broadstairs in early 1984.

I still had doubts about Doug Novick, even though I couldn't quite put my finger on what they were. I told Kerry that my biggest worry was that he looked at me in a sexual way. We jointly came to the conclusion that I was fearful of men in general.

I left Kendall House carrying a small bag of clothes and possessions and Patch my hamster in a cage. It was the greatest feeling on earth walking out of there for what I assumed to be the very last time. How often I had dreamed of this moment! On the other hand, there was something anti-climactic about the whole experience. As I looked back at its dismal exterior, I realised that the sad, lonely years I had spent inside that building were lost to me forever. I could never get them back. The pain would always be with me. One day the scars might heal, but there was no turning back the clock.

I stuck my head out of Doug Novick's car window as he

drove me away. 'Goodbye forever!' I screamed into the wind. Laughter bubbled up inside me. I was free! No more injections, no more Sick Bay, no more Harriet or Dr Peri – and no more Bridget. Yet the very thought of them all depressed me, despite the fact that I had finally escaped them. Images of what I'd suffered flashed through my mind. I hunkered down in my seat and spent the rest of the journey brooding.

I felt very shy when we arrived at the house. I just wanted to shut myself away. So after playing with the children a bit and cooing over the baby, I asked if I could go to my bedroom. Pam said that would be fine.

At first I spent most of my days in there. I needed my own space. It was so weird to be removed from the sights, sounds and smells of Kendall House that it was going to take a bit of time to adjust. With no routine to keep to, I played records and lay on the bed trying to blank out my most painful memories. And, like every teenage girl, I dreamed of falling in love, preferably with someone who looked like Christopher Reeve in *Superman*. I went downstairs for meals and to watch television in the evenings. Sometimes I'd play with the kids, chat to the lodgers or help Pam prepare food. But I kept my distance from Doug. There was just something about him that made my skin prickle.

His stepson Martin said that Doug had broken his arm in a rage once. He had then made him lie to his mother Pam about what had happened, so that he didn't get the blame. 'He told me to say it was an accident,' Martin told me. I didn't like the sound of that. I became even warier of Doug.

One night Doug, Pam and I sat down to watch a horror film. Halfway through, Pam yawned and announced she was going to bed. I stayed, caught up in the plot and desperate to see if the heroine would escape the forces of evil. There were lots of scary bits and I gasped out loud quite a few times.

'Don't be frightened,' Doug said. 'It's only a film.'

'I know, but look!' I pointed at the screen. The heroine was now being chased by something or somebody unknown, in the woods, in the dark, in the middle of the night. I was on the edge of my seat, nervously chewing my nails.

'Come and sit on my lap,' he said, patting his thigh.

I hesitated. Good memories of sitting on Dad's lap clashed with my natural aversion to Doug, but in the end I went for it, thinking that perhaps it would be a bonding experience. Plus, I was really scared. The film was reaching a terrifying climax and I imagined that it would be a comfort to sit with him, that he was offering a place of safety. How stupid and naïve I was.

I went over and sat on his knee. I felt uncomfortable immediately. I couldn't concentrate on the film. I just kept thinking, Why didn't I stay where I was? But I didn't move. I didn't want to seem rude or ungrateful.

I felt his hand slide down my back. A shiver of revulsion went through me. The woman in the film screamed. He started touching my legs. I tried to move away, but he held me firmly down. I could feel that he had an erection. He put his hands between my legs. I pulled away. I got off his lap and went straight up to bed without looking at him.

Disgusted by the memory of his touch, I wouldn't come out of my bedroom the next day. I wanted to run away while he was at work and Pam was out, but they locked the kitchen when they were out and my hamster and money were in there. The Novicks were keen on locking rooms. Their bedroom was always locked, as was the lodgers' room.

The first chance I had, I rang Kendall House. 'I don't like Doug. I think he's a pervert,' I told Harriet.

'I thought something like this would happen,' she replied. 'Now stop being silly. It's all in your head.'

I put the phone down and burst into tears. I had hoped so much that my nightmares were at an end.

One morning as I was taking a bath, I heard Pam call goodbye on her way out. 'I'll be back in a couple of hours. Don't forget to feed the dog,' she reminded Doug.

'Get going now, or you'll be late,' he replied.

I ducked my head under the bath water at the sound of his voice and held it under for as long as my lungs allowed. When I emerged into the steamy air, I heard a tap on the bathroom door. I ignored it and ducked back under the water.

There was another tap on the door, louder and more urgent than the previous one. 'Open the door. Your sister is on the phone,' he said.

I hadn't heard the phone ring. I didn't trust him. So I said nothing. But he started knocking harder on the door, insisting that Bernadette was waiting to speak to me. 'Don't keep her hanging on, she's in a phone box!' he said.

Perhaps it is true, I thought. Not wanting to miss the chance of speaking to Bernadette, I stood up, reached for a towel and wrapped it around me. I put my dressing gown over the top and fastened it at the waist.

I unlocked the bathroom door and stepped onto the landing. He was waiting for me. He grabbed me and pulled me across the landing. 'Don't!' I said. 'What about Bernadette?'

He dragged me towards the lodgers' room and unlocked the door with his key. He pushed me inside. I'd never been in the room before. There were two beds along the left side of the wall.

I was petrified. I froze with fear as he slammed the door.

He lunged at my dressing gown and tried to pull it off. I wrapped my arms around my body, trying to keep it in place, but he was so solid and strong that there was nothing I could do to stop him. Tears streamed down my face as he forced me onto the bed. He made me turn over so that he couldn't see my face. I cried out and begged him not to touch me. I tried to push him away and turn myself back over, but he forced me down flat.

He put an arm round my waist, pulled me up towards him and raped me. I screamed but no sound came out. He stroked my back as he repeatedly hurt me. Pain shot through me as he pushed and forced himself inside me. The more I struggled the more force he used. I begged him to get off. He kept telling me that he didn't want to hurt me, but he was hurting me terribly. I bit into the sheets as a way of coping with the pain.

He raped me several times. I don't know how long it went on for, but it was not a brief moment, it was ages. There was nothing I could do to stop him. He was too strong. Eventually it was over.

I pulled my towel over me, to cover myself up. Tears were still pouring down my face and I felt like my insides were going to drop out. I made a break for the door and got out of the room. As I ran to the bathroom, I saw blood running down my legs. I locked myself in the bathroom and sat on the toilet. I was bleeding really badly. I rocked in pain and cried so hard that I thought I'd never stop crying.

When at last I heard Pam come home, I left the bathroom and crept to my bedroom. He'd been there. My dressing gown was strewn on the bed.

I went on bleeding and had to use a pad to absorb the blood. All I could think about was taking Patch my hamster out of his cage and cuddling him. I barricaded my door with a chair and a chest of drawers. Pam called me down for tea but I ignored her. I felt that it was far better to starve than go downstairs and see his nasty face. I was in pain and I felt dirty. I knew hate, but I never knew hate like I felt it that day.

I played it as safe as I could from then on, making sure that I was never alone with him. I hated catching his eye, but I had to keep a look out for him at all times. I was obsessed by the thought that everything I owned was locked away in the kitchen. I knew that there was no way I could leave without my hamster. And if I did leave, where would I go? My family couldn't have me. The Whattlers loved having me to stay but it wasn't a permanent option. I had no other friends.

I tried calling Kendall House again, from a phone box down the road. Kate answered. 'Can you call me back?' I said, my voice cracking with emotion.

Harriet, rather than Kate, called back. 'What is it this time?' she said.

Sobbing, I told her that Doug Novick had done something very bad to me and I needed to go to the police.

'No, you do not need to go to the police,' she said crossly. 'You will go back to the house and stop being such a baby. When will you grow out of making up stories?'

So I went back. What choice was there?

Doug was always staring at me, smirking. I had nowhere to run and he knew it. He disgusted me. I felt like retching all the time he was around. One day, as he was cleaning the patio windows, he spat several times on the glass and delightedly watched his spittle dribble downwards, before wiping it off with some newspaper. 'Joanna' by Kool and the Gang was playing on the stereo. I wanted to puke.

Another time, Pam asked me to get some cheese from the larder. She was in the sitting room with the kids. Doug followed me in and pinned me against the larder wall. His rottweiler was lying on the floor. Doug started touching me. It was only when his wife called me that he took his fingers out of my knickers and let me go.

He raped me again in his bedroom while the baby lay in her cot sleeping. He put his hand over my mouth so that I didn't wake her. Out of the blue his stepson Martin walked into the bedroom.

Doug jumped off the bed and launched himself at the bedroom door. 'Get out!' he yelled. 'If you ever come in here again, if you ever say anything about what you saw in here, I will kill you!'

Martin never said a thing.

I rang Kendall House again from the phone box using coins I'd found down the side of the sofa. I cried my eyes out down the phone, but the response was always the same. 'Stop being stupid, go back to the house and behave.'

One of the lodgers found me in tears on a bench near the phone box. 'What is it, Teresa?' he said, his voice full of concern.

All I could say was, 'That man . . . he hurt me . . .'

'Do you mean Doug? Has he raped you?' he said.

Shocked that he had guessed the truth just like that, I managed to nod a yes.

'You must go to the police,' he said. 'There was a girl here before you. She ran away and was never traced again. I always wondered about her. I definitely thought something funny had been going on.'

He gave me some money to call the police, but my voice faltered when I came to speak to the duty sergeant. I just couldn't say it. I was too scared of the repercussions.

I stopped eating. I stopped sleeping. All I could think about was running away. I wondered whether my mum's relative Karen would take me in. I kept her phone number on me at all times, just in case.

Then my chance finally came. Doug, Pam and the kids left the house to go swimming, forgetting to lock the kitchen door. I rang Karen.

'I've got to get out of here. It's really bad. Can I come to you?'

To my relief she said yes. I almost fainted with gratitude. She asked if I had enough money to pay my bus fare. I admitted that I didn't. 'Get yourself down to the local bus station. Tell them I'll meet you at the other end and pay your fare,' she said.

I grabbed Patch's cage and a couple of other things and left the house without even shutting the front door. I walked as fast as I could in the direction of the bus station, racked with fear. What if they caught me? What would Doug do to me? I knew that he would be at swimming a while longer, but I had to hurry.

The wait for the coach to Watford was agonising. I kept scanning the bus station for Doug's thick-set figure, come to get me and take me back to hell. Finally the coach arrived. The driver let me on. We pulled out of the station. I burst into tears.

There was a nice young guy sitting next to me. I poured my heart out to him. He listened attentively, full of compassion. 'At least you're free now,' he said, patting me on the arm.

Karen met me at the bus depot at other end. She paid my fare and took me back to her house. I was in such a daze that

I barely noticed the peeling wallpaper or dirty, smelly carpets.

Karen was so nice to me that night. When we heard the ice cream van outside the house, she said, 'Would you like an ice cream?'

I didn't answer. My mind kept drifting to images of Doug raping me. I was still bleeding and in a lot of pain. My tummy was swollen. I started being sick.

Karen told her husband Trevor that instead she was going to take me to the petrol station to get an ice cream, so that we could have a private chat. On the way back I blurted out everything that had happened. She was aghast and full of sympathy.

The next day she took me to her GP for a pregnancy test. At the time we didn't know that Doug had had a vasectomy. She then informed Wandsworth Social Services and Kendall House of my whereabouts. They both insisted that I return to the house in Broadstairs.

'No way is she going back there to be raped again!' Karen said. She contacted her social worker Jo, who backed her up, although strangely she didn't report my rape claims to the police.

I was so grateful to Karen for taking the lead. I felt incapable of thought or action. It was as if I were in a trance. The shock of what Doug had done to me overruled everything. I could barely interact with Karen, Trevor or her kids. I left everything to her and blanked the world out.

But it gradually became clear that I had gone from the frying pan into the fire. Karen and Trevor were good about saving me from Doug Novick, but their charity went no further than that. I began to realise that it was in their interests to have me living with them because I provided free baby-sitting and cleaning services.

At first I was devoted to them, but in time the scales fell away from my eyes. The house was always cold. The heating was only ever on when Karen and Trevor were home. It didn't matter to them that I was freezing and could see my breath in the air.

The outhouse and back garden resembled a junkyard. They were full of car and bike parts and tyres. It was like a bikers' paradise. The house was dirty and there was rarely any food in the kitchen, although the makeshift bar in the dining room was always well stocked with booze.

Beer cans in hand, swearing and cursing and as loud as could be, they always managed to attract attention. I had to face the fact that I had moved in with what most people would consider to be neighbours from hell. They were the local problem family. Every neighbourhood has at least one – and, round here, they were it.

It was as unhappy a home for me as my dad's had been. Karen was not the nice person I had longed for her to be. She and Trevor made me go out to work and give them my wages in lieu of keep. I got a job in a leisure centre two miles from their house and they made me walk there and back in the dark, except on Fridays, when they'd be waiting outside in the car to collect my wages. I also sold Avon products door to door, and Karen got the commission.

One day I tried to run away. Trevor spotted me and dragged me back into the house by my hair. Once inside, Karen screamed at me that I was an ungrateful cow. 'I saved you from that foster father and this is how you repay me!'

I felt total and utter despair. Wherever I went, my life was hell. There was no stability, no love, no care and no freedom anywhere. There was no me. It was always about what everyone else wanted.

It got so bad that I approached Karen's social worker, Jo. She suggested that I return to Kendall House after she rang Kendall House and had a long chat with Mrs Tarwin, who had been promoted. Jo negotiated a temporary return for me, which stipulated that I wouldn't be drugged or locked up, and that I could go out by myself when I wanted to. I was ever so grateful to her. Anything was preferable to Karen and Trevor's house. It was a war zone. What's more, the rape allegations against Doug Novick had to be dealt with.

Mrs Tarwin picked me up. As we drove away, I didn't look back once. I never contacted them again. Mrs Tarwin took me to the Whattlers' house for the night. Aunt Betty and Uncle Don were terribly concerned about me. They believed everything I said about what Doug Novick had done to me. They offered every imaginable support. I loved them for it.

I was still bleeding and in pain. My condition seemed to be getting worse, rather than better. I didn't say anything to anyone at Kendall House, because I knew they wouldn't care. They'd just say that it was all in my head. Instead I took myself to the casualty department at the local hospital.

I cried miserably as I waited my turn, crippled with pain. Seeing how distressed I was, a nurse took me to a room on my own. She was so nice to me, I couldn't bring myself to tell her what was wrong. I was ashamed and embarrassed, and the pain was so debilitating that I could hardly speak anyway.

An Indian doctor came to examine me. He asked me my name and where I lived, but I was too scared to tell him. He tried to calm me down. 'I can't tell what's wrong if you don't let me have a look at you,' he said softly.

I flinched at the very thought of being touched down there, but I lay on the bed and let him prod my stomach.

When he felt my lower abdomen, I shrieked in agony. The nurse took my temperature. 'It's rather high, doctor,' she said.

Eventually I agreed to an internal examination. The nurse held my hand as he inserted a speculum. I wriggled in pain as he inspected me. 'Who has done this to you?' he asked in a firm but kind voice.

'I'll get in trouble if I tell you,' I replied.

'It won't be you who gets into trouble, it will be whoever has done this,' he assured me.

After I'd got dressed, he told me that my vagina and cervix were badly torn, as was the neck of my womb. I had an infection that had spread to my fallopian tubes, causing salpingitis, a serious inflammatory infection of the ovaries that can cause infertility. He recommended a short stay in hospital.

But I had to get back to Kendall House. If I stayed out any longer they would assume I had run away and I'd be in big trouble. 'At least let me report this to the police,' the doctor said. 'A crime has very obviously been committed here.'

'No, please!' I begged. Reluctantly he let me leave, taking copious antibiotics and painkillers with me.

Back at Kendall House, Nicole rushed up to me. 'Your foster parents are here!' she said.

I reeled in shock. The next thing I knew, Mrs Tarwin was calling me upstairs to the staffroom on the second floor. I walked in to find Doug and Pam Novick, Dr Harris, Miss Woods and Mrs Tarwin sitting in a circle. Dr Harris was a psychiatrist. He was standing in for Dr Peri.

All eyes fell on me as I entered the room. Without any preamble whatsoever, Miss Woods said, 'Sit down, Teresa. We need you to state your allegations against your foster father.'

I shuddered visibly. I was terrified out of my wits at the sight of Doug Novick. It was horrific being in the same room as him. 'Where's my social worker?' I asked.

'She is on holiday. Unfortunately, we are compelled to conduct this meeting in her absence.' I noticed that Miss Woods was speaking with unusual precision, and throwing her voice like an amateur actress. Little did I know that she was secretly taping the meeting.

'Sit down, Teresa,' Mrs Tarwin said. I looked wildly around the room. The only spare chair was the one next to Doug Novick.

'Not there,' I said.

'Sit down now!'

I did as I was told, my head spinning. Doug shifted uncomfortably in his seat and I cringed, expecting him to leap up and hit me. I could hardly believe what was happening. Here was the man who had raped me so badly that, earlier that very day, a doctor had wanted to report him to police.

'Now, clearly state your complaint against Mr Novick, please.'

I said nothing. I was too scared to move or speak.

'Let me just take Teresa outside for a five-minute break,' Mrs Tarwin said. She took hold of my hand and led me out of the room.

In order to involve the police, Teresa, you have got to say what your foster father did to you. If you don't tell us now, we won't be able to help you.'

I desperately wanted to see justice done. I couldn't bear the idea of Doug Novick getting away with it, especially when I was in so much pain. I asked to be excused to go to the toilet and promised to return.

In the toilet, I took out one of the bottles of painkillers that the doctor had given me. I pondered whether to take them. Once again, I didn't want to go on living. Suddenly I started knocking back pills, as many as I could cram into my mouth and swallow in one go. But then Mrs Tarwin came to find me. I hid the bottles behind the toilet and went back to the staffroom.

As I entered the room, I pointed at Doug Novick and screamed, 'You raped me and you hurt me!' What did it matter what I said now? By morning I would be dead. I ran out of the room in floods of tears.

Nicole came to find me. She cuddled me and asked me what was wrong, but I asked her to leave me on my own. Shortly after the tablets started to work I went into a daze. Mrs Tarwin asked me if I'd taken anything because I didn't look well.

'Yes, I hope it kills me so that none of you can hurt me anymore,' I yelled. I started running around in rage and fury, but then dropped to the floor in a dead faint.

When I came to, I was totally floppy, so Mrs Tarwin and a member of staff called Sally held me up and walked me to the local hospital in an attempt to keep me conscious. I heard Mrs Tarwin tell Sally that it was all an act, as usual. 'She loves attention. That's all she lives for,' she said, thinking I couldn't hear.

Not surprisingly, the pills soon wore off. After all, my body had been used to far worse in the past. The main side effect was that I couldn't stop crying. A psychiatrist evaluated me. He said I was a simple girl, but not mentally ill or disturbed.

It took Miss Woods two whole months to report my allegations to the police. Finally a policeman from Gravesend police station came to interview me at Kendall House. Not a policewoman, as was later logged at the station, but a policeman. *He* saw me in Miss Woods's office. After spending ages with Miss Woods, he gave me five minutes, barely listening to what I had to say. 'You don't have a leg to stand on,' he concluded. And that was that.

I will never forget those words. That's the story of my life, I thought. I ran out of Miss Woods's office so that he wouldn't see me cry.

CHAPTER EIGHTEEN

One good thing came out of my time at Karen and Trevor's – and that was their friend James. He was such a lovely guy and we built up a good friendship. There were no secrets between us. I told him everything that had happened to me. Eventually he became my boyfriend.

We didn't have sex. I was scared and he didn't want to rush me. Plus, I still had loads of problems down there as a consequence of the rape. Still, we kissed and cuddled a lot and he made me feel loved every time he held me.

His family didn't like me, but we didn't care. They were very well off and his parents were snobbish. His dad was always making snide comments about me when I went to their house in St Albans.

One evening, during a game of Trivial Pursuit, I answered a question correctly.

'JRR Tolkien!' I said.

'So you know something, then,' James's dad said, eyebrows raised.

James's mum told him off for that.

Finally I left Kendall House early in 1984. First I stayed at a place called Rivendale, and then I moved to Newhaven, where the staff were nice and I was treated like a human. At

Newhaven I was encouraged to write poetry and paint. The staff were hugely supportive of me in every way, especially Elaine and Sue.

I had written a poem at Kendall House, but my grammar and spelling were so appalling that it barely made any sense. A member of staff at Newhaven helped me to set it out properly, explaining the grammar as we went.

'This is very good,' she said, when we'd finished. 'You've definitely got a way with words.' I was so unused to receiving compliments that I walked around with a big grin on my face for days afterwards.

Newhaven was housed in one of the outbuildings of what had once been Friern Barnet Hospital in North London. I really liked it there. I was given my own little flat within the building. At last, freedom and my very own space! I grew up emotionally, and learned how to be independent. I learned a lot, in fact. My self-esteem soared.

The other girls were really naughty. I remember one of the staff went mad in a group meeting and said, 'Considering the kind of life Teresa's had, where she's come from and all those drugs she's been on, how is it that she behaves better than you lot, who didn't go through all of that?'

Although Kendall House had told Karen's social worker that they wouldn't drug me when I went back there after living at Karen's, in actual fact they had insisted that I continue with a certain level of medication, just as they had when I went to the foster home. So the staff at Newhaven had to see me through extreme withdrawals when I arrived there. It wasn't a pretty sight. I vomited everywhere, collapsed all the time and often couldn't get out of bed. It took weeks and weeks to get those drugs out of my system, or perhaps even longer – it's hard to remember. It got worse before it got better. After three years on heavy medication, it's not surprising that my body reacted so violently. I went through hell. But, my God, was it worth it.

I went back to being a normal girl again. It was amazing. I no longer had mood swings. I didn't once think about suicide during this time and I didn't self-harm again. The staff at Newhaven told me that these impulses had been a direct consequence of the drugs. Now I was off the drugs, I was myself again.

That's not to say that life was suddenly a bed of roses, of course. I was still very fragile and haunted by horrific memories of abuse. My struggle to come to terms with what had been done to me at Kendall House was only just beginning and I often found it hard even to contemplate what had gone on there. I tried to block it out of my mind, but it wasn't always possible. At least my mind wasn't fogged up though. At least I wasn't being injected or beaten up or raped anymore. Life was finally worth living.

James and I became ever closer. His kindness was wonderful. I was on my period a lot of the time as a result of the salpingitis, and my periods were incredibly painful, but he was very understanding and never tried to push me into having sex.

One night, during a rare break from bleeding, we got drunk together. The big day had come. Since I didn't want to go on being scared of men and sex, that night we took things further, and one thing led to another. Unfortunately no one had explained about contraception. Sex education had simply passed me by.

Inevitably I fell pregnant. I was over the moon – until a social worker told me that I had to have a termination.

'Why?' I asked.

'You are still only seventeen and still in the care of Wandsworth Social Services. When you are eighteen, you may do what you wish. Until that time, you must play by our rules. If you don't have a termination voluntarily, I'm afraid that Social Services will take steps to compel you to have one.'

I burst into tears. I was only a few weeks off my eighteenth birthday. 'The upside is that if you agree to it, we will be in a position to award you a holiday grant,' she continued. It was an extraordinary trade off. I wish I had contacted the local newspaper, or one of the tabloids. They would have had a field day, surely.

Reluctantly, I went to my GP and said I needed an abortion. 'Are you sure this is what you want?' she asked me.

Clearly I didn't want it. But what the doctor didn't realise was that I'd been through so much abuse at Kendall House that I was mortally scared of Wandsworth Social Services. I dreaded to think what they would do to me if I didn't comply. I had visions of being locked away in a mental hospital, for life. I had heard that poor Annie from Kendall House had been sent to an adult psychiatric institution. Poor old Georgie too. My freedom was too valuable to me to risk anything like that.

So I told the doctor, 'Yes, this is what I want.' And I had the abortion.

I went on holiday with Bernadette almost immediately afterwards. I hated myself. I hated Wandsworth. I couldn't bring myself to see James ever again.

I couldn't stop thinking about the baby I had lost. When I was given a one-bedroom flat in Tottenham, North London, only weeks afterwards, I felt utterly deceived. Surely I could have kept the baby?

Life got better though. I met a wonderful guy. I fell head over heels in love with him and experienced feelings I didn't even know existed. It was overwhelming. I couldn't get enough of him.

By now my dad had been diagnosed with cancer. I knew he was dying and threw myself into caring for him. We began to grow closer than we'd ever been, which made me very happy, despite my sadness at his illness. He often came to visit me and we spent hours chatting and laughing. We still had our moments, but most of the time things were good.

Christmas 1985 was fantastic. Bernadette, David, Dad and I went to Auntie Rachel's house. Rachel was Dad's sister. I enjoyed every minute of it, even though I'd been feeling sick for a couple of weeks and didn't much feel like eating a full turkey dinner.

'I bet a hundred to one that you're pregnant,' Auntie Rachel said in a quiet moment.

'Not a chance,' I laughed. 'With my periods?'

I did a test. It was positive. I was overjoyed. A whole new world opened up before my eyes. I was going to become a mother and I wanted this baby more than anything. My only worry was telling Dad, because he disapproved of children outside marriage.

Sure enough, when I told him he went ballistic. I hadn't intended to say anything, but it just slipped out one night while I was at his flat. 'You whore, you piece of trash, opening your legs without thinking!' he shouted. 'I bet that idiot you call a boyfriend won't help you now!'

It was the worst I'd ever heard him in terms of swearing. He hit me and told me to fuck off out of his house. 'You're no longer a child of mine!' he screamed.

I was very upset. I hadn't expected such a strong reaction, but I had no choice but to leave, even though it was late and I had a terrible feeling that the trains back to North London had stopped running.

I walked to the station and shivered as I waited in the freezing cold for the next train, which wasn't due for several hours. A drunk man nearby kept trying to talk to me. He scared the crap out of me. A tall black man with kind eyes walked up. He was wearing a British Rail uniform.

'What are you doing at an empty station in the middle of the night? There are no trains. You are putting yourself in great danger,' he said.

'My dad's thrown me out because I'm pregnant! I've got to get home to Tottenham but there aren't any trains until morning,' I blurted out.

'OK. Stay put,' he said and walked away.

I didn't feel scared. You could tell he was a good man. He came back with a big overcoat and wrapped it around me. When he was able to leave work, he drove me in his car to his parents' house. Taking my hand, he led me up to his bedroom. I got into his bed, still shivering with cold and feeling hungry yet sick – pregnancy sickness. He brought me some biscuits, which I ate greedily. He gave me a big cuddle and left me to sleep.

When I woke up this wonderful guy took me downstairs again. There were lots of people milling around. They turned out to be his family and church friends. They were so polite to me, even though I looked really rough. They gave me a cup of tea and biscuits before their son drove me back to the station so that I could get a train. I will never forget his or his family's kindness and concern.

Dad stopped talking to me after that, but my brother

David started coming to see me. He'd take me to Sainsbury's in Wood Green and help me back home with the shopping bags. By then I had huge cravings. I couldn't stop staring at the shelves of pickled onions. David bought me several jars, along with lots of other food. I was amazed; he actually paid for it! At the checkout he put his arm round me and said, 'You need to eat for two now, little sister. And proper food, eh? Not just biscuits and crisps.'

I felt a wave of tiredness overtake me, so David flagged down a cab. 'Ta da!' he sang, taking out a jar of pickled onions and opening it. We were about halfway home.

I grabbed the jar and ate one onion after another until there were none left. I was like a crazy animal.

Back at home, David emptied my bins and cleaned up the flat. 'Put your feet up,' he said. 'I'll make us a salad.' I scoffed it down so quickly, he couldn't stop laughing.

He left me curled up in a chair reading a Sheila Kitzinger book about pregnancy that I'd checked out of the library. I'd lost all my education at Kendall House, so it was hard to read it, but I painstakingly put the words together, and the pictures provided a lot of information. That night I had the most wonderful feeling of butterflies in my tummy. The next day the butterflies were stronger. I was thrilled when I realised that it was my baby moving around.

I didn't smoke or drink during my pregnancy. I was obsessed with this thing growing inside me. But one day I got very upset thinking about how I wouldn't be able to help my child with his or her homework. I wouldn't know where to begin. I was thick. So I started getting more books from the library and re-educating myself. I stopped swearing and took better care of myself. With this child inside me, I felt alive for the first time in my life.

My labour came and the father held my hand and saw me through every step of it. By now we both knew that the relationship wouldn't be continuing, but there were no hard feelings. I was happy to be a single mother.

With my last push, I gave birth not only to my first child but also to a new life for me.

By now I had a small circle of friends who lived nearby, so I knew I wouldn't be too lonely. Some of them came to visit me and my gorgeous new son Daniel in hospital. Much to my amusement, my friend Dave took him out of his crib and held him up to the window. The other guys gathered round. 'That's Tottenham football ground over there,' Dave said, nodding at the stadium. 'You'll be a football player because you've got such big feet.' Daniel promptly weed on him. He had already started making his mark.

It was time to go home with my new son. I was as happy as a person could be. My sister Bernadette and Auntie Rachel arrived, closely followed by – lo and behold! – my dad. Bernadette and Rachel were all oohs and aahs. Dad kept his distance. It broke my heart to see how thin and ill he looked.

All of a sudden, Bernadette took Daniel out of his crib, marched over to Dad and plonked him in his arms. Dad had no choice but to hold him, and he started crying. He cuddled Daniel like there was no tomorrow. He didn't want to hand him back. He had fallen in love with this new being, this new child, his own flesh and blood.

'What's his blood group?' he asked.

'It's funny you should ask because it's different to mine – it's A negative,' I said.

Then Dad really began to sob. It turned out that all these years he had suspected that I wasn't his child, because my blood group wasn't the same as his. Apparently Mum had started an affair with a man down the road around the time of my conception. (Or that's what Dad claimed. You could never tell with those two. They drove each other to distraction.) Since I resembled Mum so much more than I did him, he had become sure over time that I wasn't his. But Daniel's unusual blood group convinced him that I was his child because it was the same as Dad's.

His attitude to me changed completely. He became the proudest dad and granddad in the world. He immediately stopped drinking and smoking. He insisted on being a part of his grandson's life. I had waited all my life for him to be a proper dad to me – and this was it.

He regularly travelled all the way from south-west London – where he now lived – just to be with us for an afternoon, and I took Daniel to see him as often as I could. Dad often babysat for me. He bought Daniel toys and constantly played with him. He loved his grandson so much that when Daniel got his first tooth through, he came all the way to Tottenham and then took him all the way to the Fox and Hounds in Putney just to show his drinking friends his grandson's first tooth. Then, ill as he was, he travelled all the way back with him to me in Tottenham. That night he stayed the night and started bleeding really badly. I did my best to nurse him and make him comfortable.

Bernadette and I became a lot closer too and in the summer we took Dad and Daniel on holiday to Butlins. We had an absolute scream. I've got pictures of them riding on the choo choo train, of Daniel perched on Dad's knee and Dad pushing Daniel's pram. There was always a fight about who was going to push that pram and most of the time Dad won.

Back at home, Dad started to stay with me more as his

health deteriorated. We did the crossword together every day and always had a laugh over it. He would tease me about my crap ironing and insisted that he washed and ironed all of Daniel's clothes. I've got pictures of Dad and Daniel next to the cake I baked on Daniel's first birthday. It was an amazing time. I was finally getting to know my dad properly.

Sadly, he died shortly after that. Just before he passed away, he told Auntie Rachel, 'I hope Teresa forgives me for letting her down when she needed me.'

Of course I forgave him. He had made up for everything tenfold in those last couple of years. He had become my trusted friend, as well as a proper dad.

Losing him was the most painful experience I'd ever been through. It seemed so unfair that I'd got my dad back only to lose him again. At his funeral, I wept and wept.

On the way home, I stared into my sleeping son's face. It struck me that Daniel had given me back the father I'd lost for all those years. He'd given my dad the chance to make up for everything that had gone wrong. And he'd also given me my life back.

I had every reason to go on living. Sad as I was over my father's death, I had every reason to be happy.

Daniel was now my life.

EPILOGUE

I am now 40. I have three wonderful children, fifteen gorgeous cats, two naughty dogs and a budgerigar. I work as a volunteer with DEStiny (Disability Enterprise Support) CIC and have organised a petition to get the Statute of Limitations Act changed, at http://petitions.pm.gov.uk/statutebarred/. It is important that we unite in helping to bring about the changes needed to improve the lives of vulnerable people and children.

It has taken many years to come to terms with what happened to me while I was growing up. There are still so many unanswered questions.

For a long time I didn't talk about the terrible abuse I suffered at Kendall House because I was worried that no one would believe me. I also hoped that the pain and memories would fade in time, but they didn't. So in 1992, I decided to try to track down my files, or at least find out if they still existed.

Wandsworth Social Services refused to cooperate, so my social worker at the time suggested that I go to a solicitor, which I did. It was subsequently acknowledged that the first investigation into the rape allegation against Doug Novick, the foster father, had been inadequate. As a result, the police reopened their investigation into the rape, as well as Kendall House.

But Wandsworth Social Services still refused to make my files openly available to the police, to my solicitor or to me. The council initially said that it would make part of the files available to my social worker and me, but the Kendall House files were not included in this offer. When my solicitor requested full access, not only was it denied but the previous offer was also withdrawn. This hampered the police inquiry. One police officer wrote:

'I am troubled that a public service such as Wandsworth Social Services is not open to external scrutiny and the fact that they appear to be able to hinder and undermine a current criminal inquiry is most unsatisfactory.'

I went to see my local MP, Neil Gerrard, and he brought my case up in Parliament on 25 October 1994. He criticised Wandsworth Council on several counts, from their refusal to give me access to my files to their attitude to the rape allegations against Doug Novick. He was very concerned that Wandsworth did not treat my claims seriously. Here's an extract from his speech (he refers to me as 'my constituent'):

'In 1984, my constituent was placed with a foster parent and, shortly afterwards, she alleged that the man had raped her. The way in which that complaint was dealt with was dreadful and Wandsworth Council has more or less admitted that since. The rape allegation was not immediately reported to the police and, worse than that, a few days later my constituent was forced to confront the man who she alleged had raped her, and his wife, without the presence of a social worker. The files show that the social worker was away on holiday at the time. Shortly afterwards, the Social Services department agreed that, if she did not withdraw her allegation, it would write to the police and ask them to investigate. It is clear from the paper in which it agreed to do that that it had already made up its mind. The paper states:

"When we receive formal notification from them [the police] that the allegations will not be proceeded with because of lack of evidence, the Department's records will need to be amended so that it is absolutely clear that her allegations were totally unsubstantiated and merely a fantasy."

Clearly, the department had made up its mind. It did not believe her and it was not going to refer the matter in any serious way to the police.'

Neil Gerrard also seemed very worried by the way Wandsworth continued to withhold information from the police. He said:

'The problem all along has been the refusal of Wandsworth Social Services to make its files openly available . . . the continued refusal cannot but suggest that there is something to hide. Moreover, pressure has been put on my constituent to drop the case. In direct telephone conversations with senior Wandsworth Social Services officers, she has been told, "Forget all that stuff from years ago and just get on with your life", sometimes in a quite unprofessional manner.'

The law on access to files has since been changed, although it remains a sad fact that only a small percentage of children in care ever manage to get access to their full files when they leave.

It took me twelve years to get hold of my Wandsworth files and when I finally got them, they were incomplete. (They also included a report on another Kendall House girl that should not have been in my files.) But there is enough evidence in the information that has been released to reveal the many mistakes the council made in the course of my childhood from the day my parents first contacted them.

They left me in the care of my violent father and kept sending me back to him between homes, even when they knew he had not paid the electricity bill, but they wouldn't let my mum have us because she'd had a breakdown. Mum wasn't violent to us. Many times she begged to see us and wasn't allowed to. So many times my dad asked for help and didn't get it. My parents had their problems and Social Services were supposed to help, but the council turned out to be the worst of the worst. It was not a system that cared. It was not a system that helped. It was a system that let children and families down.

Why was I sent to Kendall House? There was no valid reason. I wasn't naughty, I wasn't aggressive; I was liked and got on with most people. My schooling was average and the Social Services were trying to find excuses to put me where I didn't belong. Convenience? Who knows, but I do know that every evaluation I had prior to Kendall House made it clear there was nothing wrong with me mentally. In the end Wands-worth put me in Kendall House regardless. They took me out of a home I was happy in (Miss Foley's) and put me in the home from hell.

In my files there is a letter from Dr M A Sevitt, consultant psychiatrist at Long Grove Hospital, to Mrs White at the Inner London Education Authority, dated 19 June 1980, written during their discussions about where it would be best to send me to complete my education:

'I am writing following our Case Conference of Thursday last week to confirm that we are recommending a boarding school placement for Theresa [sic]. We feel that Theresa would be best placed at a small ordinary boarding school and will not require a maladjusted provision.'

The Inner London Education Authority agreed that a 'small ordinary boarding school' would be suitable for me. Social Services were copied in on the correspondence. Yet they insisted that Kendall House, with its drugs and punishments regime, its locked doors and its intake of violent and disturbed girls, was the right place for me. Why did they not tell me what it was like there? Did they have a vested interest in sending me there? In my files, five boarding schools are listed as placement possibilities for me, not including Kendall House. I was never supposed to be locked away.

There were newspaper reports even before 1980 slamming the drug regime at Kendall House. Complaints had been made by various individuals and establishments about Kendall House, but Wandsworth Social Services continued to put girls there. Why were none of my dad's complaints investigated, and why was he not told that I was being given drugs? The girls' complaints were also ignored. Miss Woods and Dr Perinpanayagam had free reign to do as they liked, and the devastating results included mental, physical and sexual abuse.

As soon as I learned that there were records of my time at Kendall House written by the staff, I rang all the archive centres in Kent and the surrounding areas to see if someone other than Wandsworth was holding a set. No joy. Then one day, out of the blue, I had a phone call from an archivist to say that she had found my Kendall House file.

I'm not sure what I was expecting, but I was astounded to see that my file logged every single day I spent at Kendall House from June 1981 onwards. I couldn't believe what I was reading. There in black and white was an account of the drugs I was given and the abuse I suffered. It wasn't always reliable – the staff reported day-to-day incidents from their own warped perspective and there was quite a lot of covering up. What struck me above all were the lists of daily drugs and dosages I was forced to take.

As Neil Gerrard MP pointed out in his speech to parliament, the recommended Valium dose for children and teenagers, even in exceptional circumstances, is in the range of 5 to 10 mg, yet I was being given daily doses of up to 80 mg in tablet form – and 100 mg intravenously, which was combined with other serious drugs well over recommended adult doses. It is a wonder that my body was able to process these amounts. I could easily have died.

Other medicines I was forced to take included some extremely strong antipsychotic drugs, some of which were used to treat schizophrenia. Considering that I had not been diagnosed with any form of mental illness whatsoever, it seems extraordinary that I was being 'treated' with these powerful medicines. Or was I simply a guinea pig for drugs trials? Was it possible that Dr Perinpanayagam was attempting to induce symptoms of schizophrenia in me using psychotropic drugs like Valium, in order to then treat me in a series of tests using antipsychotic drugs? It sounds farfetched, but I often ask myself, what other explanation could there be?

The drugs he used on us turned healthy girls into something they were not. Girls who arrived after me, like Danielle and Annie, came into Kendall House with clear eyes and complexions. Within days they looked ill and haunted. The drugs created a whole new me, a person who became almost unrecognisable to my family.

Why was I drugged less than twenty-four hours after I arrived at Kendall House? There was absolutely nothing in my past history or records to suggest that I required medication, and nothing in my Kendall House file to suggest that I was being disruptive. In fact that first night all I did was sleep. The psychiatrists who had assessed me prior to going to Kendall House found me to be mentally healthy, despite my unstable background. So why was I given Valium from the start? Surely it could not simply have been because I complained about being locked up.

Bridget and Tina were genuinely aggressive and disturbed, so why weren't they drugged?

My initial meeting with Dr Peri on my second day at Kendall House lasted five minutes, which obviously wasn't long enough for a psychiatric evaluation of any serious kind. Miss Woods had already made me take some medication, so the meeting with Dr Peri must have been just a formality.

Who was DR Perinpanayagam? This is his official title:

MBBS, FRC Psych, DPM, DCN, consultant psychiatrist and tutor, University of London, psychotherapist to the Home Office.

In other words, he was a highly qualified and highly respected psychiatrist and psychotherapist, a position he seriously abused.

Kendall House was not licensed to be a secure unit, nor were the staff authorised to administer the kind of drugs they were doling out. Why were untrained staff allowed to give out drugs without reference to a GP? Surely it was illegal?

An inspection visit in June 1984 by the Department of Health and Social Security (DHSS) found an alarming number of irregularities in the way Kendall House was run. The stocking and storage of medication was heavily criticised, as was the way the drugs were given. The Department report to Kendall House stated that:

'It must be absolutely clear that *no* drugs, except for

simple, non-prescribable drugs, must be administered except with the direct involvement of either the general practitioner or Dr Harris [who replaced Dr Peri at the meeting to discuss the allegation against Doug Novick].'

According to the law, only a GP or doctor is permitted to administer prescription drugs like Valium. So the injections I was given at the hands of Harriet and Mrs Tarwin, aided by Shirley, Matthew, the bookkeeper and various teachers and members of staff were not legally given, setting aside the fact that undue force and cruelty were used when they pinned me down and injected me.

The drugs I was forced to take at Kendall House included: Sparine (sedative and antipsychotic), Kemadrin (used to treat symptoms of Parkinson's Disease), Droleptan (antipsychotic, discontinued), Haloperidol (used to treat schizophrenia and mania), Disipal (used to treat symptoms of Parkinson's Disease, not recommended for use in children), Depixol (used to treat schizophrenia and mania), Largactyl (used to treat mania), Phenergan (antihistamine), Sernace (used to treat schizophrenia and mania), Normison (sedative, similar to Valium). I presented many of the side effects of these drugs, from dizziness and trembling to nausea, loss of appetite and mood swings.

Samples of my blood and urine were taken – usually by Harriet – every two weeks, but the results of the tests were not logged with my GP or any of the local hospitals. Why not? Where were the samples sent and where were the results of the tests kept? Could it be possible that Dr Peri was using those results for his own, unauthorised, research?

Why were ninety-nine per cent of the drugs administered to me not registered with my GP? And why were untrained staff like Miss Woods and Mrs Tarwin allowed to request powerful prescription drugs from the local GP and get them without a consultation with the patient?

Why did the police never look into my complaints of drugging and abuse when they picked me up after I had run away?

What are the long-term effects of drugs like the ones I was given? A common birth defect in children born to mothers who use psychotropic drugs in or prior to pregnancy is a cleft palate, and my daughter was born with this and Pierre Robin syndrome. My second son was born blind, but fortunately recovered his sight after two years. Coincidence? It seems likely that there is a link. I have never used any drugs during, prior to or since my pregnancy. The only time I was on those drugs was at Kendall House.

The 1984 DHSS report also said: 'We still remain concerned about the amount of internal locking of doors . . . in particular the continued practice of locking the door between the ground floor and first and second bedroom floors at night is not warranted . . . this does constitute a 'restriction of liberty'.

Kendall House did not have permission from any governing body to lock up the girls in this way; in which case, surely, it was responsible for falsely imprisoning the girls there.

An earlier DHSS report in 1983 ordered Kendall House to open up the detention room and Sick Bay, stating that girls must not be locked within either room. Kendall House assured the DHSS by letter that the rooms had been turned into offices. Clearly this was not the case. My files show that I was still being restrained in the detention room and Sick Bay in 1983.

Other major DHSS concerns included 'the inadequate

provision of qualified teaching staff'. The teaching curriculum was deemed to be 'too limited and traditional' and 'to have a number of serious deficiencies'.

In actual fact, the curriculum barely existed. Educational standards at Kendall House were farcically low.

The Department made a number of recommendations for change in Kendall House, including the removal from the premises of all non-prescription drugs. Perhaps if they had made their inspection a few years earlier, I would not have been subjected to daily overdoses.

Another huge question in my mind concerns my allegations of sexual abuse while I was in Sick Bay. In a letter dated 23 February 1983, Miss Woods wrote to the local GP saying:

'I enclose copy of report on anal swab taken from Teresa Cooper. It is likely that she has been sexually abused.'

It seems extraordinary that Miss Woods would make a written acknowledgement of this, when at no point did she acknowledge to me that she was taking my claims seriously. She accused me of making up stories and said that it was 'all in your head, Teresa', but this letter shows that she appeared to know a lot more than she was letting on.

It also seems incredible that not one member of staff reported my allegations of sexual abuse to the police, even after they had logged a wide range of physical problems I endured as a result of the abuse. Instead there almost seemed to be a conspiracy to keep my claims – and the evidence – contained within Kendall House. Otherwise, why did they do the swabs and examinations in house? Why all the secrecy?

Why was I given an anal stretch in hospital? I can only assume that it didn't occur to the medical staff that my injuries were sustained as a result of anal rape. They must have assumed that I had a medical problem that was causing rectal tears and fissures. Of course, I was too drugged up to have any say and the Kendall House staff spoke for me. I can only guess at the lies they told the doctors.

The foster father situation was terrible too; a serious failure by Wandsworth and Kendall House. Doug Novick was based in Kent, and he was prosecuted in later years for crimes against another person he was caring for. He is on the Social Services register and is not allowed to look after children or adults again. If Wandsworth had taken my rape allegations seriously, perhaps he wouldn't have had the chance to abuse again. As it was, they gave him free reign.

Despite numerous attempts to take legal action against Wandsworth, with full support from the legal aid board, I was unable to get around the fact that I was statute barred. The statute of limitations sets forth a maximum period of time, after certain events, that legal proceedings based on those events can be initiated. Because I had mentioned the abuse to my social worker many years before I started proceedings (and here 'abuse' refers to everything that happened at Kendall House and with the foster father) the maximum period of time had expired (six years) and I could not take civil action.

The Statute of Limitations Act crippled me, as it does many victims of abuse, by preventing me from taking civil action against my abusers and the local authorities. It blocks any redress for the abuse suffered and also prevents sufferers from getting recognition of what they went through. The care system failed many survivors of historic abuse and the Statute of Limitations Act puts survivors through further abuse by not allowing them the right to a fair hearing. The civil law as it stands contradicts fair law when it comes to survivors of child abuse. I feel strongly that the law must be changed so that it supports the abused and not the abusers and I am currently campaigning for that change.

The Criminal Injuries Compensation Authority refused me the right to seek compensation under the exceptional circumstances clause, despite all the evidence. No matter what route I took, they prevented any compensation claim.

Through the many years that I have been trying to seek some form of justice, not one of those involved in the abuse I suffered has shown remorse. I will not give up seeking an apology from those who had a duty of care for me and failed me.

The cruel regime at Kendall House is one that no child should endure and these regimes need to be highlighted in order to bring about much needed changes. The abuse I suffered violated every description of the word 'care' and it wasn't normal to be treated like that in the care system. Like many survivors we were put in care to protect us from abuse and bad family situations, but we were subjected to abuse in the care system that in many cases far outweighed any abuse we suffered at home.

My mum and dad are both dead, Mr and Mrs Whattler too. Bernadette now works abroad. I haven't had contact with my brother David for more than ten years. I don't see or speak to Karen, my mum's relative.

Last year I contacted Jules again and our friendship is stronger than ever.

Annie, the girl whose tortured screams I heard while I was locked up in Sick Bay, committed suicide in 1987 by jumping in front of a train. I am in contact with Amanda, Annie's best friend and we have a good friendship.

I heard that Georgie was bundled off to a psychiatric hospital, but has since been released into the community.

I don't know where Bridget is, or what happened to Nicole. I haven't tried to find out.

The Council of Social Responsibility is now known as the Church of Social Responsibility. The church helped me to get hold of my Kendall House files and is currently aiding other Kendall House ex-residents in the search for their files.

I went to have a look at Kendall House recently. Back in the 1980s it closed down as a girls' home and was turned into rooms for the homeless, but it is now derelict. Standing on the pavement outside, I felt horrible. The windows were dirty. It looked dead. It was dead. There was no life in it. It's just a house now, just broken down bricks and mortar. The staff are no longer there; the girls aren't there. I didn't go inside. I felt relieved when I drove off. It was good to get home to my children and all my pets, where I am happy.